# Obion County Tennessee

## Court *of* Pleas & Quarter Sessions

### - 1834-1836 -

By:
Works Progress Administration

Southern Historical Press, Inc.
Greenville, South Carolina

This volume was reproduced from
A personal copy located in the
Publisher's private Library

All rights reserved. No part of this publication may be reproduced,
stored in a retrieval system, transmitted in any form, posted
on to the web in any form or by any means without
the prior written permission of the publisher.

Please direct all correspondence and orders to:

**www.southernhistoricalpress.com**
or
**SOUTHERN HISTORICAL PRESS, Inc.
PO Box 1267
375 West Broad Street
Greenville, SC   29601
southernhistoricalpress@gmail.com**

Originally published: Nashville, TN 1941
ISBN #0-89308-972-9
All rights Reserved.
*Printed in the United States of America*

OBION COUNTY

COURT OF PLEAS & QUARTER SESSIONS

1834-1835

(p-1)　　State of Tennessee)　　Court of Pleas & Quarter Sessions
　　　　　Obion County　　　　)　　January Term 1834.

　　　Be it remembered that at a Court of Pleas & Quarter Sessions begun & held at the Courthouse in the town of Troy, County & State aforesaid on Monday the 6th day of January A. D. 1834 present at worshipful John Parr, Seth Bedford, Willis Caldwell, John Harpole, Benj. Totten, William Downey, Jesse Daugherty, William Wilkinson, Henry D. Logan.

　　　Richard B. Brown produced in open court a commission as a Justice of the Peace for said County and took the oaths of office.
(Issued)

　　　Wm. C. Edwards proved the killing of two wolves within this county over six months old & it is ordered by the court that the same be so certified.
(Issued A. T. H.)

　　　John P. Wright proved the killing of one wolf within this county over four months old which is ordered by the court to be so certified.

　　　Moses D. Harper proved the killing of one wolf over four months old in Obion County which is ordered by the Court to be so certified &c.
(Issued)

　　　John Williams proved the killing of two wolves over four months old in Obion County which is ordered by the Court to be so certified.
(Issued)

　　　Jesse Williams proved the killing of one wolf in Obion County over four months old which is ordered by the Court to be so certified.
( Issued)


(p-2)　January Term 1834.

　　　Ordered by the Court that George W. Macey be appointed overseer on the Mills Point road from the Weakley County line near Tottens Wells to the four mile tree in the room of Elias Edwards removed and that all the hands that worked under said Edwards work under him & that he keep the same in repair as a first class road.

　　　Ordered by the Court that James Wadkins be appointed overseer on the Mills Point road from the widow Daltons to the state line in the room of Robert Dickison, resigned, & that he have the same hands that worked under Dickerson, to wit:　Jerome Wadkins, William Snider, John Moses, Samuel Moses, Washington Moses, Claybourn Taylor, Eli Bapham, James Bapham, Andrew Moore, James Moore, Tully Estridge, Willie Skeggs, John Snider, Madison Cole, James Jones, B. D. Logan, William Saunders, Charles Nice, James Davis,

Thomas Wright & John Stanford and all other hand with in said bounds and that he keep the same in repair as a first class road.
( Issued 23rd Jan. 1834)

Ordered by the Court that James I. McCollum be allowed one dollar and fifty cents for services performed for the county and that the Trustee pay the same out of any monies not otherwise appropriated.
(Issued 23rd of Janry 1834)

(p-3) January term 1834

Ordered by the Court that it be certified to the Trustee of Obion County that James I. McCollum served this court five days at the October term 1833 as constable.

Ordered by the court that Joseph Wilson be appointed overseer of the Dyersburg road from the town of Troy to the four mile post in the room of Stephen Macey removed and that he have all the hands that worked under said Macey & keep the same in repair as a first class road.

Ordered by the Court that Porter & Partee be released from the payment of all County tax as retail merchants on the license recently obtained by them over and above five dollars.
(Issued 24th Janry 1834)

Ordered by the court that A. W. & W. Ross be released from the payment of all County tax as retail merchants on the license recently obtained by them over & above five dollars.

The last will & testament of Andrew Linn was this day produced in Open Court and the due execution thereof duly proved by the oaths of James Harper & Jonathan Whiteside subscribing witnesses thereto & ordered recorded.

Ordered by the Court that the road from Troy by R. B. Browns, Widow Harper & Robt Harper to the Mills Point road at Thomas Buchannons be kept up & that James B. Hogge be appointed overseer thereon & keep the same in repair as a second class road & that he have R. B. Browns & hand, Widow Harpers & James T. Brown & hand.
(Issued 23rd Jan 1834)

(p-4) Monday January term 1834

Ordered by the Court that the following taxes be given for the year 1834, to wit:

| | |
|---|---|
| For County Contengences of each 100 acres of land | 12½ |
| On each white pole | 12½ |
| On each slave | 25 |
| On each town lot | 25 |
| On each stallion half the season of 1 mare | |
| On each tavern with license | $ 5.00 |
| On each retail store | $ 5.00 |
| On each Jack half the season of 1 mare | |
| On each four wheeled pleasure carriage | $ 4.00 |

| | |
|---|---|
| On each 2 wheeled Do | .50 |
| For Courthouse tax | |
| On each 100 Acres of land | 18 3/4 |
| On each town lot | 37½ |
| On each slave | .25 |
| On each free poll | 12½ |
| On each stud horse or Jack half the season of 1 mare | |
| On each retail store | $ 5.00 |
| On each tavern with license | 5.00 |
| On each four wheeled pleasure carriage | 1.00 |
| On each 2 Do | .50 |
| For the payment of Jurors | |
| On each 100 acres of land | 6¼ |
| On each town lot | 12½ |
| On each free poll | .06¼ |
| On each slave | .12½ |
| On each stallion or Jack ¼ the season of 1 mare | |
| On each retail store | $ 2.50 |
| On each tavern | 1.50 |
| On each four wheeled pleasure carriage | 1.25 |
| On each 2 Do | .50 |

& that each suit be taxed $1.00 to pay the Quorum Court.

(p-5)   Monday, January term 1834

Ordered by the Court that the following persons be appointed to take lists of taxable property in the following companies, to wit:

John Harpole in Capt. Hill's Company
Willis Caldwell in Capt. Henry's Company
John Parr in Capt. Nelm's Company
Richard B. Brown in Capt. Head's Company
James Henderson in Capt. Vaughn's Company
H. J. P. Westbrook in Capt. Asbrook's old Company
William Downey in Capt. Watson's old Company
Seth Bedford in Capt. Brown's Company

Ordered by the Court that Willis Caldwell, John Parr & Benjamin Totten, Esqrs. be appointed Justices to hold the Quorum Court for the present year.

Ordered by the Court that the commissioners of County Revenue in settling with Joel L. Enloe as Sheriff receive as vouchers any receipts, orders or notes executed by Thomas Allen, Dennis Cochran & Jesse Edminson or either of them.

Ordered by the Court that Joel L. Enloe be allowed forty six dollars thirty two cents the amount of the costs in the case of Marr Vs Enloe & that the Revenue Commissioners allow him a credit for the same.

This day Daniel St John was duly and constitutionally elected Constable for the next ensuing two years whereupon the said Daniel St John came into Court & executed bond with William A. Maxwell, Joel L. Enloe & R. B. Brown his security & took the oaths of office.

Willis Cathey came into Court & resigned his office as constable for Capt. Brown's Company.

(p-6) Monday, January term 1834.

Charles Sinkler was this day duly elected Constable for the next two ensuing years in Capt. Head's Company. Henry D. Logan was this day duly elected Constable for the next two years in Capt. Brown's Company.

Ordered by the Court that John L. Doxey, A. W. O. Totten & Seth Bedford be appointed Commissioners to settle with the present and all former commissioners for the town of Troy and report the same to the next term of this Court and that the Sheriff give notice to all concerned.

Ordered by the Court that the following persons be appointed Common School Commissioners in the following companies, to wit:

William A. Maxwell for Capt. Hill's Company
Alfred Lornax for Nelm's Company
Willis Caldwell for Henry's Company
Sanford Bramblet for Brown's Company
R. B. Brown for Head's Company
William Downey for Watson's old Company
Wm. M. Wilson for Vaughn's Company
Henry Applewhite for Ashbrook's old Company

Ordered by the Court that the following be the tavern rates for Obion County, to wit:

each diet 25 cts., 12½¢ for lodging, 25 cts. for horse feed, 37½ for horse per night.

(p-7) Monday, January term 1834.

12½ cts. per half pint for whiskey, 25¢ Do for rum, 25 Do for wine, gin, brandy.

Ordered by the Court that the following be the rates of ferriage at Nelms ferry, to wit:

12½ cts. for man & horse, 6¼ cts. for footman or single horse, 50 cts. for each waggon within the banks.

Ordered by the Court that the following be the rates of ferriage at Kentens ferry, to wit:

12½ cts. for man & horse, 6¼ cts. for footman or single horse, 50 cts. for each wagon, 3 cts. per head per cattle, hoggs or sheep, 37½ cts. for each carryall, 25 cts. for each cart & team, 50 cts. for each four wheeled pleasure carriage, 25 cts. for each gig.

Wm. Hutchinson )
To            )
Theodore Staley)

This day Wm. Hutchinson, the grantor, came into Court and acknowledged a deed of conveyance to Theodore Staley for fifty two acres of land, to be his act and deed for the purposes therein specified which is ordered to be certified for registration, ordered by the Court that Joel S. Enloe Shff. be allowed a credit by the commissioner for the tax on Studhorses for the former years & that he be furnished with a duplicate by the clerk & proceed to collect the same.

(p-8) Tuesday, January term 1834.

James H. Davis resigned as Deputy Clerk for this Court.

Ordered by the court that court adjourned until tomorrow morning 9 o'clock.

John Harpole, Jr.<br>B. Totten, Jr.<br>Willie Caldwell

Tuesday January 7th 1834.

Court met pursuant to adjournment.

This day came Jane A. Linn by attorney filed her petition & it appears to the Court therefrom that Andrew Linn has departed this life & his last will and testament was duly proved in this Court & that said Linn in his said last will & testament has nominated Robert Harper, his sole executor & that said Harper has failed to accept or renounce the execution of said will and that said Jane A. Linn is the only heir & devise. It is therefore ordered by the court that William Miller be appointed Receiver of all the goods & chattels, rights & credits of said estate and that he have & possess all the power & privileges that may be necessary for the safety & profit of said estate until the next term of this court and that he execute bond with security for the (p-9) faithful performance of his duties as receiver & that the said Robert Harper be summoned to appear here at the next term of this Court & either accept or renounce the execution of said will. Whereupon the said William Miller came into Court & executed bond with Richard B. Brown & Robert Harper his securities.

The Sheriff returned into Court venire facias awarded at the last term of this Court executed on all the persons therein named except Daniel F. Moore, James B. Holloman, William Jackson, Joseph Taylor & Lanford Norrid & the following Jurors appeared to wit: William Miller, Samuel Hutchinson, James B. Hogge, Edward Norrid, John Holloman, Samuel Reeves, Elisha Parke, Benjamine Garrison, James L. Brown, Lewis Foust, James Wilson, William Carter, Moses D. Harper, Robert Harper, Willis Hogge, Gideon Kirksey, out of which number the following persons were drawn as a grand jury, to wit: William Miller, Samuel Hutchinson, James B. Hogge, Edward Norrid, John Holloman, Samuel Reeves, Elisha Parker, Benjamin Garrison, James L. Brown, Lewis Foust, James Wilson, William Carter and Moses D. Harper. Whereupon William Miller was appointed foreman of the grand jury and after being sworn Daniel St John was sworn to attend the grand jury & they retired to consult of presentments &c.

Tuesday, January Term 1834.

State )
Vs )
W. F. Scott )

On Motion of William F. Scott who was fined at the last term of this Court for failing to attend as a Juror. It is ordered by the Court that the said fine be released on payment of costs. It is therefore considered by the Court that the State of Tennessee recover of said Defendant the costs about this suit in this behalf expended.

Joel S. Enloe was this day duly elected Sheriff for the County of Obion for the term of two years whereupon the said Joel S. Enloe came into Court and executed bond agreeably to law with William M. Willson, Moses D. Harper, William Carter, A. L. Harris and James M. Ross his securities and took the Oaths of office.

Charles Sinkler who was on yesterday elected constable came into Court & executed bond agreeably to law with R. B. Brown, Jesse Daugherty & Joel S. Enloe his securities & took the Oaths of office.

(p-10)  (Torn out of book)


(p-11)  Tuesday January term 1834.

Jubilee M. Bedford was this day duly elected Trustee for the County of Obion for the term of two years.

Samuel D. Wilson Clerk of this Court produced in Court the receipt of the Treasurer which was ordered to be recorded & is in the word & figures following, to wit:

Treasury office Dec. 23rd 1833 Rec'd of Sam D. Wilson Clerk of the County Court of Obion County one hundred & five dollars & 22 cts. the full amt. of Revenue due for the year ending the first of October 1833 according to the Revenue commissioners report.

Jas. Caruthers, Treasurer.

10522

Henry D. Logan came into Court and resigned his office as Justice of the Peace for Obion County.

Henry D. Logan who was yesterday elected constable came into Court and executed bond agreeably to law with Seth Bedford, J. M. Bedford, Joel S. Enloe and William M. Wilson his securities and took the oaths of office.

(p-12)  Tuesday January term 1834.

State        )
Vs           )   Fine
James B. Holloman)

On motion of the Defendant who was fined at the last term of this court for failing to attend as a Juror it is ordered by the Court that the said fine be released and that the State of Tennessee recover of said Defendant the costs about this suit in this behalf expended.

On motion of the attorney general it is ordered by the court that a subpoena issue against Alexander Edmunds to come into Court instantee & give evidence before the grand jury in behalf of the State against Lewis Foust and -- Hamilton.

Samuel D. Wilson Clark &c produced in Court a receipt from the Trustee of Obion County which was ordered to be recorded & is in the word in figures following, to wit:

State of Tennessee)   Trustee, Office
Obion County      )   Rec'd January 6th 1834

From Saml. D. Wilson Clark of the County Court for the County aforesaid twenty four dollars 37½ cts. the County revenue collected by him for the preceding year.

                                    John C. Wilson
                                    Trustee of Obion Co.

On motion of Jubilee M. Bedford and James H. Davis revenue Commissioners leave is granted them till the next term of this court to make their report.


(p-13)   Wednesday, January term 1834.

Jonathan Badgett )
Vs               )   Sci fa
Saml. L. McDaniel)

On motion of the Deft. it is ordered by the Court that the fine assessed in this case at the last term of this Court be released on payment of cost wherefore it is considered by the Court that the Plaintiff recover of the Defendant his costs about his suit in this behalf expended.

And the Court adjourned till tomorrow morning 9 o'clock.

                                    B. Totten, J. P.
                                    John Parr, J. P.
                                    Willis Caldwell, J. P.


Wednesday, January 8th 1834.

Court met pursuant to adjournment, present Benj. Totten, Willis Caldwell & John Parr, Esqr.

State          )
Vs             ) Sci Fa forfeiture
James Walker & Lucy D. Walker)

On motion of the Defendant by their attorney it is ordered by the Court that the forfeiture of the recognisance in this case be set aside on payment of costs. It is therefore considered by the Court that the State of Tennessee recover of the Defendants the costs about this suit in this behalf expended and that the defendant be taken &c.


(p-14)   Wednesday January 8th 1834


State        )
Vs           ) Riot
James Walker)

This day came the attorney general on the part of the State & the Defendant in his own proper person and moved the Court to quash the Indictment which motion was overruled and on motion of the attorney general it is ordered that this cause be continued till the next term of this Court & that the Defendant be recognized in the sum of $250 to make his personal appearance at the next term of this Court to answer said charge.


James Lewis  )
Vs           ) Debt
Joseph Wilson)

This day came the plaintiff by his attorney and the Defendant though solemnly called came not but made default. Wherefore it is considered by the Court that Plaintiff recover of the Defendant one hundred and fifteen dollars the debt in the declaration mentioned and also the further sum of thirty seven dollars ninety five cents the damages adjudged by said Court to said plaintiff by reason of the detention thereof and also his costs by him about his suit in this behalf expended and that execution issue &c


Mathew Young    )
Vs              ) Debt Sci Fa
Adams & Bedford)

By consent of parties it is ordered that this cause stand continued till the next term of this Court.


(p-15)   Wednesday January 8th 1834


Samuel D. Wilson         )
Vs                       ) Debt Sci Fa
Adams & Bedford admrs. &c)

By consent of parties it is ordered by the court that this cause stand continued till the next term of this court.


James L. Brown )
Vs             )   Debt
Joel S. Enloe  )

    This day came the parties by their attorneys & thereupon came a Jury of good & lawful men, to wit: William Miller, Saml Hutchinson, James B. Hogge, Edward Norrid, John Holloman, Samuel Reeves, Elisha Parker, Benj. Garrison, Lewis Foust, James Wilson, William Carter and Moses D. Harper who being elected tried & sworn the truth to speak upon the issue joined upon their oaths do say that the Defendant is indebted to the Plaintiff in the sum of two hundred and five dollars and assess his damage by reason of the detention thereof to fourteen dollars & seventeen cents wherefore it is considered by the court that the Plaintiff recover of the Defendant the said sum of two hundred and five dollars the debt aforesaid and also the sum of fourteen dollars 17 cts. the damages aforesaid by the Jury aforesaid in manner & form assessed as aforesaid and also his costs by him about his suit in this behalf expended which Judgment the Defendant prayed an appeal to the Circuit Court to be holden for said County on the 2nd Monday in --


(p-16)   Wednesday Jany term 1834

May, next- which was granted on his entering into bond with security as required by law whereupon the Defendant entered into bond with Littleton Hubbard & Andrew S. Harris his security conditioned as the law directs.


State          )
Vs             )   Indictment for selling liquor
Cornelius Sheeks)

    This day came the solicitor on behalf of the State and the Defendant in his own proper person and the Defendant by his Attorney moved the Court to quash the Indictment herein which motion was by the Court overruled and on motion of the solicitor it is ordered that this cause be continued.


State                          )
Vs                             )   Indictment Affray
George Fentress & Edward Robins )

    It is ordered by the court that this cause be continued and that an alias capias issue


Samuel Crockett admr. &c )
Vs                       )   Assumpsit
Charles McAlister        )

    This day came the parties by their Attorneys and thereupon came a Jury of good & lawful men, to wit: Robert Harper, Archibald Lockett,

John Ross, Alexander Polk, Littleton Hubbard, Cornelius Sheeks, Willis Hogge, William H. Guy, Horace Head, Wm A. Brown, A. C. Hubert & Grastly Mansfield who being elected, tried and sworn the truth to speak upon the issues joined upon their oaths do say that the said (p-17) Defendant did undertake and promise as therein the said Plaintiff declaration is alledged and assess the said Plaintiffs damage to fifty dollars 43/100 3/9 cts. wherefore it is considered by the Court that the Plaintiff recover of the said Defendant the aforesaid sum of fifteen dollars 43/100 3/9 cts. the damages aforesaid by the Jury aforesaid in manner & form assessed as aforesaid and his costs about his suit in this behalf expended and that execution issue &c

It appearing to the court that Enos Hay had died intestate William Andrews was appointed administrator of his estate and came into Court with Grastly Mansfield his security and acknowledged a bond to the governor as the law directs in the sum of six hundred dollars whereupon on motion it is ordered by the Court that the said administrator sell all the goods and chattels of said estate on a credit of 12 months taking bond and sufficient security for the benefit of said estate and return a true account of the sales of said estate to the next term of this Court & that he give 15 days notice of the time & place of said sale.

McSwing & Cassedy )
Vs )
I. S. & I. M. Ross)

Defendant filed his plea herein & by consent of parties it is ordered that a Commission to take depositions issue to either party & that he give legal notice &c

(p-18) Wednesday January 8th 1834

Nathan C. Pinson & Joel Pinson)
Vs )
Seth Stroud ) Debt

This day came the parties by their attornies and thereupon came a Jury of good and lawful men, to wit: William Miller, Samuel Hutchinson, James B. Hogge, Edward Norrid, John Holloman, Samuel Reeves, Elisha Parker, Benjamin Garrison, James S. Brown, Lewis Foust, James Wilson & William Carter who being elected tried and sworn the truth to speak upon the issue joined upon their oaths do say that the defendant owes & is indebted to the Plaintiffs in the sum of one hundred and ten dollars and assess their damage by reason of the detention thereof to three dollars eighty five cts. wherefore it is considered by the Court that the Plaintiff recover of the defendant the sum of one hundred and ten dollars the debt in the declaration mentioned also three dollars 85/100 cts. the damage by the Jury assessed as aforesaid together with their costs by them about their suit in this behalf expended and that execution issue &c.

William Cunningham ) Debt
Vs )
James F. Bedford, John Farr and Seth Bedford)

11

This day came the parties by their attornies the worshipful Willis Caldwell, Benj. Totten and William Wilkinson presiding & holding said Court and thereupon came a Jury, to wit: William Miller, Samuel Hutchinson, (p-19) James B. Hogue, Edward Norrid, John Holloman, Saml. Reeves, Elisha Parker, Benj. Garrison, James S. Brown, Lewis Foust, James Wilson & William Carter who being elected tried and sworn the truth to speak upon the issues joined upon their oaths do say that the said Defendants have not paid the debt in the declaration mentioned but do owe the same and assess the Plaintiffs damage by reason of the detention thereof to four dollars and fifty cents wherefore it is considered by the Court that the plaintiff recover of the defendants one hundred dollars the debt in the declaration mentioned and also four dollars fifty cents the damages by the Jury assessed as aforesaid together with his costs and that execution issue &c

Lonsdale Walton & Co.)     )
Vs     ) Debt
James Hogge     )

This day came the parties by their attorneys and their upon came a Jury of good & lawful men, to wit: William Miller, Samuel Reeves, Edward Norrid, John Holloman, Elisha Parker, Benj. Garrison, James S. Brown, Lewis Foust, James Wilson, William Carter, Moses D. Harper & Robert Harper, who being elected tried and sworn the truth to speak upon the issues joined upon their oaths do say that the Defendant doth owe the Plaintiff one hundred & eighteen dollars and assess their damage to six dollars and (p-20) twenty seven cents by reason of the detention thereof wherefore it is considered by the Court that the Plaintiffs recover of the Defendant the aforesaid sum of one hundred and eighteen dollars for his debt aforesaid & six dollars & 27/100 cts. the damages assessed as aforesaid and also his costs about his suit in this behalf expended and that execution issue &c

G. W. Wood & A. M. L. Mc Bean)
Administrators &c     )
Vs     ) Case
William Wilkinson     )
the worship John Parr

This day came the parties by their attorneys the worshipful John Parr, Benj. Totten & Willis Caldwell presiding & holding said Court & thereupon came a Jury of good and lawful men, to wit: Gideon Kirskey, Robert Harper, Willis Hogge, A. K. Hogge, Archibald Lockett, John Parr, Hugh Shelton, James Harper, William Hamilton, Ezekiel Carter, Philip Field & John Long who being elected tried & sworn the truth to speak upon the issue joined upon their oaths do say that the said Defendant did not undertake & promise in manner and form as the said Plaintiff in their said declaration have alledged whereupon it is considered by the Court that the Defendant recover of the Plaintiff his costs about his suit in this behalf expended to be levied of the goods & chattels of the intestate in their land to be administered &c.

Thomas Allison     )
Vs     ) Debt Certiorari
G. W. Wood & A. M. L. Mc Bean, admrs. &c)

This day came the parties & consented that this cause should be placed on the trial docket at the next term of this court.

(p-21) Wednesday, January term 1834.

Jonathan Badgett )
Vs ) Sci Fa
H. D. Logan )

On motion of the Defendant by atty. it is ordered that he be released from all further liability in this cause & it is considered by the court that the Defendant recover of the Plaintiff his costs by him about his suit in this behalf expended and that execution issued &c.

On motion of Albert Moore by his attorney it is ordered by the Court that Jubilee M. Bedford, Samuel L. Teater & A. S. Harris be appointed commissioners to settle with the said Albert Moore as administrator of Peter Moore dec'd and report to be next term of this Court.

On motion of L. Adams & Seth Bedford it is ordered by the court that William U. Watson, Jas. H. Davis & A. S. Harris be appointed commissioners to settle with the said Adams & Bedford as administrators of Jonas Bedford dec'd & report to the next term of this Court.

William W. Watson came into court and by consent of Joel S. Enloe, Sheriff was qualified as deputy Sheriff for Obion County.

Jubilee M. Bedford who was yesterday elected Trustee for Obion County came into Court with Joel S. Enloe, Seth Bedford, William M. Wilson & A. S. Harris his securities and acknowledged a bond to the Chairman of the County Court & his successor in the sum of four thousand dollars conditioned as the law directs & was duly qualified &c (p-22) and the Court adjourned till tomorrow morning 9 o'clock.

B. Totten, J. P.<br>Seth Bedford, J. P.<br>Willis Caldwell, J. P.

Thursday, January 9th 1834

Court met pursuant to adjournment present the worshipful Benjamin Totten, Seth Bedford & Willis Caldwell.

Saml. Crockett, admr. )
Vs ) Case
Charles McAlister )

This day came the Defendant by his attorney and prayed and appeal in this cause to the next circuit court to be holden for Obion County which is granted on his giving bond and security as required by law whereupon the said Defendant with Jubilee M. Bedford and Samuel Hutchinson executed & acknowledged bond as required by law.

State )
Vs ) Riot
James Walker )

This day came the Defendant & John McDaniel his security & acknowledged themselves indebted to the State of Tennessee in the sum of two hundred and fifty dollars each to be levied of their respective goods & chattels, lands & tenements but to be void on condition that the said Defendant makes his personal appearance at the next term of this Court to answer the State of Tennessee in a charge for rioting.

(p-23)   Thursday, January term 1834.

Wood & Mc Bean, admrs. &c )
Vs ) Case
John Farr )

This day came the parties by these attornies and thereupon came a Jury of good & lawful men, to wit: William Miller, Samuel Hutchinson, James B. Hogge, Edward Norrid, John Holloman, Samuel Reeves, Elisha Parker, Benjamin Garrison, James S. Brown, James Wilson, William Carter & Moses D. Harper who being elected tried and sworn the truth to speak upon the issues joined upon their oaths do say, we of the Jury fined for the Plaintiff $58.31¼ cts. in damages and on motion of the Defendant by his attorney ordered that the verdict of the Jury as aforesaid be set aside and held for nought and that a new trial of this cause be granted &c.

Jesse Edmondson )
Vs )
Madison C. Johns )

This day William M. Wilson, J. P., returned into court an execution in favor of Jesse Edmondson against Madison G. Johns for fifty dollars & 75 cts. debt with interest from the 6th day of April 1833 & costs with the following return to wit: No personal property found in my county levied on one town lot in the town of Troy No. 38, 9th of January 1834.

Joel S. Enloe, Shff.

Wherefore it is considered by the Court that said lot be condemned to be sold and that an exponas renditis issue &c.

9th Thursday January term 1834

Lonsdale Walton & Co. )
Vs ) Debt
James Hogge )

This day came the defendant by his attorney and prayed an appeal to the next Circuit Court for Obion County which is granted on his entering into bond with security as required by law whereupon the said defendant came into court with Samuel Hutchinson and A. M. L. McBean his securities

& acknowledged bond as required by law.

Jones Jones )
Vs ) Debt Certiorari
James F. Bedford & John Matheny )

On motion of the Defendant by their attorney it is ordered by the Court that the execution in this cause be quashed & that a procedendo be awarded to John Harpole Esquire directing & commanding him to give & allow said Defendants all the benefit of a stay of execution from the time of the rendition of said Judgement that the law gives them & it is considered by the Court that the Defendant recover of the Plaintiff their costs by them about their suit in this behalf expended & that execution issue &c.

Rosanah Harper )
Vs ) Debt
James M. Ross, Joel S. Enloe )
& Richard B. Brown )

This day came the parties by their attornies & the Plaintiff Benjamin Totten, Seth Bedford & Willis Caldwell each presiding by attorney moved the court for leave (p-24 not noted) (p-25) to amend the return of the coroner on the summons herein which was granted and done accordingly.

Rosanah Harper )
Vs ) Debt
James M. Ross, Joel S. Enloe )
& Richard B. Brown )

This day came the parties by their attornies & the Plaintiff by Benj. Totten, Willis Caldwell & Seth Bedford Esqrs. presiding the attorney moved the court for leave to amend the declaration herein which motion was overruled by the court and thereupon the Plaintiff moved the court for leave to dismiss this cause which was granted whereupon said cause was dismissed & leave granted to the Plaintiff to withdraw the bill single filed by him in this cause & it is further considered by the court that the Defendants go hence without and recover of the Plaintiff their costs by them about their defence in this behalf expended & that execution issue &c.

Ordered by the court that the grand Jury be discharged.

G. W. L. Marr )
Vs ) Debt
Seth Bedford )
William Wilkinson )

The Defendant came into Court Willis Caldwell & Benj. Totten, Esqrs. presiding and acknowledged himself indebted to the Plaintiff in the sum of one hundred & eight dollars wherefore it is considered by the court that the Plaintiff recover of the defendant one hundred & eight dollars the debt afsd. together with his costs by him about his suit, (p-26) in this behalf expended and by consent of parties it is ordered that execution be stayed for eleven months from this date.

George W. L. Marr )
Vs ) Debt
Willis Caldwell )

The Defendant came into Court William Wilkinson, Benjamin Totten, & Seth Bedford Esqrs. presiding and acknowledged himself indebted to the plaintiff in the sum of one hundred & five dollars wherefore it is considered by the court that the plaintiff recover of the Defendant the sum of one hundred and five dollars the debt aforesaid and also his costs by him about his suit in this behalf expended and it is agreed by the parties that the execution be stayed for eleven months from this date.

Ordered by the court that the traverse Jury be discharged.

James B. Hogge, assignee &c )
for the use of Henry Kiger )
Vs ) Debt Sci Fa
Adams & Bedford, admrs. &c )

By consent of parties this cause is continued till next term.

(p-27) Thursday January term 1834

Jonathan Badgett )
Vs ) Debt Sci. Fa.
Robert Dickerson )

Ordered by the court that this cause be continued till the next term of this court.

Ordered by the court that William U. Watson, James H. Davis & Daniel StJohn be appointed commissioners to settle with John C. Wilson the former Trustee for Obion County & report to the next term of this court.

Seth Bedford, Esqr. came into court William Wilkinson, Willis Caldwell & Benjamin Totten Esqrs. presiding & resigned his office as a Justice of the peace for Obion County.

By consent of Joel S. Enloe, Sheriff of Obion County Seth Bedford was duly qualified as Deputy Sheriff for Obion County.

(p-28) Thursday, January term 1834.

Ordered by the court that the following persons be appointed Inspectors of the election for Delegates to the convention to be held on the first Thursday & Friday in March 1834 at the following places, to wit: At the precinct Bird's old place. John Harpole, John S. Doxey & David Thompson at Troy. Richard B. Brown, William Wilkinson and James Henderson at the widow Davidsons, H. I. P. Westbrook, John Williams & Hugh A. Shelton, at Norrids old place, William Downey, Edward Norrid, Starkey Pervis. At Richard T. Merriwethers, Richard T. Merriwether, Evan Sholly & R. W. Stone.

Ordered by the court the following persons good & lawful men of the County of Obion be summoned by the Sheriff to be and appear at the next term of the Circuit Court to be held for said county at Troy on the second Monday in May next as grand and petit Jurors, to wit:

1. Benjamin Totten
2. John Harpole
3. David Thompson
4. John Whitesides
5. Martin Tally
6. Edward Jones
7. John Huzza
8. Willis Caldwell
9. Joseph Meadows
10. Obadiah Roberts
11. Jonas Bedford
12. John McGee
13. John Parr
14. Alfred Lomax
15. Ezekiel Carter
16. John Gore
17. Thomas M. Harper
18. William Carmack
19. William Wilkinson
20. John P. Wright
21. Samuel Simpson
22. Beryl Tanner
23. H. I. P. Westbrook
24. William Downey
25. Frederick Taylor
26. Jeremiah Norrid

(p-29)   Thursday January term 1834

And that Charles Sinkler & Daniel St. John constables be summoned to attend said circuit court.

Ordered by the court that the following good and lawful men of the County of Obion be summoned to appear here at the next term of this Court on Tuesday after the first Monday in April next as grand and petit Jurors, to wit:

1. John Jones
2. Levi Cook
3. Jesse Cook
4. Lion Hill
5. James Elder
6. Saml. Henry
7. Benj. Sheeks
8. Jesse Sheeks
9. James H. Guy
10. Thomas W. Dean
11. Robert Dickerson
12. Thomas Taylor
13. John Polk
14. John Linn
15. Henry Pryor
16. William Haslip
17. John Taylor
18. Joseph Wilson
19. Thomas Tanner
20. Porter A. Davis
21. Abram Herring
22. Benj. Farris
23. Alexander Allen
24. Theodore Staley
25. Anderson A. Cunningham
26. William T. Whiteside

And that Henry D. Logan & William Calhoun be summoned as constables to attend said court

James F. Bedford )
Vs                       )
Henry D. Logan  )   Debt Certiorari
& Benj. D. Logan)

On motion of the Defendants it is ordered by the Court that an alias certiorari be awarded commanding the Justice below to bring up the papers in this cause to the next term of this court. (p-30) And the court adjourned till tomorrow morning 8 o'clock.

                                B. Totten, J. P.
                                Willis Caldwell, J. P.
                                D. B. Brown, J. P.

Friday January term 10th 1834.

Court met pursuant to adjournment. Present Richard B. Brown, Benj. Totten & Willis Caldwell, Esqrs.

William T. Baldridge      )
Assignee of A. A. Kinkannon)
Vs                        )   Debt
Phillip Fields            )

This day came the Plaintiff by his attorney and the defendant though solemnly called came not but made default therefore it is considered by the Court that the Plaintiff recover of the Defendant the sum of seventy three dollars 38¼/100 the debt in the declaration mentioned are thirty five dollars 12½cts. the damages adjudged to him by said Court by reason of the detention thereof and also his costs by him about his suit in this behalf expended & that execution issue &c. And the court adjourned till court in course.

                                B. Totten, J. P.
                                Willis Caldwell, J. P.
                                R. B. Brown, J. P.

(p-31) Monday April 7th 1834.

State of Tennessee)   Court of Pleas & Quarter Session
Obion County      )   April term 1834

Be it remembered that at a Court of Pleas & Quarter Sessions begun & held at the Courthouse in the town of Troy for the County of Obion in the State of Tennessee on the 7th day of April being the first Monday in the same A. D. 1834. Present the worshipful Benjamin Totten, John Harpole, John Parr, Willis Caldwell, R. B. Brown, H. I. P. Westbrook and James Henderson commissioners and assignee to hold said term qualified accordingly.

Stancel Moore came into court and proved the killing of a wolf in the limits of this County over four months old and it was ordered by the Court five Justices being present that he receive out of the Treasury agreeable to the statutes of the State of Tennessee in such cases made and produced.

I. Nuton came in to open court and proved the killing of two wolves in the limits of this county over four months old and thereupon on motion it was ordered by the court, five Justices being present, that the State of Tennessee pay him therefore according to law.

(p-32)   April term 1834.

It being made to appear to the court that Polly Parr, on the day -- of A. D. 1834 departed this life in the limits of Obion County and she made no deposition by will of her goods & chattels, rights & credits thereupon on motion it was ordered by the court that William Parr, be appointed Administrator of all and singular the goods and chattels, rights & credits which were of the said Polly Parr dec'd and that he have the rights & incur the liability of that office and thereupon the said William Parr intered into bond as administrator. John Parr his security & took the oath prescribed by law. And the said William Parr administrator as aforesaid filed in court an inventory of the goods & chattels, rights &c of the said deceased.

William Parr, administrator of all & singular the goods and chattels, rights &c which were of Polly Parr dec'd have moved the court for an order to sell two negro girl slaves belonging to said estate, to wit: Peggy, five years of age and Emelin, about three years of age, that a division among the heirs & legal representatives of said Polly Parr dec'd may be made and it was therein ordered by the court that said Administrator sell the said negroes upon a credit of twelve months giving legal notice of the terms & place of such sale & that he take bond and security for the purchase money.
(Letters issued 14th April 1834.

(p-33)   April term Monday 7th 1834.

Jesse S. Ross returned into court his resignation as a Justice of the Peace with his papers which was ordered by the court to be void.

Jourdan Hassell by his attorney came into court as administrators of the estate of J. G. Houghton, Dec'd of all and singular the goods and chattels of said estate and by petition in writing sworn to &c here moved the court to sell two slaves Peter & his wife, Meryah, for the purpose of satisfying claims that yet remain due against said estate. It was therefore ordered by the court that said Administrators sell the said negroes accordingly on six months credit giving legal notice.
(Copy issued to Hassell 1st Aug. 1836)

R. B. Brown returned into court a list of taxable property in Captain Head's Company which was ordered to be received and recorded.

James Henderson returned into court a list of Taxable property in Capt. Vaughn's Company which was ordered to be received and recorded.

William Downey returned into court a list of taxable property in Capt. Watson's old company which was ordered to be received and ordered to be recorded.

John Harpole returned in court a list of taxable property in Capt. Hill's company which was ordered by the court to be received and recorded.

(p-34)   April Term 1834, Monday 7th.

State of Tennessee)
Vs             )
Samuel L. McDaniel)

Ordered by the Court that the clerk of this Court is hereby instructed not to issue an alias execution on the case of Jonathan Badgett against Samuel L. McDaniel which suit was commenced by Sci Fa because the court was of the opinion that they had not the power to tax the Defendant with the case.

State     )
Vs        )
John Mosier)

Ordered by the court that the excuse of said Defendant is sufficient to exhonorate him for further trouble or damages and that he the Defendant go without pay.

William U. Watson by request of James Bedford Ranger of this County was qualified as Deputy Ranger.

Jesse S. Ross by Joel S. Enloe his agent came into Court and resigned his commission as Internal Improvement Commissioner for the County of Obion.

(p-35)   Tuesday April 8th 1834.

Court adjourned until tomorrow morning eight o'clock.

Willis Caldwell, J. P.<br>
B. Totten, J. P.<br>
R. B. Brown, J. P.

Court met agreeable to ajournment present the worshipful Benjamin Totten, Willis Caldwell & R. B. Brown, Esqrs.

A deed of bargain and sale for 250 acres of land from Joseph Wilson to Amosa Webb was produced in open court and acknowledged by the said Joseph Wilson and ordered by the court to be certified for registration.

A deed of bargain and sale from Joseph Wilson to Amosa Webb for 100 acres of land was acknowledged by the sale Joseph Wilson an ordered by the court to be certified for registration.

The State of Tennessee)
Vs                    )
Daniel Brown          )

Daniel Brown having been summoned as a Jurior at the October term of this court 1833 and failing to appear was ordered by the court that

Sci Fa should issue against him whereupon the said Daniel Brown came into court and the court being of opinion that his excuse was sufficient ordered that he should be dismissed and that the Defendant go without pay.

(p-36)   Tuesday April 8, 1834.

Joel H. Dyer Solicitor General being absent and upon motion it was ordered by the court that Felin Parker Jr. one of the attornies of this court be sworn in as solicitor protem which was done accordingly.

The Sheriff returned into court the venire facias awarded at that term of this court executed on all the persons therein named except Robert Dickinson and the following Jurors appeared, to wit:

| | | | |
|---|---|---|---|
| 1. | John Jones | 13. | Abram Henning |
| 2. | Levi Cooke | 14. | Harry Pryor |
| 3. | Jesse Cooke | 15. | Wm. Haselip |
| 4. | Sion Hill | 16. | John Taylor |
| 5. | James Elder | 17. | Benjamin Farris |
| 6. | Samuel Henry | 18. | Thomas Tanner |
| 7. | Benjamin Sheeks | 19. | Porter A. Davis |
| 8. | James H. Guy | 20. | Joseph Wilson |
| 9. | Thomas W. Dean | 21. | A. A. Fosllen |
| 10. | Thomas Taylor | 22. | Theodore Staley |
| 11. | John Polk | 23. | A. A. Cunningham |
| 12. | Jesse Sheeks | 24. | William T. Whiteside |

Out of which number the following persons were drawn as a grand Jury, to wit:

| | |
|---|---|
| Joseph Wilson | Jesse Cook |
| Henry Pryor | A. A. Cunningham |
| Thomas Tanner | William Haislip |
| William T. Whiteside | James Elder |
| A. A. Fosler | Theodore Staley |
| John I. Taylor | Samuel C. Henry |
| Thomas W. Dean | |

Whereupon Joseph Wilson was appointed (p-37) fourman of the Grand Jury and after being sworn William Calhoon was sworn to attend on the Grand Jury and they retired.

Whereas it appears to the satisfaction of the court that Andrew Lynn has departed this life leaving a Last Will and Testament in which he appointed Robert B. Harper his Executor whereupon it is ordered by the court that letters testamentary issue to said Robert B. Harper upon his giving bond and security in the sum of seven thousand dollars whereupon the said Robert B. Harper came into court & entered into bond with James Harper, Samuel Hutchison, John Lynn and Samuel L. Tetter securities and took the oath prescribed by law.

Ordered by the court that John Lynn be excused from attending as a Juror at this term of the court.

A Deed of bargain and sale from John S. Docksey to Daniel Brown was produced in court and execution thereof proven by the oaths Daniel St. John and Benjamin Totten the subscribing thereto and ordered to be certified for registration.

Ordered by the court that William W. Watson, J. M. Bedford and W. S. S. Harris be appointed commissioners to settle with Jordan Hossitt administrator of John C. Horton deceased (p-38) and that they report to this court.

James F. Bedford )
Vs ) Certiorari
B. D. Logan & )
H. D. Logan )

This day came the parties by their attornies and the Plaintiff by his attorney moved the court to dismiss the Defendant Certiorian and upon agreement being had thereon and the matters of law answering thereon being fully understood by the court it is understood by the court that the Defendants petition for writs of certiorari and Supercedias be dismissed and it is further considered by the court that the Plaintiff recover of the Defendants the sum of a twenty dollar debt the sum recovered in the court below and the sum of one dollar and fifty cents damages sustained by reason of the detention thereof and also his costs by him in and about his suit expended and on motion it is further considered by the court that the Plaintiff have judgment against Joseph C. Culperson & Charles McAlister jointly with the Defendants for his debt damages and cost aforesaid and that execution issue accordingly &c. Willis Caldwell, Benjamin Totten and Richard B. Brown, Esqrs. presents and presiding, whereupon the Defendants prayed an appeal in the nature of a writ of error to the Circuit Court for said County.

(p-39). April Term A. D. 1834.

Benjamin Totten )
Vs ) Debt
George W. L. Marr )

This day came the parties by their attornies, John Parr, Willis Caldwell & Richard B. Brown, Justices of the Peace in & for Obion County, presiding and holding said Court and thereupon came a jury of good and lawful men, to wit: John Long, Levi Cook, Benjamin Sheeks, James H. Guy, Cornelius Sheeks, William Carmach, Samuel Hutchinson, Sion Hill & Abraham Herrin, Thomas Taylor, John Polk and Benjamin Farris who being elected tried and sworn the truth to speak upon the issue joined, upon their oath do say, that said Defendants have not paid the debt in said Plaintiffs said declaration alledged, but that said defendants owe and are indebted to said Plaintiff in the sum of seventeen hundred and sixty two dollars four and two third cents, as said Plaintiff hath alledged and they do assess said plaintiff damages, by reason of detention thereof to seventy eight dollars and fifty cents besides costs.

It is therefore considered by the court that said Plaintiff recover of said defendants seventeen hundred and sixty two dollars four and two third cents the debt aforesaid, found to be due & owing as aforesaid and seventy eight dollars and fifty cents, the damages aforesaid by the Jury aforesaid found and assessed in manner and form aforesaid and also his costs by him in an about his suit in this behalf expended.

And thereupon the said defendants by attorney here pray and appeal in the nature of a writ of error to the Circuit Court to be holden for said County of Obion at the Courthouse in Troy on the second Monday of May next (p-40) which was granted upon said defendants entering into bond with Joseph Wilson and Lewis Foust as their securities to prosecute said appeal with effect &c.

Samuel Nelson )
Vs ) Debt
Lucy Byrd )

This day came the parties by their attornies, and thereupon came a jury of good and lawful men, to wit: John Jones, Levi Cook, Benjamin Sheeks, James H. Guy, Thomas Taylor, John Polk, Benjamin Faris, Cornelius Sheeks, William Carmack, Samuel Hutchinson, Sion Hill & Abraham Herring, who being elected, tried and sworn the truth to speak upon the issue joined upon their oaths do say that said Defendant has not paid the debt in said Plaintiffs declaration mentioned as said Plaintiff has alledged by reason of detention thereof to two dollars and twenty five cents besides costs.

It is therefore considered by the court that said Plaintiff recover of said Defendant one hundred dollars, the debt in said declaration mentioned and two dollars & 25¢ the damages aforesaid by the jury aforesaid in manner and form aforesaid assessed and also his costs, by him in and about his suit in this behalf expended and that execution upon &c.

(p-41) April Term A. D. 1834.

John C. Wilson )
Vs )
Horace Head & ) Debt
Samuel D. Wilson )

This day came the parties by their Attornies and thereupon came a jury of good and lawful men, to wit: John Jones, Levi Cook, Benjamin Sheeks, James H. Guy, Thomas Taylor, John Polk, Benjamin Farris, Cornelius Sheeks, William Carmack, Samuel Hutchinson, Sion Hill, Abraham Herrin, who being elected tried and sworn the truth to speak upon the issues joined upon their oaths do say that said Defendant Wilson did assign to said Plaintiff the said writing obligatory in said Plaintiffs declaration mentioned as said Plaintiff hath alledged, and that said defendants have not paid said Plaintiff the said money in said Plaintiffs declaration mentioned, but that they owe and are indebted to said Plaintiff in the sum of one hundred and fifty dollars and they do assess his damages by reason of detention thereof to two dollars & fifty cents besides costs.

It is therefore considered by the court that said Plaintiff recover of said Defendants one hundred and fifty dollars the debt aforesaid and two dollars & 50¢ the damages aforesaid by the Jury aforesaid in manner & form aforesaid assessed & also his costs by him in & about his suit in this behalf expended.

And thereupon said defendants prayed an appeal to the Circuit Court to be holden for said County of Obion, on the second Monday of May next, which was granted upon their entering into bond with James M. Porter and A. M. L. McBean (p-42) securities for prosecuting said appeal with effects &c.

Samuel H. Cole )
Vs ) Covenant
Littleton Hubbard )

This day came the parties by their attorneys, and thereupon came on to be heard the Plaintiff demurrer to Defendant second and third pleas, by heirs in this behalf pleaded, and the matters of law arising thereon being seen and by the court fully understood, it seems to the court here that the law is with the Plaintiff & that said demurrer ought to be sustained.

It is therefore considered by the court that said pleas be overruled and for nothing extended & that said demurrer be sustained.

And thereupon came a jury of good and lawful men to try the issue of fact between the said parties in this behalf, to wit: John Jones, Levi Cook, Benjamin Sheeks, James H. Guy, Thomas Taylor, John Polk, Benjamin Farris, Cornelius Cheeks, William Carmack, Samuel Hutchinson, Sion Hill & Abram Herrin, who being elected tried and sworn the truth to speak upon the issue joined, upon their oaths do say that said Defendant did not pay to said Plaintiff in $20.00 current money the said sum of money in the covenant in said Plaintiffs said declaration mentioned, but that he broke said Covenant as said Plaintiff hath alledged and they do assess the said plaintiffs damages by reason thereof to two hundred and eighteen dollars besides costs.

Therefore it is considered by the court that said Plaintiff recover of said Defendant two hundred and eighteen dollars the damages aforesaid by the Jury aforesaid, in manner (p-43) and form aforesaid assessed and also his costs by him in this behalf empended and that execution issue &c.

Frederick Johns & )
John H. Kelton, admrs. )
of Wm. L. Thompson, dec'd ) Debt
Vs )
David Thompson )

This day came the parties by their attorneys and thereupon came a jury of good and lawful men, to wit: John Jones, Levi Cook, Benj. Sheeks, James H. Guy, Thomas Taylor, John Polk, Benjamin Farris, Cornelius Sheeks, William Carmack, Samuel Hutchinson, Sion Hill, Abraham Herring, who being elected, tried and sworn the truth to speak upon the issue joined upon their oath do say that said Defendant has not paid the debt in said

Plaintiff's declaration mentioned, nor has he set off against the same, but that detains from Plaintiff one hundred and forty dollars and they assess the Plaintiffs damages for detention thereof to nine dollars 18 3/4 cts. besides costs.

Thereupon it is considered by the court that said Plaintiff recover said Defendant one hundred and forty one dollars the debt aforesaid and nine dollars 18 3/4¢ the damages aforesaid & also their costs by them in this behalf expended.

Frederick Johns &  )
John H. Kelton, admrs. )
of W. L. Thompson, dec'd) Debt
Vs )
David Thompson )

This day came the parties by their attornies and thereupon came a jury of good (p-44) and lawful men, to wit: John Long, Levi Cook, Benjamin Sheeks, James H. Guy, Thomas Taylor, John Polk, Benjamin Farris, Cornelius Sheeks, William Carmack, Samuel Hutchinson, Sion Hill & Abraham Hennin who being elected tried and sworn the truth to speak upon the issue joined upon their oath do say that said Defendant has not paid the Plaintiffs Intestate the debt in said Plaintiffs declaration mentioned, but that he distrain from the said Plaintiff the sum of two hundred dollars as said Plaintiffs have obliged and they do assess said Plaintiffs damages by reason of detention thereof to four dollars & 10¢ besides costs.

It is therefore considered by the court that said Plaintiff recover of said defendants the said sum of $200 the debt aforesaid, and $4.10¢ the damages aforesaid by the jury aforesaid in manner & form aforesaid assessed & also his costs by them in & about this suit in this behalf expended.

Enus W. Wood & )
A. M. L. McBean, admrs.)
of A. C. Pagan, dec'd.) Debt Certiorari
Vs )
Thomas Allison )

This day came the parties by their attornies & thereupon by consent it was ordered by the court that this cause be continued to the next term of this court.

(p-45)   April Term 1834

McEwing & Cassady)
Vs )
Jesse S. Ross & ) Assumpsit
James M. Ross )

This day came the parties by their attorneys and the said Plaintiff by attorney here dismiss their said suit and here say they intend no further to prosecute the same.

Therefore it is considered by the court that said cause stand dismissed and that said defendants recover of said plaintiff their costs by them in & about their defence in this behalf expended and that execution issue &c.

G. W. Wood            )
A. S. M. McBean, admrs.)  Debt
Vs                    )
John Parr             )

This day came the parties by their attornies and thereupon by concent of parties it was ordered that this cause be continued to the next term of this court.

It appearing to the satisfaction of the court that Jane A. Linn requested that Joel A. Enloe should be her guardian, it was ordered by the court that he be appointed and that he enter into bond in the sum of seven thousand dollars with William Miller, William W. Watson and Joseph Wilson his securities and took the oath prescribed by law.

(p-46)   April Term 1834

The State of Tennessee)
Vs                    )  Affray
Edward Roberts        )

This day came the Defendant and moved the court for a continuance of this cause and by consent of the attorney General it was ordered by the court that it be continued to the next term of this court.

The State    )
Vs           )   Sci Fa
John Hublett )   as Juror

This day came the Defendant and made his excuse for his non attendance as a Juror at the October term of this 1833 court which was considered by the court to be sufficient therefour it was considered by the court that he be discharged and go without pay.

A Bill of sale from Stancil Moore to Lonsdale Watson was duly acknowledged in Open Court and ordered to be certified for registration.

J. M. Bedford, W. S. S. Harris & William U. Watson who were appointed commissioners to settle with Jourdan Hassel as administrators of J. C. Horton, dec'd. produced in Open Court a settlement which was ordered by the court to be rec'd. and recorded.

(p-47)   April Term 1834.

John McClure )
Vs )
W. S. S. Harris )

This day came the parties by these attornies and upon motion of the Defendants it was ordered that the Plaintiff give additional security for the prosecution of this suit the court allowing him until tomorrow evening to bring in his security.

State )
Vs ) Affray
George W. Fentress )

This day came the solicitor in behalf of the State and read his prosecution to which the Defendant pled not guilty and thereupon came a Jury of good and lawful men, to wit: John Jones, Levi Cook, Benjamin Sheeks, Thomas Taylor, John Polk, Benj. Farris, Cornelius Sheeks, James L. Brown, Saml. E. Allen, Benj. Ross, B. H. Linn who being elected tried & sworn the truth to speak upon the matters of traverse joined upon their oaths do say that the Defendant is not guilty in manner & form as charged in the indictment.

Whereupon it is considered by the court that the Defendant go hence without pay & that the said County of Obion pay the costs of this prosecution and that the clerk issue a copy of this order to the Trustee &c.

(p-48) Tuesday April Term-1834.

John Linn )
Vs )
Tyra Dabney )

This day came the Plaintiff by his attorney & filed his petition in writing & moved the court for Writs of Certiorari & Supersedes in this cause which was ordered by the court to be issued agreeably to the prayer of said petition on his giving bond with security agreeably to law.

State )
Vs )
David W. Pound )

By consent of parties this cause is continued until the next term of this court.

James B. Hogge, assignee &c )
for the use of Henry Chiger ) Sci Fa
Vs ) Motion to quash
Seth Bodford & Lysander Adams, admrs. )

This day came the parties by their consent and the Defendants here moved the court to quash the proceedings in this cause, and the matters of law arising out of the said motion to dismiss being argued and by the court, here fully understood, it seems here to the court that the law is with the Defendant. It is therefore considered by the court that the proceedings in said cause be quashed, that the Defendants (p-49) go hence thereof without pay and recovers of the said James B. Hogge the Plaintiff and of the said Henry Chiger for whose use the action is brought the cost of this suit, in this behalf expended.

    Court thus adjourned until tomorrow 8 o'clock.

                            B. Totten, J. P. in all Tuesdays minutes, except in the suit Benjamin Totten Vs George W. L. Marr & Joel S. Enloe.
                            Willis Caldwell, J. P.
                            John Parr, J. P.
                            H. B. Brown, so far as respects the suit of Benjamin Totten by G. W. L. Marr & Joel S. Enloe.

    Court met pursuant to adjournment of proclamation being proceeded to business.

Frederic John &  )
John H. Kelton, admrs.  )
of Wm. L. Thompson, dec'd.)    Trespass in this case
Vs  )
David Thompson  )

    This day came the parties by their attorneys, and thereupon the said Plaintiff here dismiss their said suit in this behalf, & say they intend no further to prosecute the same and that the consideration upon which the suit is brought is satisfied & Deft. asumes the cost &c.

    Therefore it is considered by the court that this cause stands dismissed and that the Plaintiff recover of Defendant the cost of court in this behalf &c.

(p-50)  April Term 1834.

Frederick Johns,  )
John H. Kelton, admr.  )
of Wm. L. Thompson, dec'd.)    Debt
Vs  )
David Thompson  )

    This day came the parties by their attorneys & thereupon by consent of parties it is ruled and ordered by the court that execution upon the judgment, which the plaintiff recorded against Defendant at the present Term of this court, for one hundred & forty one dollars debt & $9.18¢ damages & costs be stayed and enjoined until the expiration of three months from & after the date hereof &c.

Frederick Johns,               )
John H. Kelton, admrs.         )
of Wm. L. Thompson, dec'd.)    Debt
Vs                             )
David Thompson                 )

This day came the parties by their attorneys and thereupon by consent of parties, it is ruled & ordered by the Court, that execution of the judgment obtained by the Plaintiff against the Defendant for the sum of two hundred dollars debt & $4.10¢ damages & costs be staid and enjoined for the term of three months from & after the date thereof.

(p-51)   Wednesday April Term 9th 1834

This day before the worshipful Benjamin Totten, Willis Caldwell & John Parr, Justices of Obion County sitting & holding a Court of Pleas & Quarter Sessions for said County of Obion came into court Joel S. Enloe Sheriff and Collector of public taxes of said County and makes and presents here to the court a report in due form of Law of Sundries tracts of Land and parts of tracts of Land & Town Lots lying and being in the said County of Obion which have been given in for Taxes upon which remain due and unpaid, for the year 1833, and who for the owners and claimants thereof have no goods or chattels within said County on which to distrain for said taxes which report is here received by the court and it is ordered by the Court that the Clerk record said report which is done and reads as follows, to wit:

I, Joel S. Enloe, Sheriff and collector of the public Taxes for the County of Obion do hereby report to the court the following tracts and parts of tracts of land and town lots, the taxes upon which for the year 1833 remain due and unpaid, and that the respective owners and claimants thereof have no goods or chattels within my County on which I can distrain for said taxes, to wit:

John R. Eaton heirs, one tract of 1000 acres granted by the State of North Carolina by Grant number 147 to Abner Nash lying in the 3 & 4 Range and 7th Section, 13th District, taxes $5.62½ cents, Clerks fee $1.40, Sheriff's fee $1.00, Printers fee $1.50.

John R. Eaton heirs one tract of 1318 3/4 acres granted by the State of North Carolina to Abner Nash by grant number 150 for (p-52) 1000 acres lying in the 3 & 4 Range and 8th Section, 13th District, taxes $7.41 cents, Clerks fee $1.40 cents, Sheriff's fee $1.00, printers fees $1.50 cents.

Thomas R. L. Eaton one tract of 1000 acres granted by the State of North Carolina to Abner Nash by grant by grant no. 143 lying in the 3 &44 Range and 8th Section, 13th District, Taxes $5.62½ cents, Clerks fees $1.40 cents, Sheriffs fees $1.00, printers fees $1.50 cents.

Thomas R. L. Eaton one tract of 1175 acres granted by the State of North Carolina to Abner Nash for 1000 acres by grant number 152 lying in 3 & 4 Range & 7th Section, 13 District.  Taxes $6.60 cents, Clerks fees $1.40 cents, Sheriffs fees $1.00, Printers fees $1.50 cts.

Sarah A. and Susan Eaton one tract of 1278 acres granted by the

State of North Carolina to Abner Nash by grant number 138 per 1000 acres, lying in the 3 & 4th Range & 7 & 8th Section, 13th District, Taxes $7.18 cents, Clerks fees $1.40 cents, Sheriffs fees $1.00, printers fees $1.50 cents.

(p-53) William Flemming 313 acres part of a track of 3000 acres granted by the State of North Carolina to William Haughlett by grant no. -- dated 10th July 1788. Taxes $1.75 cents, Clerks fees $1.40 cents, Sheriffs fees $1.00, printers fees $1.50 cents.

Sarah A. and Susan Eaton one tract of 1000 acres granted by the State of North Carolina to Abner Nash by grant number 146 lying in the 3 & 4th Range & 8th Section, 13th District. Taxes $5.62½ cents, Clerks fees $1.40 cents, Sheriffs fees $1.00, printers fees $1.50.

(p-53) William Fleming one tract of 313 acres part of a tract of 3000 acres granted by the State of North Carolina to William Hublett by grant no. -- dated 10th July 1788. Taxes $1.75, Clerks fee $1.40, Sheriffs fee $1.00, printers fee $1.50.

Archibald Henderson one tract of 72 acres entry no. 466 lying in the 3rd Range, 2nd Section, 13th District. Taxes 40 cents, Clerks fee $1.40, Sheriffs fee $1.00, Printers fee $1.50.

John C. Hamilton one tract of 1128 acres part of a 5000 acre tract entered by Hugh Martin no. of entry 119, lying in the 8th Range and 6th Section. Taxes $5.34, Clerks fee $1.40, Sheriffs fee $1.00, printers fee $1.50.

Edward Hickmans heirs 640 acres, no. of entry 487 lying in the 5th Range, and 8th Section, 13th District. Taxes $3.11, Clerks fee $1.40, Sheriffs fee $1.00, printers fee $1.50.

I. P. and E. Hickman one tract of 100 acres no. of entry 480 lying in the 4th Range and 6th Section, 13 District. Taxes $3.10, Clerks fee $1.40, Sheriffs fee $1.00, printers fee $1.50.

(p-54) William Lyth 631 2/3 acres an undivided part or balance of a tract of 848 acres entry by I. C. McLemore and Lythe by entry no. 416 lying in the 9th Range, 8th Section, 13th District balance paid taxes $3.56½, Clerks fee $1.40, Sheriffs fee $1.00, printers fee $1.50.

John McAdams 100 part of a 1000 acre tract granted to Edward Harris by grant no. 14 lying in the 7th Range & 8th Section, 13th District. Taxes 56¼ cts., Clerks fee $1.40, Sheriff fee $1.00, Printers fee $1.50.

Michial McLeann 500 acres part of a tract entry in the name of G. W. L. Marr lying on the Mississippi River. Taxes $2.81¼, Clerks fee $1.40, Sheriffs fee $1.00, Printers fee $1.50.

John P. Mathews one tract of 500 acres formally owned by P. Parmer laid off out of a 1000 acre tract granted to Edward Harris lying in the 7th Range and 6th Section, 13th District. Taxes $2.81¼, Clerks fee $1.50

Sheriff fee $1.00, Printers fee $1.50.

G. W. Campbell one tract of 1000 acres part of William & Thomas, D Porter Hubletts tract of 3000 acres. Taxes $5.12½, Clerks fee $1.40, Sheriff fees $1.00, Printers fee $1.50.

(p-55)   April Term 1834.

John Page one tract of 400 acres. Taxes $2.35, Clerks fee $1.40, Sheriff fee $1.00, Printers fee $1.50.

Washington Shelton 400 acres. Taxes $2.25 cents, Clerks fee $1.40, Sheriff fee $1.00, Printers fee $1.50.

Joel R. Smith 200 acres part of a tract of 1834 acres entered in the name of A. Little, Taxes $7.12½ cents, Clerks fee $1.40, Sheriff fee $1.00, Printers fee $1.50 cents.

William Townsend one tract of 200 acres entry number 477 lying in the 3 Range & 9th Section, 13th District. Taxes $1.12½ cents, Clerks fee $1.40, Sheriffs fee $1.00, Printers fee $1.50.

I. P. & A. Taylor one tract of 640 acres entry number 144 lying in this 7th Range & 8 Section, 13th District. Taxes $3.60 cents, Clerks fee $1.40, Sheriff fee $1.00, Printers fee $1.50.

Edward Thurslys heirs one tract of 2020 acres being the balance of an original tract not conveyed away of 2500 acres entered in the name of Edward Thursly by no. of entry 9th Section, Range 5. Taxes $11.35, Clerks fee $1.40, Sheriffs fee $1.00, Printers fee $1.50.

(p-56)   April Term 1834.

Edward Thurslys heirs one tract of 1520 acres the balance of a tract not paid of 1900 acres. Entry in the name of Edward Thursly by entry no. 419 lying in the 9th Range and 8th Section 13th District. Taxes $8.50, Clerks fee $1.40, Sheriffs fee $1.00, Printers fee $1.50.

James Taylor one tract of 1000 acres granted by the State of North Carolina to Abner Nash by grant number 141 lying in the 3rd & 4th Range and 8th Section, 13th District. Taxes $5.62, Clerks fee $1.40, Sheriffs fee $1.00, Printers fee $1.50.

James Whitesell one tract of 274 acres. Entry number 211 lying in the 6 Range and 6th Section, 13th District. Taxes $1.50, Clerks fees $1.40, Sheriffs fee $1.00, Printers fee $1.50.

Hugh Ritcheys heirs one undivided fifth part of a tract granted by the State of North Carolina to J. G. and T. Blount by grant number 327 dated 10th of July 1788 for 1000 acres and annexed of said Blounts to Hugh Williams. Taxes $1.12½, Clerks fee $1.40, Sheriffs fee $1.50, Printers fee $1.50.

Hugh Ritcheys heirs one undivided fifth part of a tract granted by the State of North Carolina to J. G. & T. Blounts by grant number 217.

(p-57) dated 10th July 1788 for 1000 acres and by said Blounts conveyed to Hugh Williamson. Taxes $1.12½, Clerks fee $1.40, Sheriffs fee $1.00, Printers fee $1.50.

Hugh Ritcheys heirs one undivided fifth part of a tract granted by the State of North Carolina to J. G. & T. Blount by grant number 240 dated 10th July 1788 for 1000 acres and by said Blounts conveyed to Hugh Williamson. Taxes $1.12½, Clerks fee $1.40, Sheriff fee $1.10, Printers fee $1.50.

Hugh Ritcheys one fifth of an undivided tract granted from the State of North Carolina to John G. & Thomas Blount by grant no. 189 dated 10th July 1788 for 1000 acres and being conveyed to Hugh Williamson. Taxes $1.12½, Clerks fee $1.40, Sheriffs fee $1.00, Printers fee $1.50.

Hugh Ritcheys heirs one undivided fifth part of a tract of 1000 acres granted by the State of North Carolina to J. G. & Thomas Blount by grant no. 232 dated the 10th of July 1788 and said Blounts convey to Hugh Williamson. Taxes $1.12½, Clerks fee $1.40, Sheriffs fee $1.00, Printers fee $1.50.

Hugh Ritcheys heirs one undivided fifth part of a tract of 3000 acres grant from the State of North Carolina to J. G. & Thomas Blount by grant no. 234 dated 10th of July 1788 and by said (p-58) Blounts conveyed to Hugh Williamson. Taxes $3.37½, Clerks fee $1.40, Sheriffs fee $1.00, Printers fee $1.50.

Hugh Ritcheys heirs one undivided fifth part of a tract of 2000 acres granted by the State of North Carolina to J. G. & Thomas Blount by grant no. 246 dated 10th of July 1788 and conveyed by Blount to Hugh Williamson. Taxes $2.25, Clerks fee $1.40, Sheriffs fee $1.00, Printers fee $1.50.

Hugh Ritcheys heirs one undivided fifth part of a 1000 acre tract granted by the State of North Carolina to J. G. & Thomas Blount by grant no. 205 dated 10th July 1788 and by said Blount conveyed to Hugh Williamson Taxes $1.12½, Clerks fee $1.40, Sheriff fee $1.00, Printers fee $1.50.

Hugh Ritcheys heirs one undivided fifth part of a tract of 1000 acres granted by the State of North Carolina to John G. & Thomas Blount by grant no. 328 dated 10th of July 1788 and by said Blounts conveyed to Hugh Williamson. Taxes $1.12½, Clerks fee $1.40, Sheriffs fee $1.00, Printers fee $1.50.

Hugh Ritcheys heirs one undivided fifth part of a tract of 1000 acres granted by the State of North Carolina (p-59) to John G. & Thomas Blount by grant no. 172 dated 10th of July 1788 and one of said Blounts conveyed to Hugh Williamson. Taxes $1.12½, Clerks fee $1.40, Sheriffs fee $1.00, Printers fee $1.50.

Hugh Ritcheys heirs one undivided fifth part of a tract of 1000 acres granted from the State of North Carolina to John G. & Thomas Blounts by grant no. 252 dated 10th July 1788 and by Blounts conveyed to Hugh Williamson. Taxes $1.12½, Clerks fee $1.40, Sheriffs fee $1.00, Printers fee $1.50.

Hugh Ritcheys heirs one undivided fifth part of a tract of 1000 acres granted by the State of North Carolina to John G. & Thomas Blount by grant

No. 174 dated 10th of July 1788 and by said Blounts conveyed to Hugh Williamson, Taxes $1.12 cts., Clerks fees $1.40 cts., Sheriffs fees $1.00, Printers fee $1.50.

Hugh Ritcheys heirs undivided fifth part of a tract of 1000 acres granted by the State of North Carolina to J. G. & T. Blount by grant No. 236 dated 10th July 1788 and by said Blounts conveyed to Hugh Williamson. Taxes $1.12 cts., Clerks fee $1.40, Sheriffs fee $1.00, Printers fees $1.50.

Hugh Ritcheys heirs one undivided fifth part of a tract of 1000 acres, granted by the State of North Carolina to J. G. & T. Blount by grant number 227 dated 10th day of July 1788, and by said Blounts conveyed to Hugh (p-60) Williamson. Taxes $1.12½, Clerks fees $1.40, Sheriffs fees $1.00, Printers fees $1.50.

Hugh Ritcheys heirs one undivided fifth part of a 5000 acre tract granted by the State of North Carolina to John G. & Thomas Blount by grant number 232 dated 10th July 1788 & by said Blounts conveyed to Hugh Williamson. Taxes $5.02, Clerks fees $1.40, Sheriffs fee $1.00, Printers fees $1.50.

Hugh Ritcheys heirs, one undivided fifth part of a 5000 acre tract, granted by the State of North Carolina to J. G. & T. Blounts grant No. 2813, grant dated 10th July 1788 & by said Blounts conveyed to Hugh Williamson. Taxes $0.50½, Clerks fee $1.40, Sheriffs fees $1.00, Printers fee $1.50.

           Joel S. Enloe, Sheff
           & Collector of Obion Cty.

Whereupon it duly appearing to the satisfaction of the Court here that Justices of the peace one for each Captains Company in said County had been duly appointed to take and receive lists of taxable property & polls within said County for the year 1833. That said Justices so appointed respectively proceeded accordingly to take and receive the same, and made and return thereof unto said Court and that the same have been duly recorded by the Clerks of this Court, and it furthermore appearing here to the satisfaction of the Court from an inspection of the said record so much by the Clerk as aforesaid that therefore giving tracts of land and parts of tracts of (p-61) land are upon and from a part of said recorded lists and are lying and being in the said County and that the Clerk had within the time and in the manner prescribed by law made out and delivered to said Sheriff and Collector of Taxes, a list of Taxable property and property from said recorded lists and that said lands are liable to the small amount of taxes charged on each, and that all other matters and things required by law in this behalf to be done and performed, have been duly done and performed. It is therefore considered by the Court that judgment be and it is hereby entered against the aforesaid tracts and parts of tracts of land in the name of the State for the sum annexed to each, being the amount of Taxes, costs and charges fue severally thereon for the year 1833, and it is ordered by the Court that said small tracts of land and parts of tracts of land, or so much there of as shall be sufficient of each of them to satisfy the Taxes, costs and charged annexed to them annually be sold as the law directs.

And also here before the Justices aforesaid sitting and holding a Court as aforesaid comes Joel S. Enloe, Shff. and collector of the public Taxes for the County of Obion here into Court, and makes and presents hereunto Court, a report in due form of Law of Sundries tracts and parts of tracts of land and seven lots lying and being in said County of Obion which were -- given in for the Taxes for the year 1833, (p-62) and are liable to double Tax for said year which Taxes remain due and unpaid and wherefor the owners or claimants have no goods and chattels within said County on which to distrain for said double taxes, which said report is recorded by the Court is ordered by the Court that the Clerk receive said report which is here done in words & figures as follows, to wit:

I, Joel S. Enloe, Sheriff and Collector of the public Taxes for the County of Obion, do hereby report to Court the following tracts of land and parts of tracts of land Town Lots as having been omitted to be given in for Taxes for the year 1833 that the same is liable to double Taxes, that the double Taxes therein remain due and unpaid and that the respective owners or claimants thereof have no goods or chattels within my County on which I can distrain for said double Taxes, to wit:

One tract of land supposed to contain 1200 acres granted by the State of North Carolina to William T. Lewis by grant No. 330 for 1500 acres part of which 1500 acres is cut off by the Kentucky line lying in the 4th Range and 9 & 10 sections, 13th District. Of this report 159 3/8 acres given in and paid by Samuel L. McDaniel. Taxes $13.40 cents, Clerks fee $1.40, Sheriffs fee $1.00, Printers fee $1.50.

(p-63) One tract of land containing 500 acres entree in the name of George Wilson by Entry No. 353, 4 Range & 9 Section, 13 Dist. Taxes $5.62½, Clerks fee $1.40, Sheriffs fee $1.00, Printers fee $1.50. (fee received into office $2.40¢)

One tract of land containing 85 acres entered in the name of Daniel Montgomery by entry No. 513 lying in the 4 & 5 Range & 9th Section. Taxes 96¢, Clerks fee $1.40, Sheriffs fee $1.00, Printers fee $1.50.

One tract of land supposed to contain 1128 acres granted by the State of North Carolina to James Coor by grant No. 72 dated 10th July 1788 for 1000 acres lying in the 5th Range & 6th Section, 13th District. Taxes $12.68¢, Sheriffs fee $1.40, Printers fee $1.50.

One tract of land supposed to contain 1128 acres granted by the State of North Carolina by grant No. 85 dated -- day of July 1788 for 1000 acres lying in the 5th Range, 6 Section, 13th District. Tax $12.64, Clerks fee $1.40, Sheriffs fee $1.00, Printers fee $1.50.

(p-64)  April Term 9th 1834.

One tract of land containing 640 acres No. of entry 2, entered in the name Thomas McWrey lying in 6th Range and 7 Section, 13 District. Taxes $7.90, Clerks fee $1.40, Sheriffs fee $1.00, Printers fee $1.50.

One Tract of land containing 640 acres entered in the name of Archibald G. Anderson by entry No. 332 lying in the 5th Range, 8 & 9 Sections, 13th District. Taxes $7.20, Clerks fee $1.40, Sheriffs fee $1.00, Printers fee $1.50.

One undivided part or balance consisting of 802 acres of a tract of 1002 acres entered in the name of Andrew Barnett by entry No. 102 lying in the 5th Range and 9th Section, 13th District, balance paid by John C. McLemore. Taxes $1.69, Clerks fee $1.40, Sheriffs fee $1.00, Printers fee $1.50.

One tract of land containing 200 acres entered in the name of Thomas Wilson by entry No. 387, lying in the 5th Range & 9th Section, 13th District. Taxes $2.25, Clerks fee $1.40, Sheriffs fees $1.00, Printers fees $1.50.

(p-65)   April Term 9th day 1834.

One tract of land containing 640 acres entered in the name of Mickel Hackney heirs by entry No. 670, lying in the 5th & 6th Range, 6 Section, 13 District. Taxes $7.20, Clerks fee $1.40, Sheriffs fee $1.00, Printers fee $1.50.

George W. Campbell 2000 acres the balance of a tract of 2500 acres entered by said Campbell by entry No. 5 in 6 & 7 Range, Section 6 & 7, 13 District. After deducting 500 acres by John C. McLemore & wife, Taxes $22.30, Clerks fee $1.40, Sheriffs fee $1.00, Printers fee $1.50.

Samuel L. Winston one tract of 250 acres of land a part of a 5000 acre tract entered in the name of Joseph Winston lying in 6th Range and 9th Section, No. of entry -- 13 District. Taxes $2.81½, Clerks fee $1.40, (p-66) Sheriffs fee $1.00, Printers fee $1.50.

Lewis Winstons 500 acres laid off into a tract of 5000 acres entered in the name of Joseph Winstons lying in the 6th Range & 9 & 10 Section, 13th District. Taxes $3.62½, Clerks fees $1.40, Sheriffs fee $1.00, Printers fee $1.50.

Joel Laudettes 63 1/3 acres balance of a tract of 230 acres conveyed by A. L. Harris to said Laudetts after deducting 166 2/3 acres paid by him. Taxes 70 cts., Clerks fees $1.40, Sheriffs fee $1.00, Printers fee $1.50.

One undivided part or balance consisting of 3360 acres of a tract of 3840 acres entered in the name of Benjamin Stedman by entry No. 650 made 14th December 1822, lying in the 10th Range & 6 Section on the bank of the Mississippi in 13th District. Taxes $39.80 cents, Clerks fee $1.40, Sheriffs fee $1.00, Printers fee $1.50, balance paid John C. Mc Lemore.

Fountain Winston one tract of 500 acres laid off to said Winston out of a 5000 acres tract entered in the name of Joseph Winston by entry number 386 lying in the 6 Range, 9 & 10 Section, 13th District. Taxes $5.62½, Clerks fee $1.40, Sheriffs fee $1.00, Printers fee $1.50.

(p-67)   One tract of land containing 25 acres entered in the name of John Wood by entry number 1000 lying in Ragne --, 9th Section, 13th District. Taxes 28 cents, Clerks fee $1.40, Sheriffs fee $1.00, Printers fee $1.50.

Joseph Winston 5000 acres entry No. 386 lying in the 6th Range and 9th & 10th Section, 13 District excepting out of this report 1000 acres claimed by Fountain Winston, 400 acres by Joseph Williams heirs, 200 acres by Isaac Parks, 250 acres by Saml. L. Winston, 500 acres by Lewis Winston, 600 acres by Sarah Dalton, which leaves 1650 acres to be sold, for taxes (p-68) Taxes $18.56¼, Clerks fee $1.40, Sheriffs fee $1.00, Printers fee $1.50.

One tract of land containing 3840 acres entered in the name of the President & Trustees of the University of North Carolina by entry No. 656 lying in the 6 & 7 Range & 7 Section, 13th District and conveyed by them by Deed to James H. Wood, Thomas, Pete and Mathew Dabney, dated December 27th 1830. Taxes $43.00, Clerks fee $1.40, Sheriffs fee $1.00, Printers fee $1.50.

Daniel Masons heirs one tract of 640 acres entered in the name of Bryant Watson by entry No. 4 lying in the 7th Range & 7 Section, 13 District. Taxes $5.20, Clerks fee $1.40, Sheriffs fee $1.00, Printers fee $1.50.

One tract of land containing 640 acres entered in the name of William Scoggins by entry No. 430 lying in the 6th Range and 8th Section. Taxes $7.20, Clerks fee $1.40, Sheriffs fee $1.00, Printers fee $1.50.

One tract of land containing 150 acres entered in the name of Josias Anthony by entry No. 391 lying in the 6th Range & 9th Section & 13th District. Taxes $1.68, Clerks fee $1.40, Sheriffs fee $1.00, Printers fee $1.50.

(p-69) April Term 1834.

One tract of land containing 489¼ entered in the name of William E. Anderson by entry No. 357 lying in the 6 Range and 9 & 10th Section, 13th District. Taxes $5.50, Clerks fee $1.40, Sheriffs fee $1.00, Printers fee $1.50.

One tract of land containing 134 acres entered in the name of Callow Wheeton by entry NO. 1855 lying in the 7th Range & 6th Section, 13 District. Taxes $1.40, Clerks fee $1.40, Sheriffs fee $1.00, Printers fee $1.50.

One tract of land containing 640 acres entered in the name of Thomas Henderson by entry No. 368 lying in the 7th Range, 6 Section, 13 District. Taxes $7.20, Clerks fee $1.40, Sheriffs fee $1.00, Printers fee $1.50.

One tract of land containing 284 acres entered in the name of Daniel McKinley by entry No. 450 lying in the 7th Range & 7th Section, 13 Distric Taxes $3.20, Clerks fee $1.40, Sheriffs fee $1.00, Printers fee $1.50.

(p-70) April Term.

One tract of land containing 266½ acres entered in the name of Ann and Henry by entry number 686 lying in the 6 & 7 Range and 9th Section, 13 District. Taxes $3.00, Clerks fee $1.40, Sheriffs fee $1.00, Printers fee $1.50.

One tract of land containing 640 acres entered in the name of Jno. Anderson by entry number 363 lying in the 7th Range and 9th Section, 13th District. Taxes $7.20, Clerks fee $1.40, Sheriffs fee $1.00, Printers fee $1.50.

One tract of land containing 640 acres entered in the name of Hardy Winford entry number 364 lying in the 7 Range & 9th Section, 13th District. Taxes $7.20, Sheriffs fees $1.00, Clerks fees $1.40, Printers fees $1.50.

John C. Hamiltons heirs 640 acres entered in the name of Edmund Diggs entry number 429 lying in the 7th Range & 9th Section, 13 District. Taxes $7.20, Clerks fee $1.40, Sheriffs fee $1.00, Printers fee $1.50.

One tract of land supposed to contain 833 1/3 acres being that part of a tract of 2500 acres granted by the State of North Carolina to Ephsium McLain by grant number 159 which lies in Obion County in the 8th and 9th Range and 6th Section, 13th District. Taxes $9.37, Clerks fees $1.40, Sheriffs fees $1.00, Printers fee $1.50.

(p-71) April Term 1834.

Jonathan Hampton one tract of land containing 1500 acres granted by the State of North Carolina to William T. Lewis by grant No. 166 lying in the 8th Range and 9th Section, 13 District. Taxes $16.87, Clerks fees $1.40, Sheriffs fees $1.00, Printers fee $1.50.

William M. Berryhill one undivided part or balance consisting of 605 acres of a tract of 756 3/4 acres entry number 422 lying in the 9 & 10 Range and 7th Section, 13th District. Taxes $6.80, Clerks fees $1.40, Sheriffs fee $1.00, Printers fee $1.50.

One undivided part or balance consisting of 152 acres of a tract of 197 acres entered in the name of William Hitly heirs by entry number 425 lying in 9th Range, 7th Section, 13th District. Taxes $17.10, Clerks fees $1.40, Sheriffs fee $1.00, Printers fee $1.50.

One tract of land containing 600 acres being that part of a tract of 1200 acres granted by the State of North Carolina to Hubert Holmes by grant number 371 which lied in Obion County lying in the 3 & 4 Range and 6 Section, 13th District. Taxes $6.75, Clerks fee $1.40, Sheriffs fee $1.00, Printers fee $1.50.

One tract of land containing 200 acres being that part of a tract of 600 acres granted by the State of North Carolina to Anna -- by grant number 33 which lies in Obion County in the 3 &4th Range and 6th Section, 13 District. Taxes $2.25, Sheriffs fee $1.00, Printers $1.50, Clerks fee $1.40.

One tract of land containing 120 acres entered in the name of Alvin D. Williams by entry number 712 lying in the 4 Range and 6th Section, 13 District. Taxes $1.45, Clerks fee $1.40, Sheriffs fee $1.00, Printers fee $1.50.

(p-72)   April Term 1834.

One tract of land containing 1000 acres entered in the name of Isiah P. Hackett by entry number 497 lying in the 5th Range and 7 & 8th Sections, 13th District. Taxes $11.12½, Clerks fee $1.40, Sheriffs fee $1.00, Printers fee $1.50.

One tract of land containing 1854 acres entered in the name of Joseph Kerr by entry number 442 lying in the 9 & 10 Range, 6 & 7 Section, 13 District. Taxes $20.87, Clerks fee $1.40, Sheriffs fee $1.00, Printers fee $1.50.

One tract of land containing 1500 acres entered in the name of name of William Murphy by entry number 432 lying in the 8 & 9th Range and 7th Section, 13 District -- out of this report 102 acres paid in by McLemore which leaves 1398 acres reported. Taxes $15.72, Clerks fees $1.40, Sheriffs fee $1.00, Printers fee $1.50.

One tract of land containing 191 acres entered in the name of Trust & McMillan by entry number 143 lying in the 6 Range, 7 Section, 13 District. Taxes $2.14, Clerks fees $1.40, Sheriffs fee $1.00, Printers fee $1.50.

One tract of land containing 1000 acres granted by the State of North Carolina to John G. & Thomas Blount by grant number 244 dated 10th of July 1788 lying in the 3 & 4 Range and 6th Section of the 13 District. Taxes $11.12½, Clerks fee $1.40, Sheriffs fee $1.00, Printers fee $1.50.

Isham Boyce heirs 640 acres entered in the name of John Linell by entry number 711 lying in the 8 & 9th Range and 9th Section, 13 District. Taxes $7.20, Sheriffs fee $1.00, Clerks fee $1.00, Printers fee $1.50.

Isham Boyce heirs 640 acres entry number 712 in the name of Jno. Lenell lying in the 8 & 9 Range and 9th Section, 13th District. Taxes $7.20, Clerks fees $1.40, Sheriffs fee $1.00, Printers fee $1.50.

One tract of land containing 2500 acres entered in the name of Robert Naul by entry No. 535 lying in the 10 & 11th Range and 6th Section of the 13 District. Taxes $28.12½, Clerks fee $1.40, Sheriffs fee $1.00, Printers fee $1.50.

One tract of land containing 1000 acres granted by the State of Tennessee to Edward Harris by Grant number 14, dated 10th of July 1788 lying in the 7 Range and 6 Section, 13th District. Taxes $11.12½, Clerks fee $1.40, Sheriffs fee $1.00, Printers fee $1.50.

One tract of land containing 1000 acres granted by the State of (p-73) North Carolina to Edward Harris grant number 10, dated 10th of July 1788, lying in the 7th Range and 7th Section, 13th District. Taxes $11.12½, Clerks fee $1.40, Sheriffs fee $1.00, Printers fee $1.50.

One tract of land containing 1000 acres granted by the State of North Carolina to Edward Harris by Grant number 6, dated 10th of July 1788 lying in the 7th Range and 6th Section, 13th District. Taxes $11.12½, Clerks fee $1.40, Sheriffs fee $1.00, Printers fee $1.50.

One tract of land containing 1000 acres granted by the State of North Carolina to Edward Harris by grant number 7, dated 10th of July 1788 lying in the 7 & 8th Range and 6 & 7 Section, 13 District. Taxes $11.12½, Clerks fees $1.40, Sheriffs fee $1.00, Printers fee $1.50.

(p-74)    April Term.

One undivided part or balance consisting of 1400 acres of a tract of 2000 acres entered in the name of Wheaton & Lindell by entry number 420 lying in the 9th Range & 8th Section, 13th District. Balance paid by H. McLemore & Vaughn. Taxes $15.10, Clerks fee $1.40, Sheriffs fee $1.00, Printers fee $1.50.

One tract of land of 1834 acres entered in the name of Archibald Lyth by entry number 181 lying in the 4 & 5th Range and 9th Section, 13th District, including out of this report 355 acres paid by McLemore and 200 acres given in by Joel R. Smith which leaves 1279 acres of original tract hereby reported. Taxes $14.00, Clerkd fee $1.40, Sheriffs fee $1.00, Printers fee $1.50.

Heirs of Eli Harris one tract of 168 acres being lot No.11 laid off to Eli Harris heirs by a Decree of the Chancery Court at Paris out of a grant of 1000 acres to Edward Harris granted by the State of North Carolina by grant No. 15, dated 10th July 1788 lying in the 7 & 8 Range and 6th Section, 13 District. Taxes $1.88, Clerks fee $1.40, Sheriffs fee $1.00, Printers fee $1.50.

James McColum & May, his wife, one tract of 129 acres being lot No. 12 laid off to them by a Decree of Chancery Court at Paris out of a tract of 1000 acres granted by the State of North Carolina to Edward Harris by Grant number 15 dated 10th of July 1788 lying in the 7th & 8th Range and 6th Section, 13th District. Taxes $1.45, Clerks fee $1.40, Sheriffs fee $1.00, Printers fee $1.50.

(p-75)    April Term 1834.

James McColum & wife one tract of 185 acres being Lot No. 12 laid off to them by Decree of the Chancery Court at Paris out of a Grant of 1000 acres granted by the State of North Carolina to Edwin Harris by Grant number 9, dated 10th July 1788, lying in the 7 Range and 6 & 7 Section, 13th District. Taxes $2.08, Clerks fees $1.40, Sheriffs fee $1.00, Printers fee $1.50.

Heirs of Eli Harris one tract of 250 acres being Lot No. 11 laid off to them by a Decree of the Chancery Court at Paris out of a 1000 acre tract granted by the State of North Carolina to Edward Harris by Grant number 11 dated 10th July 1788, lying in -- Range, Section --, 13 District. Taxes $2.81¼, Clerks fee $1.40, Sheriffs fee $1.00, Printers fee $1.50.

Heirs of William Harris one tract of 250 acres being lot No. 7 laid off to said heirs by a decree of the Chancery Court at Paris out of a tract of 1000 acres granted by the State of North Carolina to Edward Harris by Grant No. 16, Dated 10th July 1788, Taxes $2.81, Clerks fee $1.40, Sheriffs fee $1.00, Printers fee $1.50.

Samuel Harris 250 acres being lot No. 10 laid off to said Harris by Decree of the Chancery Court at Paris out of a tract of 1000 acres granted by the State of North Carolina to Edward Harris by grant No. 16 dated 10th July 1788. (p-76) Taxes $2.81, Clerks fee $1.40, Sheriffs fee $1.00, Printers fee $1.50.

Robert McCord 250 acres of land Lot No. 6 laid off to said McCord by a decree of the Chancery Court at Paris and out of a tract of 1000 acres granted by the State of North Carolina to Edward Harris by grant No. 16 dated 10th July 1788. Taxes $2.81, Clerks fee $1.40, Sheriffs fee $1.00, Printers fee $1.50.

James Harris one tract of land of 168 acres being lot No 1 laid off to said James Harris by a Decree of the Chancery Court at Paris out of a tract of 1000 acres granted by the State of North Carolina to Edward Harris by grant No. 4, dated the 10th July 1788, lying in the 7 Range & 6th Section, 13th District. Taxes $1.89, Clerks fee $1.40, Sheriffs fee $1.00, Printers fee $1.50.

One tract of original tract 622 acres entered in the name of Edward Harris (p-77) By entry 421 lying in the 9th Range & 7 & 8 Section, 13 District. 40 acres laid off to A. Province, 40 acres laid off to Stephenson, 40 acres laid off to M. Rosbrough, 40 acres to Abner Harris, the location intrust 126 acres given in for taxes $4.98, Clerks fee $1.40, Sheriffs fee $1.00, Printers fee $1.50.

Thomas Davidson one tract of 1100 acres being the balance of a tract of 3000 acres granted by the State of North Carolina to Thomas Davidson by grant No. 44 lying in 4 & 5 Range and 6 & 7 Section. After deducting a tract of 1400 acres paid by Samuel Ragsdale, Taxes $18.00, Clerks fee $1.40, Sheriffs fee $1.00, Printers fee $1.50.

Jane Davidson 1775 acres being the balance of a tract of 2000 acres granted by the State of North Carolina to Jane Davidson by Grant No. 52 after deducting 225 acres paid by -- lying in the 5th Range & 6th Section, 13th District. Taxes $19.81, Clerks fee $1.40, Sheriffs fee $1.00, Printers fee $1.50.

Isaac Parker one tract of 200 acres part of a tract of 5000 acres entered in the name of Joseph Winston by Entry No. 386 lying in 6th Range, 9th Section, 13 District. Taxes $2.25, Clerks fee $1.40, Sheriffs fee $1.00, Printers fee $1.50.

(p-78) April Term 1834.

One tract of land of 1000 acres granted by the State of North Carolina to John G. & Thomas Blount, Grant number 226 dated 10th July 1788 lying in the 7th Range and 8th Section of the 13th District. Taxes $11.12½, Clerks fee $1.40, Sheriffs fee $1.00, Printers fee $1.50.

Henry Winthrop 5000 acres entry number 214 lying in the 7th range & 6th Section of the 13th District on Bib Clover Lick Creek excepting out of this report 1550 acres assessed to Gideon Pillow and 1333 acres laid off to White Dunlapp and Johnson and 225 acres conveyed to Luke Lieman which leaves 1892 acres of the original tract being reported. Taxes $21.28, Clerks fee $1.40, Sheriffs fee $1.00, Printers fee $1.50.

One tract of land containing 400 acres granted by the State of North Carolina to Wlycoff & Clark grant number 57, dated 10th of July 1788, lying in the 9th Range and 7th Section of the 13th District. Taxes $4.36¼, Clerks fee $1.40, Sheriffs fee $1.00, Printers fee $1.50.

One tract of land containing 390 acres granted by the State of North Carolina to Wycoff & Clark by grant number 82 dated 10th of July 1788, lying in the 9th Range and 7th Section of the 13 District. Taxes $4.36¼, Clerks fee $1.40, Sheriffs fee $1.00, printers fee $1.50.

(p-79) April Term 1834.

Wm. C. Carmac 1 Lot in town of Troy, lot No. 8 Taxes $1.50, Clerks fee $1.40, Sheriffs fee $1.00, Printers fee $1.50.

Wm. C. Carmac 1 town lot in Troy, No. 25. Tax $11.50, Clerks fee $1.40, Sheriffs fee $1.00, Printers fee $1.50.

Jno. W. Gibson 1 town lot in Troy, No 47. Tax $1.50, Clerks fee $1.40, Sheriffs fee $1.00, Printers fee $1.50.

G. W. Gibson 1 lot in town of Troy, No. 48. Taxes $1.50, Clerks fees $1.40, Sheriffs fee $1.00, Printers fee $1.50.

G. W. Gibson 1 lot in No. 50. Tax $1.50, Clerks fee $1.40, Sheriffs fee $1.00, Printers fee $1.50.

G. W. Gibson 1 town lot in Troy No. 81. Tax $1.50, Clerks fee $1.40, Sheriffs fee $1.00, Printers fee $1.50.

Wm. Posts heirs 1 town lot in Troy, No. 9. Clerks fee $1.40, Taxes $11.10, Sheriffs fee $1.00, Printers fee $1.50.

Jerimiah Westcott one half being the South half of Lts. No. 15 in Town of Troy. Taxes $10.75, Clerks fee $1.40, Sheriffs fee $1.00, Printers fee $1.50.

Jno Lieman 1 Town Lot in Troy No. 16. Taxes $1.50, Sheriffs fee $1.00, Clerks fee $1.40, Printers fee $1.50.

J. G. Edmund 1 Town Lot in Troy No. 26. Taxes $11.50, Clerks fee $1.40, Sheriffs fee $1.00, Printers $1.50.

J. G. Edmund 1 Lot in Town of Troy No. 28. Taxes $1.50, Clerks fee $1.40, Sheriffs fee $1.00, Printers fee $1.50.

Heirs of Will Willingham one Lot in Town of Troy No. 33. Taxes $1.50, Sheriffs fee $1.00. Clerks fee $1.40, Printers fee $1.50.

Wm. Ratcliff 1 Lot in Town of Troy No. 34. Taxes $1.50, Clerks fee

$1.40, Sheriffs fee $1.00, Printers fee $1.50.

M. G. Johns 1 lot in Town of Troy No. 38. Taxes $1.50, Clks. fee $1.40, Sheriffs fee $1.00, Printers fee $1.50.

John Lieman 1 lot in Town of Troy No. 44. Taxes $1.50, Clerks fee $1.40, Sheriffs fee $1.00, Printers fee $1.50.

Wm. Willingham 1 Town lot in Troy No. 49. Taxes $1.50, Clks. fee $1.40, Sheriffs fee $1.00, Printers fee $1.50.

(p-80) April Term 1834.

One lot in Town of Troy, owner not known, number 50. Taxes $1.50, Clerks fee $1.40, Sheriffs fee $1.00, Printers fee $1.50.

One lot in Town of Troy, owner not known, number 53. Taxes $1.50, Clerks fee $1.40, Sheriffs fee $1.00, Printers fee $1.50.

One lot in Town of Troy, owner not known, number 59. Taxes $1.50, Clerks fee $1.40, Sheriffs fee $1.00, Printers fee $1.50.

Amy Ratliff 1 town lot in Troy No. 63. Taxes $1.50, Clerks fee $1.40, Sheriffs fee $1.00, Printers fee $1.50.

Jno. Polk 1 town lot in Troy No. 67. Tax $1.50, Clerks fee $1.40, Sheriffs fee $1.00, Printers fee $1.50.

James Buin 1 lot in Troy No. 70. Taxes $1.50, Clerks fee $1.40, Sheriffs fee $1.00, Printers fee $1.50.

One lot in Town of Troy, owners name not known, number 75. Taxes $1.50, Clerks fee $1.40, Sheriffs fee $1.00, Printers fee $1.50.

One lot in Town of Troy, owners name not known, No 76. Taxes $1.50, Clks. fee $1.40, Sheriffs fee $1.00, Printers fee $1.50.

One lot in Town of Troy, owners name not known, No. 83. Taxes $1.50, Clerks fee $1.40, Sheriffs fee $1.00, Printers fee $1.50.

One lot in Town of Troy, owners name not known, number 84. Taxes $1.50, Clks. fee $1.40, Sheriffs fee $1.00, Printers fee $1.50.

One lot in Town of Troy, owners name not known, number 86. Taxes $1.50, Clks. fee $1.40, Shff. fee $1.00, Printers fee $1.50.

One lot in Town of Troy, owners name not known, number 92. Taxes $1.50, Clk. fee $1.40, Shff. fee $1.00, printers fee $1.50.

One lot in Town of Troy, owners name not known, number 93. Taxes $1.50, Clk. fee $1.40, Sheff. fee $1.00, Printers fee $1.50.

(p-81) April Term 1834.

One lot in Town of Troy, owners name not known, number 95. Taxes $1.50, Clks. fee $1.40, Shffs. fee $1.00, Printers fee $1.50.

One lot in Town of Troy, owners name not known, number 94. Taxes $1.50, Clks. fee $1.40, Shffs. fee $1.00, Printers fee $1.50.

Joel Enloe, Sheriff and<br>Collector of Obion County.

Whereupon it is considered by the Court that Judgment be and it is hereby entered against the aforesaid tracts and parts of tracts of land and Town Lots in the name of the State for the sum annexed to each being the amount of Double Taxes, cash and charges due severally thereon for the year 1833, and it is ordered by the Court that said small tracts of land and parts of tracts of land and Town Lots or so much thereof as shall be sufficient of each of them to satisfy the Double Taxes, costs and charges assessed therein severally be sold as the law directs.

John McClure )
Vs ) Appeal
W. S. S. Harris)

This day came William Cathey into Court & here acknowledged himself as Security for the Plaintiff for the Prosecution of this suit, or in case he fail and the Court therein pay & satisfy all such costs & charges as may be recovered against him for services. Whereupon by consent of the parties the cause may continue till the next term of this court.

(p-82)   Ordered by the Court that the reviewed commissioners settle with John C. Wilson, former Trustee of said County of Obion, & report the same to the next term of this Court.

Ordered by the Court that the reviewed commissioners in their settlement with the Sheriff of Obion County, credit him the said Sheriff with the taxes due on 2846 2/3 acres of land, listed in 1833, but not yet collected as appears by his report &c.

Robert B. Harper Executor of all & singular the goods & chattels, rights & credits which were of Andrew Lieman, Dec'd, returned here in Court an inventory of the goods & effects, rights &c, sworn to, which was rec'd. by the Court, and ordered to be recorded.

John Parr, Justice of the Peace in & for Obion County, returned here in Court, a list of taxable property for the year 1834 in Captain Williams Company, which was received and ordered to be recorded.

(p-83)   April term 1834.

Willis Caldwell returned here in Court a list of taxable property given in for taxes, for the 1834, for Captain Henry's Company, which was rec'd. and ordered to be recorded.

State of Tennessee )
Vs ) Riot
James Walker )

  This day came the solicitors, who prosecutes for the State and the said Defendant, James Walker, being solemnly called to come into court to answer the aforesaid charged, according to the taxes and effect of his said recognisance entered into at the last term of this Court, came not but made default.

  Therefore it is considered by the Court that the State of Tennessee recover of said Defendant two hundred and fifty dollars, the amount of his said recognisance, unless he the said Defendant appear here at the next term of this Court and show cause to the contrary & that Sci. Fa issue to make known &c.

State of Tennessee )
Vs ) Riot
James Walker )

  This day the solicitor who prosecutes for the State, and the said Defendant being solemnly called came not but made default and thereupon John McDaniel, who was security of said Defendant for his appearance here at the present term of this court to answer the aforesaid charges being solemnly called to come into Court and bring with him the body of James Walker the said Defendant (p-84) came not but made default.

  Thereupon it is considered by the Court that the State of Tennessee recover of the said John McDaniel, two hundred and fifty dollars the amount of his recognisance entered into in this behalf, unless he appears here at the next term of this court and show cause to the contrary and that Sci. Fa. issue to make known &c.

State of Tennessee )
Vs ) Forfeiture
John Payne )

  This day came the solicitor who prosecutes for the State, & it being made to appear to the Court that John Payne the said Defendant was duly summoned by subpoena to appear here at the present term of this court to give evidence & testify in behalf of the plaintiff in a prosecution here pending in the name of the State of Tennessee against Cornelius Sheoks for selling spirituous liquors illegally near a place of public worship and the said John Payne being here solemnly called to come into court according to the exigence of said subpoena, came not but made default.

  Therefore it is considered by the court that the State of Tennessee recover of said John Payne one hundred and twenty five dollars by marring the premises unless he appear here at the next term of this Court and show cause to the contrary & that Sci. Fa issue &c.

(p-85) April term 1834.

State of Tennessee )
Vs ) Selling spirituous liquors near a place of Public
Cornelius Sheeks ) Worship.

Ordered by the Court that an alias capias issue against the defendant, that he be before the Court at the next term of this court to answer the aforesaid charges.

John Edmond )
Vs ) Debt
John D. Dickey )

This day came the parties by their Attorneys John Parr, Richard B. Brown & Benjamin Totten, Justices being present holding said court & thereupon by consent of parties it was ordered by the Court this cause be transferred to the Circuit Court of Obion County, to be holden in May next.

Eachbaum & Norvell )
Vs ) Assumpsit
Charles McAlister )

This day came the parties by their attorneys & thereupon by consent it is ordered by the court that a general order to take depositions be made each party, giving to the others legal notice of the time & place of taking &c.

Jonathan Badget )
Vs ) Sci-facias
Robert Dickinson )

This day came the parties by their attorneys and thereupon by consent it is ordered by the Court that this cause be continued to the next term of this court.

(p-86) April Term 1834.

Mathew Young )
Vs )
Lysander Adams & Seth Bedford, admrs. of ) Sci-Fa, Demurrer to Dafts. pleas.
Jonas Bedford, Dec'd. )

This day came the parties by their attorneys and thereupon came on the Plaintiff demurrer to Defendants plea to be agreed and it appears here to the Court that the Law is with the Plaintiff. It is therefore considered by the Court that the Plaintiff -- to the Defendants pleas be sustained and the Defendants having failed to make any other defence, it is considered by the Court that the Plaintiff have executed judgment against the Defendants for the sum of fourteen dollars & 23 cents it being the amount of the Judgment heretofore rendered in this case on the 8th day of January 1833, also the costs of said suit before the Justice of the Peace amounting to $1.00 and that he recover against said Defendants the costs of their

Sci. fa for all which execution may issue to be levied first of the goods and chattels of the Intestate in their hand are administered if any there be, and if not then to be levied of the proper goods & chattels, lands and tenaments of said Defendants.

(p-87)  April Term.

Samuel D. Wilson         )
Vs                       )   Sci fa
Lysander Adams and       )   Demurrer to Defts.
Seth Bedford, Admr.      )   Pleas.
of Jonas Bedford, Dec'd. )

    This day came the parties by their attornies and thereupon came in Defendants pleas to the agreement on Plaintiff to be assigned and it appears here to the Court it is therefore agreed that the demand be sustained that the law is with the plaintiff & Defts. make no further defence. It is therefore considered by the court that the plaintiff recover against the Defendant and have Judgment and Execution against them for the sum of seventy five dollars the Judgment rendered by the Justice on the 8th day of January 1833 with the sum of $1 the costs of said Judgment and recover against the Defendants the cost of their sci facias for all which mention shall issue to be levied first of the goods and chattels of said Intestate in their hand to be administered if any there be and if not then to be levied of the proper goods & chattels, lands and tenements of said Defendants.

    This day William U. Watson and S. S. Henry, commissioners heretofore appointed & Seth Bedford, admrs. of Jonas Bedford, Dec'd. made a petition of a settlement which is received by the Court & recorded.

(p-88)  April term 1834.

    Court adjourned until tomorrow morning 9 o'clock.

                                            B. Totten, J. P.
                                            John Parr, J. P.
                                            Willis Caldwell, J. P.

Thursday, April 10th.

    Court met pursuant to adjournment.

    Ordered by the Court that William U. Watson be appointed commissioners to attend with A. W. L. McBain and Scott Wood, Administrators of Anderson C. Payne, Dec'd. and make returns thereof with secret decree of this Court.

    Court adjourned until Court in course.

(p-89)  July 7th A. D. 1834.

State of Tennessee ) Court of Pleas and Quarter Sessions July Term, 1834.
Obion County )

Be it remembered that at a Court of Pleas and Quarter Sessions begun and held at the Courthouse in the Town of Troy in the County of Obion and State of Tennessee on the first Monday in July A. D. 1834 being the 7th day of July 1834 present the worshipful John Parr, James Henderson, Willis Caldwell, John Harpole, Benjamin Totten, Wm. M. Wilson, R. B. Brown, Wm. Downey & William Wilkinson, Justices of the Peace in and for said County commissioned and assigned to hold said term of the said court proclamation being made the court thereupon proceeded to business.

A Bill of sale from William Parr executor of the last will of John Parr, Senior, dec'd. to John Parr, Jr. for a negro man slave named Charles was produced in open Court and the executor thereof duly proven by the oath of J. C. Kindred and James Parr subscribing witnesses thereto, and thereon it was ordered by the court that the same be certified for registration &c.

A Bill of sale from William Parr executor of the last will of John Parr, senr. dec'd to John Parr, Jr. for a negro woman slave named Lucy was produced in open court and execution thereof duly proved by the oath of James C. Kindred & James Parr subscribing witnesses thereto and thereon for registration.

(p-90) July term A. D. 1834.

William Parr administrator of all and singular the goods and chattels, rights and credits of Polly Parr, dec'd. to John Parr, Jr. for two negro slaves named Peggy and Emmalin, was produced in open court and the executor thereof duly proven by the oath of J. C. Kindred and James Parr, subscribing witnesses thereto & thereon it was ordered by the court that the same be certified for registration.

William Andrews, administrator of all and singular the goods and chattels, rights and credits of Enos Hay, dec'd. produced here in court an inventory of the estate of said intestate which was received by the court & thereon the same was ordered to be recorded. And the said William Andrews administrator as aforesaid produced here in court an account and statement of the sales of the estate of said Enos Hay dec'd together with a statement thereon that certain property therein named and which is also included in the inventory aforesaid, was set apart by commissioners for the sustainance and support of the widow & children of the said Enos Hay, dec'd. for one year all which was recovered with the report of said Commissioners and was ordered to be recorded.

It being made to appear to the court that James M. Ross has departed this life, to wit as the -- day of June A. D. 1834, that at the time of his death his usual place residence was in the said County of Obion, and that he (p-91) died intestate, no other person appearing to administer on his estate, on motion, it was ordered by the Court that Richard B. Brown, a creditor be appointed administrator of all and singular the goods and chattels, rights and credits, which were of said James M. Ross, dec'd. at the time of his death, and thereon the said Richard B. Brown took the oath prescribed by law, entered into bond with security as administrator as aforesaid, and took upon himself the burden of administrative said estate.

On motion it was ordered by the Court that Moses D. Harper have leave to alter the road leading from Troy to Dresden leaving the present road at the foot of the hill one half mile west of said Harpers, running east so as to intersect the said Dresden road at the dry fork of Davidsons Creek, and he, the said Harper, binds himself to put a good bridge across the branch which it will cross by said alterations and make said road equally as good as the present.

On motion it was ordered by the Court that Catharin R. Davidson be appointed administratrix of all and singular the goods and chattels of Andrew W. Davidson, deceased, by her entering into bond with security according to law, whereupon she entered into bond in the sum of one thousand dollars with Samuel D. Wilson & William Carter her securities and took the oath prescribed by law and that letters testamentary issue accordingly.

Samuel Mosier proved in Open Court the killing of a wolf within the limits of this County (p-92) over four months old, it is therefore considered by the Court, five acting Justices present, that he receive of the Treasurer of West Tennessee according to law. It appearing to the court that Joshia Nelms has departed this life, to wit on the day of June — 1834 that the usual place of his residence at the time of his death was in Obion County and that he made no last will.

On motion it was ordered by the Court that Samuel Nelms be appointed Administrator of all and singular the goods and chattels of Joshia Nelms, deceased, on condition that he enter into bond with security whereupon he entered into bond in the sum of one thousand dollars with Francis Taylor and Samuel Hutchinson his securities and took the oath prescribed by law and that letters testamentary issue accordingly.

William Miller receiver of A. Linn, deceased, presented in Open Court an account of sixty four dollars twelve and a half cents against the estate of Andrew Linn, deceased, which was considered just by the Court and ordered by the Court to be received and recorded.

On motion it was ordered by the Court that Alfred Nelms be appointed overseer on the Trenton Road from Obion River at Fentress Ferry to the Gibson County line, and that all the hands who worked under Alfred Harget work under him and all others in said bounds and that he make the same a first class road.

On motion it was ordered by the Court that Larkin Eastridge, Josh Mosier, Samuel Mosier, Richard Davis, William Hutchinson and Daniel Law be appointed a jury of view to mark and lay off a road from Terriels Ferry on Obion River, in the direction to Mills Point, Ky. to the State line so as to pass through the neighborhood of William Hutchinson, and Richard Davis on (p-93) the State line, and that they report and make return of their view to the next term of this court.

On motion ordered by the Court that Lewis Zachery, William Miller and Jerome Miller be appointed commissioners to settle with Richard Merriwether as administrator of David Farley, deceased, estate.

Lewis Zachrey came into court & proved the killing of five wolves within the limits of Obion County under four months old, it is therefore

ordered by the Court that he receive of the Treasurer of West Tennessee according to Law, five acting Justices being present.
Issued August 15th 1834.

Samuel Reeves came into Court and moved the killing of two wolves over four months old within the limits of this County by the oath of Urias Reeves, it is therefore ordered by the Court, five acting Justices present, that he receive of the Treasurer of West Tennessee according to Law.
(Issued)

Starkey Purvis came into open court and proved the killing of one wolf over four months old within the limits of this county, it is therefore considered by the Court, five acting Justices present, that he receive of the Treasurer of West Tennessee according to the law.

James H. Davis and Jubilee M. Bedford, revenue commissioners for the County of Obion, returned into court a settlement, with Joel S. Enloe, Sheriff of said County, which was ordered by the Court to be received & recorded, which settlement was for the years 1830-1831, 1832 & 1833.
(Issued)

(p-94) On motion it was ordered by the Court that Frederick Taylor be appointed overseer on the Dresden road from Nelms ferry on Obion River to within three miles of the Weakley County line, and that all the hands that formally worked under Thomas Nelms, and all in said bounds, work under him and that he make the same a first class road.

On motion it was ordered by the Court that William O. Lindsey be appointed overseer in the Dresden Road from the Weakley County line to the three mile post from said line in Obion County, and that all the hands that formally worked under John F. Abington and in said bounds work under him and that he make the same a first class Road.

A Deed of bargain and sale for 335 acres of land from Eldridge B. Robertson to Thomas Taylor was proven in open court by the oath of Joseph Taylor and John T. Abington, subscribing witnesses thereunto and ordered by the court to be certified for registration.

Joel S. Enloe, guardian for Jane A. Linn produced in open court an Inventory of goods and chattels of the Estate of Andrew Linn, deceased, which was ordered by the court to be received and recorded.

William Parr, administrator of all and singular the goods and chattels, rights and credits of Polly Parr, Dec'd., returned into court an account of sales of said Estate, which was ordered by the Court to be received and recorded.

(p-95) Lewis Zachary, William Miller & Jerome Miller who were appointed commissioners to settle with Richard T. Merriwether as administrators of David Farley, Dec'd. returned into Court their report of a settlement which was ordered to be received and recorded.

On motion it was ordered by the Court that William F. Smith be appointed overseer on the Trenton Road from Troy to the three mile post and that all the hands that formally worked under Jesse M. Ross and in said bounds work under him and that he make the same a first class road.

On motion it was ordered by the Court that Larkin Norrid, Jeremiah Norrid, Jesse Farmer, William Carter & Richard Nelms, be appointed a Jury of view to mark out and alter the road from three quarters of a mile in the direction of Troy from Thomas Taylors so as to intersect the Dresden or present road at the bridge on Cane Creek, and that they report the next term of this court.

On motion it was ordered by the Court that Thomas Polk be appointed overseer on the Trenton road from the three mile post to Obion River at Fentress ferry, and that all the hand that formally worked under Abram Enloe and in said bounds work under him, and that he make the same a first rate road.

On motion it was ordered by the Court that the Revenue Commissioners have till the next term of this Court to settle with John C. Wilson, former Trustee of this county and it is further ordered by the court that the said commissioners (p-96) have power to issue superior writs capias and all other process which they may think expedient and advantageous to said settlement commanding said persons to be brought before them to give evidence in such matters as relates to the same and that they have the use of all books, papers, and documents belonging to the clerks office or in the hands of the Sheriff of said county and that they have power to do all and every matter and thing that they deem necessary to the speedy arrangement of said settlement and that they report to the next term of this court.

On motion it was ordered by the court that Frances Taylor, James Watkins, William Sweden, William Cunningham and Henry Logan be appointed a Jury of view to make out a road from the mouth of Indian Creek on Reelfoot Lake to James Wilsons on the Iron Bank road in the direction to Filiecand Ky., and that they report to the next term of this court.

Ordered by the Court that George W. Maxwell be appointed overseer on the Mills Point Road from the County line near Tottens Wells to the four mile post (to wit) Beginning at said four mile Tree on said road running thence North to the State line at the East Side of the Black Swamp thence East with the State line to Issac Reeves thence South and by G. B. Tottens so as to include Abram Herring, William Harpers (p-97) John Doxey and one half of said Tottens lands and from thence with the Weakley County line to the North fork of Obion River thence down said River to the North of Harris fork and from thence Northwardly to the North corner of the widow Birds plantation to the road thence down said road to the line of Judge -- 1000 acre survey thence northward to said 4 mile tree on the Mills Point road so as to leave James B. Holomons to the West including the following lands (to wit) William B. Rolls, John Carmac, Horace Allen, Ruben Walker, Seth Curlen, Lewis Cook, Allen Pryor, Grasty Munsfield, James N. Cullen, Albert Hornsby, John Hornsby, with Betty, Mark Hubbs and brother, John Huzzy, John Jones, William R. Fisher, Elizah Hay & Brothers William, Edward T. Brockwell, William A. Maxwell, Daniel Dunn, Abraham Herring and hands, William Harper, John S. Doxey and Lamas Stephen Beggs, Will Andrews, and one half of B. Tottens lands as aforesaid and all other lands in said Bounds and that he make the same a first class road and do his duty thereon for one year.

On motion it was ordered by the Court that Porter A. Davis be appointed overseer on the Totten Road from the fork of Hoosier Creek to where it intersects the Mills Point Road near Clay Creek in the room of John Mehen removed and that all the hands in the following bounds works under him (to wit) Beginning at the North East corner of the widow Byrds plantation running thence Southwardly to the mouth of Harris fork passing west of Seth Curlin thence down the north fork of Obion River to the mouth of Grover Creek and from thence a Northward course to the (p-98) to the said Tottens Road at the place where it crosses the East fork of Hoosiers and thence with said road to the beginning so as to include all the lands on the place where Samuel Wells now lives, say John W. Byrd, John Tart, Samuel Davies, Joseph Davies, A. S. Bezzy, Isham Barner, Jesse Cooke, Sion Hill, Jefferson Cook and that he do his duty for one year and make it a 2nd class road.

On motion it was ordered by the Court a majority of the acting Justices of Obion County present that James H. Davies and Jubilee M. Bedford be allowed the sum of Twenty Two dollars and seventy five cents each for settling with Joel S. Enloe, Sheriff of said County for the year 1829, 1830, 1831, 1832 & 1833 and also the further sum of five dollars each for the settling with the County and Circuit Court Clerks and that the Clerk of the County Court issue a certificate to the Trustee of said County for the same.

Whereas John Williams & Ruben Hamilton having committed an affray in the hearing of the court it was ordered by the court that the Sheriff bring them before the court forthwith for contempt of the Court and after examination of evidence in the case it was ordered by the Court that Ruben Hamilton be fined in the sum of four dollars and that he remain in custody of the Sheriff until he pay the same with cost of settlement or give security as the law directs and that John Williams (p-99) be fined in the sum of three dollars and 75 cts. and costs of suit and that he remain in custody of the Sheriff until he pay the same or give security as the law directs.

Where report proclamation being made the court went into the election of three commissioners for the County of Obion for the next ensuing twelve months as Internal Improvement commissioner and the Sheriff had counted out the votes it was declared that William Miller, Alfred Lamar, and William W. Watson were duly and constitutionally elected Internal Improvement Commissioners for Obion County for the next ensuing twelve months.

Robert B. Harper, Administrator of the last will of A. Linn, Dec'd. produced in open court an akt. of sales of the goods and chattels of Andrew Linn, Dec'd. which was ordered by the Court to be received and recorded.

On motion it was moved by the court that Samuel Hutchinson be appointed overseer on the Mills Point Road from Nelms ferry on Obion River to the farm of Alfred Lomax and that Archibald K. Hoggs and John D. Dickey and hands and said Hutchinson hands work under him and that he make the same a second class road and that he do his duty on the same for one year.

Joel S. Enloe came into Court and enter in bond the sum of ten thousand dollars as Tax Collector for the County of (p-100) Obion for the year 1834 with James Caldwell, S. L. Teater, Charles Sinkler, John

Williams, James Davis his security which was ordered by the Court to be received and recorded.

Court adjourned until tomorrow morning 8 o'clock.

B. Totten, J. P.
John Harpole, J. P.
Willis Caldwell, J. P.

Tuesday, July 8th 1834.

Court met according to adjournment proclamation being made the court proceeded to business.

Ordered by the court that the following persons be summoned by the Sheriff to serve as Grand and Petty Juriors at the October Term of this Court, they being good and lawful men in said county (to wit) Jerrome Miller, William S. Whitehead, Alfred W. Ross, James M. Porter, Joseph Meadows, Elizabeth Carter, Samuel McDaniel, John Cloar, James Mills, Samuel G. Wafford, William F. Scott, Joseph R. Edwards, Daniel Brown, William Andrews, Grastly Mansfield, Edwin T. Brockwell, William Adair, David Hubert, John M. Buchanan, William C. Edward, John C. Wilson, Thomas Hampton, John Williams, William Carter, Edward Norrid, Jonathan Nice.

And also the following persons as Constables (p-101) to wait and attend on said court at said October Term, to wit: William Edmonds & H. D. Logan.

Ordered by the Court that the following persons being good and lawful men in said County be summoned by the Sheriff of said County to serve as Grand and Petty Jurors at the next Term of the Circuit Court to be holden for this county at the Courthouse in the Town of Troy on the second Monday in November next, to wit:

1. John Parr
2. Willis Caldwell
3. Stephen Mitchell
4. Evan Shely
5. Jesse Daugherty
6. Richard T. Merewether
7. William M. Miller
8. James Henderson
9. Wilford Farris
10. Henry J. P. Westbrook
11. Joseph Wilson
12. William Wilkinson
13. William Downey
14. John Harpole
15. Benjamin Totten
16. Frederick Taylor
17. Jeremiah Norrid
18. John Polk
19. John L. Doxey
20. Alfred McDaniel
21. Abraham Henning
22. James Harpole
23. William Miller
24. Elisha Parker
25. James B. Holoman
26. John White

And that be also summoned Daniel StJohn & James Caldwell as Constables to attend as said Court.

Ordered by the court that a tract of land of 480 acres in the name of George Mansfield Range 7, Sec. 8th, reported for the 1833 for double taxes be released from the payment of the single taxes costs & charges.

It appearing to the satisfaction of the court that Jesse H. Dyer solicitor General was absent on motion it was ordered by the Court (p-102) that W. W. Totten, one of the practicing attorneys of this Court be appointed solicitor pro tem whereupon he took the oath prescribed by law.

William U. Watson who was elected a commissioner as one of the board of Internal Improvement for Obion County came into Court and entered into bond in the sum of five thousand dollars, payable to William Carroll Governor & his superior in office with Joel S. Enloe, R. B. Brown, James M. Porter and William G. Edward his secretarys and took the oath prescribed by Law.

Alfred Lomax who was elected one of the Internal Improvement commissioners for the County of Obion came into Court and entered into bond to William G. Edwards and James M. Porter his securities and took the oath prescribed by Law.

William Miller who was elected one of the Internal Improvement commissioners for Obion County came into Court and entered into bond to William Carroll, governor & his superior in office, in the sum of five thousand dollars with Joel S. Enloe, Jerome Miller, and Charles Sinkler his securities and took the oath prescribed by Law.

(p-103) Tuesday, July 8th 1834.

McBean, Administrators)
Vs )
John Farr )

This day came the parties by their attornies and upon it was ordered by the Court that this cause be continued in the next term of this court.

John McClure )
Vs ) A. G. P.
William S. S. Harris)

This day came the parties by their attorneys & thereupon the Defendant by his attorney moved the Court to strike this cause from the dockett which motion upon was overruled and then this cause was continued by order of the Court till the next term.

On motion of A. G. P. Westbrook one of the securities of Angus M. L. McBean and G. W. Wood admimister of all and singular the goods and chattels rights and credits of A. C. Pagan, deceased. It is ordered by the Court that said Administrators give new security at the next term of this Court and that thereupon said Westbrook be released from all future liability.

(p-104) Tuesday July 8th A. D. 1834.

Proclamation being made by the Sheriff the Court went into the election of a corroner for the County of Obion and after they waved Court it appeared that James Davis was duly and constitutionally elected coroner of Obion County for the next two ensuing years.

Maury Smith by attorney came into Court and moved the Court for license to keep an ordinary -- at the residence in Troy and after examination of the situation and competency of the said Maury Smith was of opinion that she is entitled to license agreeable to the act of assembly in such cases made and proved.

It was therefore ordered by the Court license issued to her on condition she enter into bond and security according to law whereupon she enter with bond payable to William Cornell, governor, and his successors Jerome Miller and James Good her security.

A deed of bargain sale from the commissioners in trust for the Town of Troy to Charles McAlister for Lots Nos. 41 & 72 was produced in open court and the execution of the same duly proven (p-105) by the oaths of William A. Brown and Dennis Cochran subscribing witnesses thereon to an order by the Court to be certified for registration.

Solomon P. Gates)
Vs            )   A. F. G.
Logan & Hubert )

This day came the parties by their attorneys and thereupon on motion of Plf. by attorney it was ordered by the court that this cause be dismissed for want of jurisdiction. Therefore it appearing that this court has not jurisdiction it is considered by the Court that this case stand dismissed and that a writ of proceedings issued to the Justice be laid open to execution on his judgment and that the defendants pay the cost in this behalf expended and that Execution issue accordingly for the same.

John C. Wilson)
Vs            )   Debt
Hogge & Wilson)

This day came the parties and by consent of parties by their attornies and thereupon it is ordered by the Court that this cause be continued until the next term of this court.

Rosannah Harper                )
Vs                             )
James M. Ross, Joel S. Enloe,  )   Debt
and R. B. Brown                )

This day came the parties by their attorneys and it appearing to the satisfaction of the Court that James M. Ross has departed this life and that R. B. Brown has been appointed administrator of all and singular the goods, chattels, rights and credits of said James M. Ross (p-106) Deceased it is therefore considered by the court that this case be continued until the next term of Court and that Sci Facias Issue against the said R. B. Brown administrator to make known &c.

Cochbam & Norrell )
Vs                  )   Trespass on the Case
Charles McAllister  )

This day came the parties by their attornies and on motion by consent of parties it is ordered by the court that this cause be continued until the next term of this court.

N. B. Houser )
Vs           )   A. P. G.
Saml. Nelms  )

This day came the parties by their attornies and then upon by consent it is ordered by the Court that this cause be continued until the next term of this Court.

Jonathan Badgett    )
Vs                  )   Sci Fa.
Robertson Dickerson )

This day the parties failed to appear and thereupon it was ordered by the Court that this cause be continued until the next term of this court.

(p-107)   Tuesday, July 8th 1834.

John Linn   )
Vs          )   Certiorari
Tyra Dabney )

This day came the parties by their attornies and thereupon by consent it is ordered by the court that this cause be continued until the next term of this Court.

Jonas Davis who was elected coroner of this county came into Court and entered into bond, in the sum of twenty five hundred dollars payable to the Governor of the State of Tennessee with William W. Wilson, Joel S. Enloe, William U. Watson and Daniel St. John his securities and took the several oaths prescribed by law.
(Governor)

(p-108)

The State    )
Vs           )   Affray Continuance
Edward Holins)

This day came the Defendant by his attorney and the Attorney General for the State and thereupon by consent it was ordered by the Court that this cause be continued until the next term of this Court.

The State      )
Vs             )   For selling spirits near sanctuary
Cornelius Sheeks)

This day came the # & Defendant in his own proper person and thereupon by consent it is ordered (p-109) by the Court that this cause be continued until the next term of this Court and the Defendant thereupon acknowledged himself to owe and be indebted to the State of Tennessee in the sum of two hundred and fifty dollars and William U. Watson and Charles McAlister in the sum of one hundred and twenty five dollars each to be levied of their goods and chattels, lands and Tenaments for the use of the State but to be void on condition that the said Cornelius Sheeks make his personal appearance here # to answer said charges at this next Term of this Court # and not depart this Court without having first had & obtained.

Henry Applewhite)
Vs              )   Ca Sa
A. M. L. McBean )

This day came the parties by their attorneys and the Plaintiff by his attorney moved the Court for leave to amend the clerks certificate on the affadavid filed in this case before the clerk for a capias adsatisfacendio by inserting the name of Samuel D. Wilson Clerk before the name S. S. Harris deputy clerk and the matters of law answering thereupon by being heard and by the Court here fully understood it is ordered by Court that Amendment be made and it was accordingly done.

(p-110)   Tuesday, 8th July A. D. 1834.

Henry Applewhite)
Vs              )   Ca Sa
A. M. L. McBean )

This day came the parties by the attorney and the Defendant by his consent moved the Court to quash the casa in this cause and upon agreement being had then and the matters of law thereupon arising being by the Court heard and fully understood it is considered by the Court that his said motion be overruled whereupon the Defendant move the Court to quash the case, bond agreement being had and the matters of law being heard & fully understood by the court it appears that the law is with the Plaintiff and that his said Defendants motion be overruled.

William F. Baldridge)
Vs                  )   Casa
Phillip Fields      )

This day came the parties by their attorney and the Defendant by attorney moved the Court to quash the said casa and upon agreement being had and the matters of law arising and being by the Court heard and fully understood it appears that the Law is with the Defendant. It is therefore considered by the Court that his said motion be sustained and that said case be quashed, set aside & held for naught and that said Defendant Fields be discharged therefrom to recover after said Plaintiff his costs by him in this behalf expended.


(p-111)   July Term A. D. 1834.


George W. Wood &)
A. M. L. Mc Bean)
Admrs. of Pagan )    Certio. Moticio
Vs              )
Thomas Allison  )

This day came the parties by Attorney and thereupon on motion it was ordered by the Court that a rule be entered to show cause why this judgment by motion & the execution issued thereon in Court below should not be quashed.


The State of Tennessee)
Vs                    )   Indict. Affray
David W. Pound        )

This day came the solicitor for the State and the Defendant in person and thereon Defendant by attorney moved the Court to discharge him from said indictment, which motion on agreement had was overruled & cause continued to next term of this Court, upon Defendants entering into recognisance & thereon the said Defendant and James M. Pounds his security here in Court severally acknowledged themselves indebted to the State of Tennessee, in the sum of two hundred & fifty dollars each, to be levied of their goods and chattels, lands & Tenaments for the use of the State to be on condition that said Defendant be and appear here at the next regular Term of this Court to be holden at the Courthouse in the Town of Troy on the first Monday of October next, then and there to answer (p-112) to the aforesaid charge, and not depart thence without having first had & obtained.


David Armour &                       )
James H. Moran                       )
Vs                                   )   Debt
Angus M. L. Mc Bean,,one of the      )
Admrs. of A. C. Pagan, Dec'd.        )

The papus warrant judgment execution and proceedings had in this cause before the magistrate being filed in this court by Richard B. Brown the Justice of the Peace before the cause was tried and it appearing therefrom that Plaintiff had recovered $50 debt & 50 cts. costs thereon came the Plaintiff by attorney & suggested to the Court that this said administrator had wasted the estate of his said intestate and it appearing from the officers returned on the execution issued in that behalf, that he found no goods or chattels, rights or credits of the said Andrew C. Pagan, dec'd. in the hands of A. M. L. Mc Bean or George W. Wood, his administrators upon which to levy said execution on motion it was thereon ordered by the Court that a scire facias issue to make known to said A. M. L. Mc Bean administrators as aforesaid, that he be and appear here at the next Term of this Court to show cause &c, or why the said Plaintiff should not have judgment and execution for their debt and costs aforesaid out of the proper goods and chattels of said administrator &c.

(p-113)   State of Tennessee)
          Vs                  )   Sci Facias
          John S. Mc Donald   )

This day came the solicitor for the State & it appearing that Defendant had removed to parts unknown &c thereon it was ordered by the court that this cause be stricken from the docket & it is further ordered that the County of Obion pay the costs in this behalf according &c

The State of Tennessee)
Vs                    )   Sci Facias
John Payne            )

This day came the solicitor who prosecutes for the State and thereon the said defendant being solemnly called to come into court to show cause why the judgment mentioned in said Sci facias should not be made final, came not but made default, and it being made to appear to the court that a forfeiture had been entered against said Defendant at the last Term of this court for $125 for his non attendance as a witness in the case of the State of Tennessee against Cornelius Sheeks that the aforesaid Scire facias had issued thereon, and that it had been legally served upon & made known to said Defendant. It was therefore considered by the court that the aforesaid judgment for said forfeiture be made absolute that the state of Tennessee recover of the said John Payne the said sum of one hundred and twenty five dollars and also the costs in this behalf according & that execution issue for the same.

(p-114)   July Term 1834.

State of Tennessee)
Vs                )   Indict for selling spirituous liquors &c
Cornelius Sheeks  )

It being made to appear to the court that John Payne a witness for the State in this cause had failed and refused to attend this court to give evidence & that he is in contempt &c altho summoned by subpoena & on motion of the Attorney General, it was ordered by the Court that an attachment issued to the Shff. to take the said John Payne & have him at the next Term of this court to testify and give evidence in behalf of the State in the aforesaid cause & to clear his said contempt &c.

State of Tennessee)
Vs                )   Charge of Obstructing Lawful Process.
Linden Kirksey    )

This day came the Attorney General for the State and the Defendant in proper person & by Attorney & moved the court to discharge him from his recognisance in this behalf & from the said charge, which motion was ordered by the court & the said Defendant failing & refusing to enter a new recognisance to appear at next Term of Court to answer said charges he was therefore ordered to be & remain in the custody of the Sheriff of said county of Obion to be kept in the public jail or else wherein said court to appear at the next Term of this court to answer said charged.

And on motion it was ordered by the court that if Defendant shall enter into bond with security (p-115) in the sum of one hundred dollars to appear at the next Term of this Court to answer the said charge he shall be released from confinement.

John Hubert )
Vs ) Certiorari
Solomon P. Catoe )

This day came the Plaintiff by attorney and filed his petition in writing and moved the court for writs of Certio Moticio and supersedes in this cause to which Defendant Catoe by his attorney objected, but which was ordered by the court to be issued agreeably to the prayer of the petition on his giving bond and security as the Law directs.

Court adjourned until tomorrow 8 o'clock.

B. Totten, J. P.
Willis Caldwell, J. P.
John Parr, J. P.

(p-116) Wednesday, July Term A. D. 1834.

Court not agreeable to adjournment and proclamation being made court proceeded to business.

It appearing to the Court that Benjamin Totten is charged with taxes for 200 acres of land in Obion County for the year 1833, which is more than said Totten actually received. Therefore, it is ordered that Joel S. Enloe, Sheriff of this County, have a credit for the same in the settlement of his Public accounts, which Taxes is $1.12½.

It appearing to the Court that Selam Huntaman is charged with Taxes for 200 Servy of land in Obion County for the year 1833 more than he is actually liable for, therefore it is ordered that Joel S. Enloe, Sheriff of this County, have a credit for $1.12½ cents in the settlement of Obion for sd. year 1833.

It appearing to the satisfaction of the Court that Washington Shelton is charged with double taxes on 400 acres of land for the year 1833 on motion of his attorney it is ordered by the court that he be released from double taxes by thus paying the single tax cost and charges on the same.

(p-117) Wednesday July 9th A. D. 1834.

It appearing to the satisfaction of the Court that D. T. Caldwell is charged with double tax on 400 acres of land for the year 1833 on motion it is ordered by the Court that he be released from double Tax on condition he pay single Tax cost and charges thereon.

Ordered by the court that Owen Gilles be appointed overseer on the Iron Banks Road commencing where said road leaves the Mills Point Road to James Wilsons and all the hands that formally worked under William U. Watson work under him and that he do his duty thereon for the Term of one year.

Harry Appleshine )
Vs ) Motion for Indictment
Angus M. L. Mc Bean &) on Casa Bond.
Horace Head )

This day came the parties by attornies and defendant by attorney comes and offered the following plea, to wit: The defendant by attorney comes and defends the wrong and injury ---- the writing obligatory moved on which is read to them in these words, to wit: Also of the condition of said bond which is read to them in these words, to wit: and for plea say that they well and truly complied with said condition in said writing obligatory contained and these are ready to varify wherefore they pray Judgment.

Davis, Attorney for Deft.

(p-118) Wednesday, 9th July A. D. 1834

which plea was rejected by the Court.

Harry Applewhite )
Vs ) Motion
Angus M. L. Mc Bean)

This day came the Plaintiff by his attorney and moved the court for a judgment against Angus M. L. Mc Bean and Horace Head his security and the said Plaintiff by attorney made it to appear to the Court here that the said Plaintiff had recovered a Judgment by confession against the said A. M. L. Mc Bean and George W. Wood for the sum of ninety eight dollars and fifty cents debt before a magistrate in & for said County of Obion, to wit, on the 9th day of December 1833, that afterwards, to wit, on the 14th day of May 1834 capias adexpondendum issued from the official clerk of the County Court of said County of Obion upon the said Judgment, which was filed in said court by Henry D. Logan, Justice of the Peace of said Court, who rendered said judgment & who has since resigned his office as Justice of the Peace &c affidavid had been made as application for said capias adexpondendum as required by the statistic in such case &c that the said capias was executed upon the body of said A. M. L. Mc Bean and of said defendants to said Judgment by the Sheriff of Obion County to whom the same was directed & returned thereon that George W. Wood the other Defendant was not found, that the said Sheriff took a bond from the said Angus M. L. Mc Bean with Horace Head his security, payable to Henry Applewhite the Plaintiff in this motion according to the statute in such case &c
(p-119) condition that the said A. M. L. Mc Bean be and appear here at the

present term of this Court to pay to said Henry Applewhite the said debt, or to take the insolvent oath or to surrender up his property according to the law of the state, which said casa & bond are here in court and the said A. M. L. Mc Bean failing and refusing to come into court & pay said debt, or to take the insolvent debtors oath or deliver up his property as aforesaid.

Therefore it is considered by the Court that said motion be sustained that said Henry Applewhite recover of the said Angus M. L. Mc Bean and Horace Head his security aforesaid, in the bond aforesaid, ninety eight dollars and fifty cents for this debt aforesaid and also his costs in and about his suit in this behalf expended.

The State of Tennessee )
Vs ) Rescuing property unlawfully from Sheriff.
Dollay Kerksey )

This day came the attorney for the State and the Defendant in her own proper person and by attorney & moved the court to discharge her from the recognisance in this behalf and from the said charge which motion was overruled by the court and James Hogge leaving her security for her personal appearance here at this court and having delivered up the said Defendant to the Sheriff in the presence of the Court and by order of the Court on motion it is ordered that the said James Hogge be released (p-120) from all further liabilities and the said Defendant failing and refusing to enter into a new recognisance to appear here at the next Term of this Court to answer to said charges he was therefore ordered to be and remain in the custody of the Sheriff of said County of Obion to be confined in the public jail or elsewhere in said County so that he appear here at the next Term of this Court to answer said State of Tennessee in said charge.

And on motion it was ordered by the Court that if the said Defendant shall enter into bond with security in the sum of one hundred dollars to appear here at the next Term of this Court to answer said State of Tennessee of said charge she shall be released from close confinement.

Henry Applewhite )
Vs )
A. M. L. Mc Bean & ) Motion
Horace Head )

The Defts by attorney came into Court and tendered bills of exception Nos. 1 & 2 which then signed & sealed by the Court & ordered to be made part of the record.

A. M. L. Mc Bean & )
G. W. Wood, admrs. )
A. C. Pagan, Dec'd. ) Certiorari
Vs )
Thomas Allison )

By consent of parties it is ordered by the Court that a motion entered at the present Term of this Court to quash & to be continued to the next term of this court.

(p-121)   Court then adjourned till Court in Course.

                              B. Totten, J. P.
                              Willis Caldwell, J. P.
                              John Parr, J. P.

(p-122)   October 6th 1834.

Be it remembered that at a Court of Pleas and Quarter Sessions begun and held for the County of Obion and State of Tennessee on the 1st Monday in October being the 6th day of October A. D. 1834 present the worshipful Benjamin Totten, Willis Caldwell, John Harpole, R. B. Brown, H. L. P. Westbrook, William Wilkinson, Wilford Farris and James Henderson commissioned and assigned to hold said Court.

On motion it is ordered by the Court that Benjamin Totten be appointed chairman of this Court protem in place of John Parr absence.

Samuel D. Wilson clerk of this Court this day tendered his resignation as clerk of the County Court of Obion County which was received by the Court whereupon the Court appointed Andrew C. Harris Clerk protem of this Court until another clerk is elected to fill the vacancy occasioned by the resignation of Samuel D. Wilson former Clerk of this Court who took the oaths prescribed by law.

(p-123)   October 6th 1834.

Ordered by this court that Porter A. Davis be appointed overseer on the road from Hoosier Creek leading to the Mills Point road near Wyatt Bettys, and that Elisah Hay, Edwin Brockwell, John Jones, William B. Fisher work under him and that he do his duty for the Term of one year.
(Issued 13th Oct. 1834)

Ordered by the court that Jerome Miller, Alfred W. Ross and James H. Davis be appointed commissioner to settle with George W. Wood and Angus M. L. McBean as administrator of A. C. Pagan, Dec'd. and that they report to the next Term of this court.
(Issued 13th October)

Ordered by the court that Jerome Miller, Alfred W. Ross and James H. Davis be appointed commissioners to settle with William W. Watson as administrator of David Brown, deceased, and that they report to the next Term of this court.

(p-124)   October 6th 1834.

An account of the sale of the goods and chattels of the estate of Andrew W. Davidson, deceased, was produced in open court by the administratrix of said estate Catharine R. Davidson which was ordered by the Court to be received and recorded.

On motion it was ordered by the Court that the presinks of elections held at the house of Mary Davidson be moved to the house of John Williams and that all elections hereafter be held at said William's.

Ordered by the Court that John Williams be excused as serving as a Juror at their Term of Court.

R. B. Brown administrators of the estate of James M. Ross, deceased, produced in open court an account of the sale of the goods and chattels of said estate which was ordered (p-125) by the court to be received and recorded.

James H. Davis and William W. Watson commissioners for the County of Obion produced in open court a settlement with John C. Wilson former Trustee of said County which was ordered by the court to be received and recorded and it was further ordered by the court that said commissioners be authorized to give said John C. Wilson credit for all vouchers produced by him hereafter and such credits as shall be deemed insolvant on the Raingers books and that they report to the next term of this court.

On motion it was ordered by the Court that William Calhoon be appointed constable for Capt. Nelm's Company which was done on condition that he give bond and security as directed by law.

(p-126)  October 6th 1834.

On motion it is ordered by the Court that William C. Edwards be appointed overseer on the Road leading from Troy to B. Tottens from the East end of John Parrs lane to the main East fork of Hoosier Creek and that all the hands that formally worked under Alfred Lomax work under him and that he make the same a second class road and that he do his duty thereon for one year.

On motion of John Mc Neely by attorney it is ordered by the Court that the Trustee of Obion County pay the holder of said John Mc Neelys order one hundred and sixty five dollars the balance due him on an order drawn in his favour by Jesse Edminson one of the commissioners in Trust for the Town of Troy for two hundred and sixty five dollars dated 1st April 1833 out of the money collected by virtue of Taxes levied to defray the expenses of building the Courthouse.

(p-127)  October 6th 1834.

On motion it is ordered by the Court that David W. Farris be appointed overseer on the Road from Troy to Dyersburg commencing at Troy and working to the four mile post and that all the hands that worked under Samuel M. Simpson work under him and that he make the same a first class Road and that he do his duty thereon for one year.

Ordered by the court that Thomas Spright have leave to alter the Trenton Road so as to straighten his land now running through this plantation.

On motion it was ordered by the court a majority of the acting justices of Obion County present that Joel S. Enloe, Sheriff of Obion County, be allowed the sum of fifty dollars for exofficio services for this year.

Ordered by the court that William Adams be excused as serving as a Juror at this Term of this court.

(p-128)   October 6th 1834.

On motion it is ordered by the court a majority of the acting Justices of Obion County present that Samuel D. Wilson, former clerk of this court, be allowed forty dollars for his exofficio services for this year and that he be allowed the sum of twenty dollars for making out the Tax list for the year 1834.

On motion it is ordered by the court that James L. Mills be appointed overseer on the road leading from Mills Point to Dresden beginning at the four mile tree to Mud Creek at the State line and to have all the hand in the following bounds to wit, beginning at the four mile tree then north to the Black Swamp at the State line thence West to Culbersons on the State line thence South East to the East side of Edward Janes house thence to the East (p-129) side of William F. Scott's thence Southward to John Matheney's house thence Southwardly to the East side of M. Talley's house thence to the West side of B. Ivins plantations thence South to John Pankeys ood improvement thence East to Grove Crest bridge thence to the East side of James B. Holomons plantation thence North to the beginning and to make the same a first class road and that he do his duty thereon for one year.

(p-130)   October 6th 1834.

A deed of bargain and sale from A. S. Harris to Thomas and Simon B. Spight for Two Town Lots in Troy Nos. 5-10 & 29 was produced in open court and duly acknowledged by the said A. S. Harris and ordered by the Court to be certified for registration-Catherine R. Davidson records his stock mark a cross off the right ear and a split in the left.

On motion it was ordered by the court that Joel S. Enloe, Sheriff and Collector of the Public Taxes for the County of Obion, be authorized to receive Taxes on the property not listed for taxation for this year and that he report the same accordingly.

On motion it is ordered by the court a majority of the acting Justices of the County of Obion (p-131) present that James H. Davis and William W. Watson be allowed the sum of Twenty five dollars each for settling with John C. Wilson former Trustee of this County for the years 1830, 1831, 1832 and 1833.

On motion it was ordered by the Court that the order appointing commissioners to view out a road and mark the same from the mouth of Indian Creek to James Wilsons on the Moscow road be reviewed and that Willis Caldwell be added to the Jury.

On motion it was ordered by the Court that Lots Nos. 53 and 76 in the Town of Troy be sold by the commissioners of said Town in Trust and that they make report of the same at the next Term of this Court.

(p-132) It appearing to the court that there was a mistake in listing land of Colin Auld, for taxes for the year 1834, 1500 acres only being listed on motion it was ordered by the court that the tax list be amended by listing 15000 acres in the name of Colin Auld, in twelve tracts, situated on the North Fork of Obion River instead of the 1500 acres.

This day came James L. Mills and presented here in court a petition signed by sundry citizens of the county of Obion, praying that a Jury be appointed to sum and report whether the road leading from the state line on toward Dresden from the Reelfoot bridge to the state line cannot be so laid off & attend so as to run through the plantation of James L. Mills in a way without detriment to the public and without detriment to said Mills Plantation so as to make it run on as good ground as it now runs, and make report to next Court & ordered that William A. Maxwell, Martin Hall, Geo. W. Maxwell, Alfred Mc Daniel, John S. Davis, Jno. Jones, and Geo. White be appointed said Jury.

(p-133)  October Term 1834.

It is ordered that tomorrow be set apart for the doing of county business which is administered by this Clerk accordingly the court will also do other business an tomorrow.

Court adjourned until tomorrow morning 9 o'clock.

B. Totten, J. P.
John Harpole, J. P.
R. B. Brown, J. P.

Tuesday morning, 7th October A. D. 1834.

Court met pursuant to adjournment proclamation being made proceeded to business.

Benjamin C. Totten produced in court a license authorized to practice in the different courts in this State as an attorney at Law & on motion it was ordered that he be admitted an attorney of this court & thereupon the oaths prescribed by law were admitted to him as such.

It appearing to the court that Joel H. Dyer the Attorney General for the State is not in attendance it is thereupon ordered by the court that Benjamin C. Totten, one of the attorneys of this court be appointed Attorney General for the State during the present Term of the Court & thereupon the said Benjamin C. Totten took the oaths prescribed by law as Attorney General.

(p-134)  October 7th 1834.

The Sheriff returned into court the venire facias awarded at the last term of this court executed on all the persons therein named except

Samuel Mc Daniel and the following persons appeared, to wit:

1. William T. Whitesell
2. Jerome Miller
3. Alfred W. Ross
4. James M. Porter
5. Joseph Meadows
6. James Mills
7. Samuel G. Warford
8. William F. Scott
9. Joseph R. Edwards
10. Daniel Brown
11. William Andrews
12. Grasty Mansfield
13. E. T. Brockwell
14. William Adams, discharged
15. John M. Buchanan
16. William C. Edwards
17. John C. Wilson
18. Thomas Hampton
19. John Williams, discharged
20. David Hubert
21. William Carter
22. Jonathan Nix, discharged.

(p-135) October 7th 1834.

Out of which number the following persons were drawn as grandjury, to wit:

1. William T. Whitesell
2. Daniel Brown
3. Grastly Mansfield
4. Alfred W. Ross
5. William T. White
6. Joseph Meadows
7. William C. Edwards
8. William Andrews
9. Thomas Hampton
10. James M. Porter
11. John M. Buchanan
12. William F. Scott
13. Joseph R. Edwards
14. Jerome Miller

Whereupon William T. Whitesell was by the court appointed foreman of the grand jury and after being duly sworn and by the solicitor general cautiously and duly charged as the law directs they retired to consult &c

On motion it is ordered by the court that Jonathan Nix be excused as a Juror at the present term of this court.

(p-136) October 7th 1834.

On motion it is ordered by the court that Samuel G. Warford be excused as Juror of present Term of this Court it appearing to the satisfaction of the Court that a Stallion belonging to John M. Buchanan had been entered on the Tax list for 1834 as taxable property and said John M. Buchanan making it appear to the Court on oath that he had not kept the said horse holly for that purpose whereupon it is ordered by the court that he be released from all but one dollar and fifty cents of said Tax.

Solomon P. Catoe)
Vs            )
John Hubert   )  Certiorari

This day came the parties by attorney and the defendant by attorney moved the court to rule the Plaintiff to give security for prosecuting this suit whereupon by consent of the parties it is ordered by the court that this cause be continued until the next Term of this Court and that the Plaintiff give security to prosecute his suit by calling of the cause at the next term or that the same be stricken from the Dockett.

William Calhoun who was yesterday elected Constable for Obion County came into Court and entered into bond in the sum of one thousand dollars payable to this William Carroll, governor of the State at the time being and his successors in office with William C. Edwards and Samuel S. Calhoun his securities conditioned as the law directs.

On motion it is ordered by the court that Richard Davis, John Mosier, Saml. Mosier, Larkin Eastridge, William Eastridge, William Hutchinson and George Cunningham be appointed a Jury of view to view and mark out a road the nearest and best way from the nine mile post on Dyersburg road to Richard Davis, on the State line (p-138) in a direction to Mills point Kentucky and that they make report to the next term of this court.

On motion it is ordered by the Court that Thomas Harper be appointed overseer on the Dresden road from Troy to the four mile post and that all the hands that formally worked under Willis Hogge work under him and that he make the same a first class road and that he do his duty thereon for one year.
(Issued 14th Oct.)

On motion it is ordered by the court that Richard B. Brown serve as one of the Quorum Court during this Term.

Samuel D. Wilson former clerk of this court having tendered his resignation on the first day of this term and the same being received (p-139) on motion the court went into the election of a clerk whereupon proclamation being made the court proceeded to the election and after counting out the votes it appeared that William S. S. Harris had three votes and that Harry Applewhite had three votes and the Court proceeded to the second balloting and on counting out the votes it appeared that W. S. S. Harris had three votes and Harry Applewhite had three votes whereupon it was ordered by the court that said election be continued until tomorrow.

Samuel H. Cole )
Vs )
Littleton Hubard ) Motion
and William W. Watson )

This day came the parties by attorney and it appearing to court capias issue from the court of pleas and quarter sessions of said County of Obion on the 8th day of July 1834 and (p-140) returnable to the present term of this court at the suite of the Plaintiff against Littleton Hubbard by which the Sheriff was commanded to take the body of said Hubbard in satisfaction of the sum of two hundred and eighty dollars damages and seven dollars 12 cts. cash which was executed on the body of said Hubbard and the said Hubbard entered into bond with William W. Watson his security conditioned according to the act of 1824 for Insolvent Debtors and thereon came said Hubbard and moved for his discharge from said Ca Sa

(*Page 137)

and on examination of proof the court was of opinion that said casa had illegally issued it was ordered by the court that said Hubbard be discharged from said casa and bond and said Cole called upon the court to require of said defendant to comply with (p-141) the conditions of said bond which he refused then he moved the court for Judgment on said bond against said Hubbard and Watson for the amount of his said Ca Sa returned which the court refused to render.

It is considered by the court that the said Hubbard and Watson recover of said Cole the costs of this motion from all of which said Cole prays an appeal to the next Circuit Court of said County of Obion which was granted & he gave bond and security as the law directs.

John Parr, Chairman of County Court of Obion County )
Vs ) Motion
Joel S. Enloe, Sheriff & Collector and his securities )

This day came the attorney General who prosecutes for the State and moved the court for Judgment in favor of Plaintiff against the said Joel S. Enloe, Sheriff and Collector of the public revenues for the County of Obion for the year 1829 (p-142) and against Seth Bedford, William M. Wilson and Benjamin W. McIntosh as his securities for the sum of Two hundred dollars and two cents apart of the county taxes remaining and from Joel S. Enloe as Sheriff and Collector for said year 1829 which motion was by the court ordered to be docketed.

John Parr, Chairman of Obion County Court )
Vs )
Joel S. Enloe, Sheriff and Collector of the Public Revenues )
of Obion County and his securities. )

This day came the Attorney General who prosecutes for the State and moved the court here for Judgment in favor of sd. Plaintiff Joel S. Enloe, Sheriff and Collector of the Public Revenues for the County of Obion for the years 1830 and 1837 and against William Wilkinson and Seth Bedford two of his securities (p-143) for the discharge of his duties as collector for the sum of three thousand thirty two dollars the revenues by him collected for the County of Obion for and during the said years which he failed to pay over and thereupon said motion was ordered by the court to be docketed.

John Parr, Chairman of the County Court of Obion County )
Vs )
Joel S. Enloe, Sheriff and Collector of the Public )
Taxes for Obion County and his securities. )

This day came the Attorney General and moved the court for Judgment in favor of the said Plaintiff against Joel S. Enloe as Sheriff and Collector of the Public Revenues for the County of Obion for the years 1832 and 1833 and against R. B. Brown, Samuel L. Teater, two of his securities for the performance of his duty as collector for the sum of thirteen hundred (p-144) and thirteen dollars a part of the county taxes for the said years which the said Joel S. Enloe, Sheriff and Collector as aforesaid is liable for and fails to pay over according to law whereupon said motion was ordered by the court to be docketed an order having been issued from the July Term 1834 of this court appointing commissioners to review the Road running from Troy to Dresden beginning at the Cain Creek and intersecting the said road three quarters of a mile on the west of Thomas Taylors and said commissioners having proceeded to view same and made report it is therefore ordered by the court that said road be -- so as to leave said Taylors plantation on the North of said road.

(p-145)   Court then adjourned until tomorrow morning 9 o'clock.

                 B. Totten, J. P.
                 Willis Caldwell, J. P.
                 R. B. Brown, J. P.

Wednesday morning court met pursuant to its adjournment.

Samuel W. Cole )
Vs )
Littleton Hubbards &)
William W. Watson )

  In this cause, James L. Totten came into court and acknowledged himself the Plaintiff's security for prosecution his appeal with effect, or the payment of their costs incident on failure.

William A. Eachbaum)
C. C. Muriel )
Vs )  Continued
Charles Mc Alister)

  In this cause by consent of parties and the assent of the court, this cause is continued as on the affidavit of the Plaintiff, and a -- order taking depositions each giving lawful notice.

D. Arman & J. H. Mann )
Vs )
Angus W. L. Mc Bain, Admrs. of)  Sci Fa
Andru C. Pagan, Dec'd. )

  This day came the (p-146) plaintiff and moved the court to order a said Facias to issue upon the suggestion then made at last term of this court and it appearing that the clerk had failed to issue a said Facias returnable to this term it is ordered that a sied Facias issue on the suggestion made at last term of this court, returnable to the next term.

H. J. P. Westbrook )  Motion to be released as security
Vs )      of Admrs.
A. M. L. Mc Bain & Jno. W. Wood)

In this case H. J. P. Westbrook came into court & dismissed this motion & proceedings & said McBain as administrator of A. C. Pagan, Dec'd., comes into court & assumes the costs whereon it is commanded that said proceedings be dismissed and said McBain pay the costs of this proceeding.

Andrew C. Harris who was appointed clerk for the term of this court tendered his resignation which was accepted by the court and the said court present B. Totten, Willis Caldwell, James Henderson, W. Farris, R. B. Brown, Jno. Harper, H. J. P. Westbrook & William Richards having failed to elect a clerk on yesterday and being of opinion that they have no power to make a permanent clerk on this day and (p-147) for the convenience of suits and further disputes of this business of this court proceeded to appoint a clerk pro tem until the court shall fill the vacancies and then upon said court appointed William S. S. Harris Clerk of this court pro tem until the court shall elect a principle clerk and thereupon said Harris came into court and entered into bond required by the Statutes in such cases made & provided and took the several oaths required by law and entered upon the duties of his offices as clerk pro tem of this court.

Ordered by the court that a tract of land containing 640 acres entered in the name of Grass Brasfield be released from double taxes for 1833-1834.

Henry J. P. Westbrook, a Justice of the Peace for this county presented his resignation which is received by the court.

James Hogge ) Motion takes reliance from
Vs ) Securities of the debts.
A. M. L. McBain, as Admrs. of H. C. Pagan)

This day came the said James Hogge and suggested here to the court that he is about to be endamaged as the security of said McBain & Wood as Administrators of A. C. Pagan and on motion of said Hogge it is ordered that a notice issue to the said McBain & Wood to appear at the next (p-148) term of this court and give other security in place of said Hogge surrender said admrs. notice according to the Statutes in such cases made & provided.

State of Tennessee)
Vs ) In Riot
Cornelius Sheeks )

This day came the attorney general who prosecutes on behalf of the state and the defendant in proper person who in being charged on this indictment herein court says that he cannot gainsay the said indictment but put in open court confessed that he is guilty in manner & form as therein charged, whereupon it is considered that he make his peace with the state by the payment of three dollars and that he remain in custody of the Sheriff until said fine and the costs of this prosecution be secured and thereupon comes into open court Jesse Sheeks and acknowledges himself the defendant's securities for payment of said fine & costs.

It is therefore considered by the court that the State of Tennessee recover against said deft. & said Jesse Sheeks said fine of $3 together with the costs of this prosecution & that execution issue & the deft. go.

State of Tennessee )  In Riot - continued as application
Vs              )           of the
Walker          )           Attorney General

(p-149)   State of Tennessee )
          Vs                 )   Indict.
          Edward Robbins     )

This day comes the Attorney General who prosecutes in behalf of the State and the Deft. in proper person who are being charged in the Bill of Indictment plead not guilty and for his trial puts himself on his County and the Attorney General doth the like and thereupon convey a Jury of good & lawful men, to wit:

1. David Hubert         7. John Gene
2. James Nulls          8. S. S. Calhoun
3. William Carter       9. Thos. Allison
4. E. T. Brockwell     10. C. M. Bennett
5. John C. Wilson      11. William Minton
6. Jesse Sheeks        12. Anderson Lysander

Who being elected tried & sworn the truth to speak upon the issue joined upon their oaths do say the deft. is guilty in manner & form as charged in the Bill of Indictment and thereupon the deft. moved the court for a rule to show cause why a new trial should be granted.

State       )
Vs          )   Indict.
John Faust )

Ordered that a Capias issue against the deft. in this case returnable to the next term.

State       )
Vs          )   Motion to quash Execution.
Jno. Polk  )

This day came the defendant moved the court to quash (p-150) an execution issued against himself for the sum of $2.12½¢ and it appearing to the court that said execution is given & ordered that the same be given hold.

Geo. W. Wood & A. M. L. Mc Bain )
Admrs. of A. C. Pagan           )
Vs                              )   Assumpsit
John Parr                       )

This day came the parties by their attornies and thereupon came a Jury of good & lawful men who being elected tried & sworn the truth to speak upon the issue joined upon their oaths do say they cannot agree, whereupon they are inspired by the court from rendering their verdict until tomorrow morning.

Ordered by the court that the bond which was given by W. S. S. Harris on today as clerk pro tem of this court be recorded which bond is in the following words, to wit:

State of Tennessee, Obion County.

Know all men by these present that we, William S. S. Harris, Samuel L. Teater, Thomas Allen, John Linn, and William Edwards all of the County & State aforesaid, are held and firmly bound unto William Carroll, governor of the State aforesaid and his successors in office in the sum of ten thousand dollars for the payment of which well and truly to be made we bind ourselves our heirs &c jointly and severally firmly by these present (p-151) sealed with our seals & dated this 8th day of October 1834.

The condition of the above obligation is such that whereas the said W. S. S. Harris was this day appointed Clerk Pro Tem of the County Court for the County aforesaid of said Court now if the said William S. S. Harris shall surely keep the records of said court and shall faithfully discharge all the duties of his said office then the above obligation to be void, otherwise to remain in full force, dated above.

Test  
H. A. Garrett

W. S. S. Harris (Seal)  
Samuel L. Teater (Seal)  
Thos Allen (Seal)  
John Linn (Seal)  
William C. Edward (Seal)

Ordered by the court that the clerk pro tem take into his possession the books, papers, furniture, scrip, laws &c and all other things belonging to the County Court of this County.

And thereupon Court adjourned until tomorrow morning at 8 o'clock.

B. Totten, J. P.  
Willis Caldwell, J. P.  
R. B. Brown, J. P.

(p-152) 9th October Term 1834.

Thursday morning court met pursuant to adjournment & proclamation being made proceeded to business.

Angus L. M. Mc Bean & George W. Wood, Admrs.)  
of Andrew C. Pagan, Dec'd )  
Vs ) Motion  
Thomas Allison )

This day came the parties by their attorneys & it appearing that the motion of defendant made at last term of this court to set aside the judgment obtained by motion in this cause & to quash said proceeding & the execution that issue on the same from the court below had not been entered, by one issue of the clerk thereon by consent of parties by their attornies it is ordered by the court that said motion be now entered, to set aside & quash the judgment & the execution that issued on the same, which was obtained by motion of said Plaintiff against said Defendant, by motion, before Seth Bedford, Justice of the Peace &c for $32.98½ & upon agreement had it appeared to the court that the defendants motion in this behalf ought to be sustained. It is therefore considered by the court that said motion be sustained, that said judgment be set aside & that the execution issued thereon be quashed that said defendant go hence &c & recover his costs against said Plaintiff or administrators to be levied of the said Plaintiff intestates in their hands &c from which judgment the said Plaintiffs pray and appeal to the Circuit Court to be holden for said County of (p-153) Obion in Troy on the second Monday next, which is granted to them.

John C. Wilson )
Vs             ) Debt. - Judgt.
James Hogge &  )
Samuel D. Wilson)

This day came the parties by their attorneys and thereupon came a jury of good and lawful men, to wit: David Hubert, James L. Mills, William Carter, Edwin T. Brockwell, Phillip Fields, Thomas Allison, John Linn, James S. Brown, John Payne, William F. Smith, James Good & Gideon Kirksey, who being elected tried and sworn the truth to speak upon the issue joined in said cause between parties, upon their oaths do say that said Defendants have not paid the debt in said Plaintiffs said declaration alledged but that the said Defendants do owe the said debt to the said Plaintiff & that the same debt is three hundred & thirty three dollars & 33 1/3 cents and they do assess his damages by reason of detention thereof to thirteen dollars 33 1/3 cents besides costs.

It is therefore considered by the court that said plaintiff recover of said defendants the said sum of $333.33 1/3 the debt aforesaid and $13.33 1/3 cents the damage aforesaid by the jury aforesaid in manner & form aforesaid assessed & also his costs by him in and about his suit in this behalf expended & that execution issue for the same & debts in.

(p-154) October Term 1834.

Cornelius Sheeks)
Jesse Sheeks    )
Vs              ) Assumpsit - Continuance
Robert White    )

This day came the parties by their attorneys and thereupon by consent of parties it is ordered by the court that this cause be continued to the next term of this court & that a general order to take deposition be first entered each to give the other twenty days notice of of the time & place of taking the same both in & out of the State of Tennessee.

William W. Lea)
Assignee &c  )   Debt.
Vs           )   Continued.
Moses Parr   )

    This day came the parties by their attorneys & thereon by consent of parties it is ordered by the court that said Plaintiff be permitted to amend his declaration as he may choose & that the cause be continued for trial at the next term of this court &c.

John Linn   )
Vs          )   Certiorari - Continuance
Finey Dabney)

    This day came the parties by their attorneys & thereon by consent of parties it is ordered by the court that this cause be continued to the next term of this court &c by the Plaintiff paying costs in this cause for this term &c.

(p-155)   October Term 1854.

George W. Wood &                          )
A. M. L. Mc Bean, Administrators          )
of A. C. Pagan, Deceased.                 )   Assumpsit
Vs                                        )
John Parr                                 )

    This day came the parties by their attorneys, and thence came the jury that was on yesterday reported, to wit: William T. White, David Brown, Crasty Mansfield, Alfred W. Ross, Jerome Miller, Joseph Meadows, William C. Edwards, William Andrews, James M. Porter, John M. Buchanan, William F. Scott, Joseph R. Edwards, who now upon their oath do say that said defendant did assume & undertake in manner & form as said Plaintiffs have alledged, within three years next before the commencement of this action and they do assess said Plaintiffs damages by reason thereof to seventy two dollars & $37\frac{1}{2}$ cts. besides costs.

    Therefore it is considered by the court that said Plaintiff recover of said Defendant the said sum of $72.37$\frac{1}{2}$ cents the damages aforesaid by the jury aforesaid in manner & form aforesaid and also their costs by them in & about their suit in this behalf expended.

John Mc Clure      )
Vs                 )   Debt - Appeal from a Justice
William S. S. Harris)

    This day came the parties by their attorneys & thereon came a Jury of good & lawful men, to wit:

David Hubert, Jas. L. Mills, (p-156) William Carter, Edwin T. Brockwell, Phillip Fields, Thomas Allison, John Linn, James S. Morris, John Pagan, William F. Smith, Jas. Bood, Gideon Kirksey, who being elected, tried & sworn the truth to speak upon the matters in dispute between said parties, thereupon by consent of parties, David Hubert one of said jurors was withdrawn & a mistrial ordered to be entered & the cause stands for trial at next term.

Noah B. Hauser )
Vs ) Debt - Appeal from a Justice.
Samuel Nelms )

This day came the parties by their attorneys and thereupon came a jury of good & lawful men, to wit: David Hubert, Jas. L. Miller, William Carter, Edwin T. Brockwell, Phillip Fields, Thos. Allison, John Linn, James S. Brown, John Payne, William F. Smith, James Good, Gideon Kirksey, who being elected, tried & sworn the truth to speak upon the matters in dispute, between said parties, upon their oath do say that said Defendant owes & is indebted to said Plaintiff in the sum of twenty seven dollars & 50 cents debt & $1.35 damages are assessed by said jury for detention thereof.

Therefore it is considered by the court that said Plaintiff recover of said Defendant the said sum of $27.50 debt & $1.35 cents the damages aforesaid by the Jury aforesaid in manner & form aforesaid assessed, and also his costs (p-157) by him about his suit in this behalf expended & that execution issue &c and the Plaintiff released twenty five cents of the damages assessed as aforesaid.

Robert B. Harper, executioner of the last will )
& Testament of A. Linn, Deceased ) Assumpsit
Vs ) Judgt.
Robert White )

This day came the parties by their attorneys and thereupon came a jury of good and lawful men, to wit: John C. Wilson, William Carter, James L. Miller, David Hubert, James A. Brown, Edward T. Brockwell, William A. Brown, A. M. L. McBean, Thomas Allison, Gideon Kirksey, Mathew Young, Wm. L. Smith, who being elected, tried & sworn the truth to speak upon the issue joined in this cause upon their oaths do say that said Defendant did assume & undertake in manner & form as said Plaintiff in declaring hath alledged & they do assess his damages by reason of non-performance of that assumpsit & undertaking to the sum of seventy four dollars ninety eight cents besides costs.

Therefore it is considered by the court that said Plaintiff recover of said Defendant the said sum of $74.98¢ the damages aforesaid by the jury aforesaid in manner and form aforesaid assessed and also the costs by him about the suit in this behalf expended & that execution issue &c.

(p-158)  October Term 1834.

The State of Tennessee )
Vs                     ) Affray - Motion
Edward Robbins         )

This day came the solicitor for the State & Defendant in person & by attorney & thereupon the Defendants rule to show cause why a new trial should not be granted came on to be heard and upon agreement thereon it appeared to the court that said motion should be overruled.

It is therefore considered by the court that said motion be overruled, that the said Defendant make his peace with the State by a fine of one dollar. It is further considered by the court that the State of Tennessee recover against said Defendant one dollar the said fine & also the costs of this prosecution & that he staid commital till he give security for the same and thereon John Linn came here in court & acknowledged himself security of said Defendant for the fine & costs aforesaid and here confess judgment for the same agrees that execution may issue against him jointly with said Defendant for the fine & costs aforesaid

Ordered by the court that James L. Mills who is one of the Travis Jury, be discharged from further service at the Term.


(p-159)    October Term 1834.


William M. Wilson, Administrator  )
of David Taylor, Deceased         )
Vs                                ) Motion for Scire Facias
Jordan Hassell, Administrator of the )
Estate of Jonathan C. Haughton, Dec'd.)

The Plaintiff comes into Court and files the affidavits of William P. Ratcliff and Andrew S. Harris which are as follows, to wit:

In this cause William P. Ratcliff makes oath that in the years 1832 & 1833 he acted as deputy clerk of the court of Pleas and Quarter Sessions of Obion County, that during the time of his so acting John Hutchinson an acting Justice of said County resigned & returned his papers into the clerks office of said County, and amongst the papers so returned there was a Judgment rendered in due form in favor of William M. Wilson, Administrator of David Taylor, Deceased, against Jonathan C. Haughton for the sum of $74.21 debt and $1.00 costs of suit that after the rendition of said judgment said Haughton died and administration of his estate was granted to Jordan Hassell. He further states that a scire facias was issued by the clerk against the said Hassell as Administrator of said estate and was returned executed by the Sheriff of Gibson County by which Hassell was commanded to appear before the Clerk of the Court of Pleas and Quarter Sessions of Obion at his office in Troy, on the 13th day of July A. D. 1833, and show cause if any he had or could, why said Judgment should not be revived & the Plaintiff have execution against him, for the amount of said debt interest & costs, of the estate of said deceased, in his hands to be administered, and that accordingly on that day said Judgment was renewed against (p-160) said Hassell as administrator as aforesaid in due form of law, for the sum of $74.21 debt and the sum of $6.92 interest, and $3.12½ costs.

He further states that he has examined the papers in the office of Clerk, for the said Judgment against sd. Haughton for the scire facias against said Hassell, and for the judgment of renewal against the said Hassell, but has not been able to find them, and that he believes said papers are lost.

  Sworn to and subscribed in Open Court)
    October 9th 1834     ) Wm. P. Ratcliff
  W. S. S. Harris, Clerk pro tem )

State of Tennessee) Court of Pleas and Quarter Sessions
Obion County   ) October Term, 1834.

William M. Wilson, Administrator of the)
Estate of David Taylor, Dec'd    )
Vs               )
Jordan Hassell, Administrator of the )
Estate of Jonathan C. Haughton, Dec'd. )

In this cause Andrew S. Harris makes oath that he has made diligent search for the papers alluded to in the foregoing affidavit of William P. Ratcliff, that he has not been able to find them & that he believes said papers are lost.

                   A. S. Harris.

Sworn to and subscribed in Open Court 9th Oct. 1834.

                W. S. S. Harris, Clerk
                Pro Tem.

And also filed execution follows, to wit:

State of Tennessee:

For the Sheriff of Gibson County, Greetings. You are hereby commanded that the goods and chattels, lands and Tenements of Jonathan C. Haughton, Dec'd., in your county (p-161) to be found, which are in the hands of Jordan Hassell (administrator of the estate of said Haughton) to be administered you cause to be made the sum of seventy four dollars 21 cents, debt six dollars ninety two cents interest, three dollars 12½ cts. the fees hereon endorsed, together with all lawful costs and interests until paid to satisfy a Judgment that William M. Wilson admt. of the estate of David Taylor, Dec'd. recovered against said Hassell as admst. aforesaid before the Clerk of the court of Pleas & Quarter Sessions of Obion County, on the 13th July 1833, fail not & due return make hereof.

  Witness, Samuel D. Wilson (Clerk) of said Court at office in Troy this 18th day of July A. D. 1833.

                Samuel D. Wilson (Clerk)
  Judgment July 13th 1833, Debt        $74.21
        Interest            6.92

| | | |
|---|---|---|
| Costs before Justice Hutchinson | | $1.00 |
| Clerks Scire facias | | .50 |
| Als Sci Fa | | .50 |
| Execution & search for papers | .25 | 1.25 |
| Sheriff McLauren returning Sci Fa not found | .25 | |
| Sheriff serving Sci Fa  62½ | .87½ | 3.12½ |

And upon the back of said execution was the following endorsement:

Issued July 18th 1833:  No property found October 10th 1833.

M. McLauren, Shff.

State of Tennessee:

To the Sheriff of Gibson County, Greetings. You are hereby commanded that of the goods & chattels, lands & Tenements of Johathan C. Haughton, Dec'd. in your county to be found which are in hands of Jordan Hassells, administrator of the (p-162) estate of said Haughton to be administered you cause to be made the sum of seventy four dollars 21 cts. debt six dollars ninety two cents, interest three dollars 12½ cts. The fees hereon endorsed together with all legal interest & costs until paid to satisfy a Judgment that Wm. M. Wilson, administrator of the estate of David Taylor, Dec'd. recovered against said Hassess as administrator as aforesaid, before the Clerk of the Court of pleas & Quarter Sessions of Obion County on the 13th day of July 1833, fail not and due return make hereof.

Witness, Samuel D. Wilson, Clerk of said Court at office in Troy this 10th October, 1833.

Samuel D. Wilson, Clerk.
By A. G. Harris, D. C.

| | | |
|---|---|---|
| Judgment July 13th 1833 -  Debt | | 74.21 |
| Interest | | 6.92 |
| Cost before Justice Hutchinson | | 1.00 |
| Clerks Sci Facias | | .50 |
| Alias Sci Fa | | .50 |
| Execution & search for papers | | .25 |
| Alias Sci Fa | 37½ | 1.62½ |
| Sheriff McLauren returning Sci Fa not found | 25¢ | |
| Executing Sci Fa | 62½ | 87½ |

And upon the back of said Execution was the following endorsements, to wit:  Issued October 10th 1833.

Came to hand same day issued no property to be found in my Cty. Jan. 4th. 1834.

M. McLauren, Shff.

(p-163)  And said Plaintiff thereupon alledged that he recovered as aforesaid against Defendants for the debt damages and costs aforesaid that execution issued on the same as aforesaid & was returned no property found and thereon the said Plaintiff states and suggests here to the court that a large amount of assets came to the hands of said Hassell as administrator and that said Hassell has wasted the same and thereon he prays that scire facias may issue in favour of the Plaintiff against said Hassell, returnable to the next term of this court, commanding him (Hassell) then & there to appear & show cause if he could why the Plaintiff should not have Judgment and execution against the Defendant of his own proper goods & chattels, land & tenements, to the amount of the Judgment, damages and costs aforesaid.

And thereupon a Scire Facias was ordered by the court accordingly, returnable to the next term of this court.

The State )
Vs )
Gideon Kirksey &) Indictment.
Dolly Kirksey )

This day the grand jury returned here in Open Court a bill of indictment against the said Gideon Kirksey and Dolly Kirksey for trespass but arrives and abstraction of legal process endorsed by their foreman a true bill and then retired.

The State )
Vs ) Indictment.
Gideon Kirksey)

The Grand Jury this returned here in Open Court a bill of indictment against Gideon Kirksey for breaking jail and escaping custody endorsed by their foreman a true bill and then returned (p-164) and proclamation being made the court then adjourned until tomorrow morning 9 o'clock.

B. Totten, J. P.
Willis Caldwell, J. P.
R. B. Brown, J. P.

Friday morning 10th October, 1834.

Court met pursuant to adjournment & proclamation being made proceeded to business.

A. M. L. Mc Bean & George W. Wood,)
Administrators Andrew C. Pagan )
Vs ) Assumpsit.
John Farr )

This day came the Defendant and prayed an appeal to the next Circuit Court to be holden for Obion County on the Second Monday in November next and filed his affidavit stating that he was unable to give security to prosecute said appeal and prayed the benefit of the act of assembly of 1821 for the benefit of poor persons and thereupon the court granted an appeal as prayed for without the Defendant giving bond and security.

(p-165)    October Term, 1834.

Umphrey Davidson )
Vs              )   Motion for order.
Benjamin Farmer )

  This day came Umphrey Davidson in court and shows to the court from the papers, records & proceedings in the cause herein mentioned that he had recovered a judgment for forty two dollars & fifty cents debt also interest thereon & 50 cts. costs on the 15th day of March 1834 in the County of Weakly against Benjamin Farmer before Perry Vincent, Justice of the Peace for said County of Weakly and that execution had issued thereon in said County of Weakly against said Farmer for said sum of recovery & the interest & costs in that behalf, but that the same was unsatisfied for the want of effects in said County & that said execution had been sent certified in due form of law, by the clerk of Weakly Cty. to the County of Obion and that execution issue thereon by Richard B. Brown, Justice of the Peace in & for Obion County dated 16th August 1834 to a lawful officer of Obion County reciting the aforesaid judgment & execution & commanding the officer to make said sum of money & costs of goods & chattels of said Defendant that William W. Watson, deputy Sheriff of Obion County returned thereon that said Defendant had no goods & chattels in his county to levy said Deft. &c & that he had levied the same upon two lots of ground situated in the town of Troy in Obion County he owes on the plan of said town by lots Nos six & twenty one & said levy is dated 1st October 1834. Thereon, on motion of Plaintiff is ordered by the Court that the (p-166) Sheriff of Obion County proceed to advertise & sell said lots of ground according to law to satisfy the judgment & costs aforesaid and that an order of sale issued to him & that he report his proceedings herein to the next term of this court &c And it is further ordered by the court that Plaintiff recover of Defendant the costs of this motion.

  Ordered by the Court that the traverse Jury be discharged from further attendance this court.

Robert B. Harper, Executor of Will )
of Andrew Linn, Dec'd.              )
Vs                                   )   Asumpsit.
Robert White                         )

  This day came the parties by their attorneys & thereon the Defendant prayed an appeal to the Circuit Court to be holden for Obion County on 2nd Monday of November next, which was granted, he having entered into bond with Wm. U. Watson & R. B. Brown as security as required by law.

The State of Tennessee )
Vs                      )   Indictment Affray, Forfeiture of Recognisance.
David W. Pound          )

This day came the attorney general for the state and said defendant being solemnly called to come into court according to his recognisance entered at last term of this court to answer a charge & not depart, with bond, came not but (p-167) made default & forfeited his recognisance it is therefore considered by the court that the State of Tennessee recover of said David W. Pounds two hundred & fifty dollars the amount of his said recognisance and also the costs in & about said recognisance in this behalf expended.

State of Tennessee )
Vs ) Indictment for an Affray - Recognisance.
David W. Pounds )

This day came the solicitor for the State and it being made to appear to the court here from the records &c that James M. Pound had entered into a recognisance at the last term of this court, conditioned that David W. Pound be and appear at the present term of this court to answer the said State a charge for an affray &c and said David W. Pound being solemnly called to come into court to answer said charge & he not appearing thereon the said James M. Pound was solemnly called to come into court and bring with him the body of said David W. Pound to answer said charge, he came not but made default & forfeited his recognisance.

It is therefore considered by the court that the State of Tennessee recover of said James M. Pound two hundred & fifty dollars the amount of said recognisance and also the costs in & about said recognisance expended.

(p-168)    Rosanah Harper )
Vs )
Joel S. Enloe, R. B. Brown ) Debt.
Administrators of James M. Ross, Dec'd. )

This day came R. B. Brown against whom a scire facias was ordered at the last term of this court as administrator of James M. Ross, dec'd., and moved the court for a rule to show cause why said scire facias should not be quashed which was ordered to be entered & upon agreement thereof it appeared to the court that the same ought to be quashed.

It is therefore considered by the court that said scire facias be quashed & for nothing esteemed B. Totten, W. Caldwell & W. M. Wilson, Esqrs. presiding and thereon the Plaintiff by attorney moved the court for a scire facias against the said Richard B. Brown, administrator of James M. Ross, deceased, to issue upon the suggestion made at the last term of this court returnable to the next term which was ordered accordingly and by consent this cause is continued until the next term of this court, B. Totten, W. Caldwell & W. U. Wilson, Esqrs. presiding.

Ordered by the court that W. U. Watson, C. McAlister & A. W. O. Totten be appointed to settle with Seth Bedford administrator of John Pate, dec'd. & report to the next term.

(p-169)    It is ordered by the court that the following persons, good &

lawful men of the County of Obion be summoned by the Sheriff to appear at the next term of this court as grand & petit jurors, to wit:

1. James H. Guy
2. James N. Cullen
3. William Harpole
4. Wyatt Bettis
5. Wm. A. Maxwell
6. George White
7. Samuel Curlin
8. John Stanford
9. James Wilson
10. Abram Marbary
11. James Wadkins
12. Ezekiah Carter
13. Jerome Wadkins
14. Francis Taylor
15. Samuel Reeves
16. James Reeves
17. Robert Harper
18. James L. Brown
19. Horace Head
20. James B. Hogge
21. Benjamin Garrison
22. Geo. W. Clark
23. Wm. B. Partee
24. Thomas Allen
25. Benjamin Sheeks
26. A. A. Cunningham

And that William Calhoun & James L. McCollum, constables, be summoned to wait on the court. The court then adjourned till court in course.

        Willis Caldwell, J. P.
        B. Totten, J. P.
        R. B. Brown, J. P.

(p-170) January Term A. D. 1835.

State of Tennessee ) Court of Pleas and Quarter Sessions,
Obion County   ) January Term A. D. 1835

Be it remembered that at a Court of Pleas & Quarter Sessions begun and held at the Courthouse in the Town of Troy, County of Obion & State of Tennessee, on the first Monday of January A. D. 1835 and 59th year of American Independance, it being the 5th day of said month, present the worshipful Willis Caldwell, John Parr, William M. Wilson, Wilford Farris, John Harpole and Jesse Daugherty, commissioned & assigned to hold said term, proclamation being made the court then proceeded to hold

Jesse Daugherty )
To      )
Isham Newton )

A deed of conveyance for 250 acres of land in Obion County was duly acknowledged in open court by Jesse Daugherty, the bargainer, and ordered by the Court to be certified for registration.

Jesse Daugherty proved the killing of one wolf over four months old within the limits of this county. It is therefore ordered by the court, five of the acting Justices of the Peace present, that he be allowed agreeable to the statue in such case made and provided and that the Treasurer pay the same out of any monies in his hands not otherwise appropriated.
(Issued to P. & P.)

(p-171) 5th Monday, January Term 1835.

Jacob Faulk produced in court a wolf scalp over four months old, and proved the killing of the same within the limits of this county. It is therefore ordered by the court, five acting Justices being present, that he be allowed agreeable to the Statutes in such cases made and provided and that the Treasurer pay the same out of any monies in his hand not otherwise appropriated.

Jacob Faulk recorded his stock mark as follows, to wit: A smooth cross off the left ear and a swallow fork and under bit in the right ear.

Ordered by the court that David W. Farris be appointed overseer on the road from Troy to Dyersburg, commensing at Troy and working to the four mile post, and that the following hand work under him, to wit: William M. Wilsons hands, Joseph Wilsons hands, John C. Wilson & hands, John P. Wright, S. P. Wright, Jeremiah Leacoat, George Read, James J. McCollum & hands, Stephen Maxey, George W. Broach, Thomas Tanner, Flersion Caruthers, John Williams & sons, Richard Faris, Charles Sinkler, John Hord and hands, Thomas Dean, Horace Head, George Johnson, G. W. L. Marr & hands, and all the hands in those bounds, and that he make the same a first class road.

Ordered by the court that Richard T. Merriwether, Jesse Daugherty, Joseph Fulk, Stephen Mitchell, G. B. Colyer, William Hutchinson and William Payne be appointed a jury of review and mark out a road from Troy to Richard T. Merriwether.

(p-172) Monday the 5th, January 1835.

Ordered by the Court that James M. Spight be appointed overseer on the road from Troy to Trenton, commensing at the Obion River and working to the county line, and that all the hands that have heretofore worked on said road work under him and all the hands in those bounds, and that he make the same a first class road.

Catharine Ingram and Daniel St. John was this day appointed administrator of the estate of Benjamin Ingram, a citizen of Obion County, deceased, entered into bond and security and took the oath prescribed by law.

Clay Hannah and William U. Watson was this day appointed Administrator and Administrator of the estate of Andrew Hannah, deceased, and entered into bond and security, and took the oath prescribed by law.

A power of Attorney from Adam Huntsman to Benjamin Totten was this day produced in open court and the execution thereof was proven by the oath of Daniel St. John, one of the subscribing witnesses thereto and the death and hand writing of Ennis Hay, the other subscribing witness thereto was proven by Daniel St. John the hand writing of the said Ennis Hay, and ordered to be so certified for registration.

Ordered by the court that William Hutchinson, Jesse Daugherty &

83

Henry J. P. Westbrook (p-173) be appointed commissioners to lay off one years provisions for Clara Hanna, widow of Andrew Hanna, deceased.

Ordered by the court, five acting Justices being present, that John Cloah be appointed overseer, on the Mills Point raod, in place of James Wadkins, resigned, and that he work the same distance and bounds of hands as the former overseer, and that he keep the same in repair as a first class road. Samuel Helms this day resigned as overseer of the Dresden road.
Ordered by the court that Johathan Whiteside be appointed overseer on the Dresden road in the place of Samuel Nelms, resigned, and work the same distance and bounds of hands as former overseer, and that he keep the same in repair as a first class road.

Samuel Reeves this day produced in open court one wolf scalp over four months old, and proved by his own oath the killing of the same within the limits of this court, five acting Justices being present, that he be allowed agreeable to the Statues, in such cases made and provided, and that the Treasurer pay the same out of any monies in his hands not otherwise appropriated.

Ordered by the Court, five acting Justices being present, that John Brown be appointed overseer of the Mills Point road, from Buchannans field to Mrs. Daultons, in the (p-174) place of Sanford Bramblett, resigned, and that he work the same distance and bounds of hands, as the former overseer, and that he keep the same in repair as a first class road.

Ordered by the court, five Justices being present, that William Carmack be appointed overseer on the Mills Point road, in the the place of Jubille M. Bedford, who has this day resigned as overseer, and that he work the same distance and bounds of hands as former overseer and all the hands, and keep the same in repair as a first class road.

Ordered by the court, five Justices being present, that Seth Bedford, administrator of John Pate, Deceased, be allowed the sum of Fifty Dollars for settling up the business of said estate, to be paid out of said estate.

Ordered by the court, five Justices being present, That Jubilee M. Bedford be allowed the sum of eighty six dollars and forty cents to renumerate him for monies paid for Taxes on eight town lots in the town of Troy, belonging to the commissioners in trust for said town, and that the County Trustee pay the same out of any monies in his hands not otherwise appropriated.

Ordered by the court, five Justices being present, that James Davis, coroner of Obion Dounty, be allowed the sum ten dollars for holding two Juries of inquest over the bodies of Joseph (p-175) Wallace and Berry Doffel, and that the County Trustee pay the same out of any monies in his hands not other appropriated.

Ordered by the court, five Justices being present, that James M. Porter & Wm. B. Porter (merchants) be allowed the sum of fifteen dollars for a Record Book furnished by them for Obion County, and that the Trustees pay the same out of any monies in his hands not otherwise appropriated.

Ordered by the court, five Justices being present, that the commissioners in trust for the town of Troy sell all the unsold town lots, of said town on the second day of April Court 1835 on a credit of twelve months taking bond and security from the purchasers.

Ordered by the court that the following Justices be appointed to take a list of taxable property in the different Captains companies in Obion County, to wit: Benjamin Totten in Captain Hill's old company, Willis Caldwell in Captain Henry's and Captain Adams' companies. John Parr in Captain Nelms' company, William Wilkinson in Captain Head's company, Wm. Hutchinson in Captain Darnal's company, James Henderson in Captain Vaughn's company, William Downey in Captain Watson's old company and that they make returns at the next term of this court.

Ordered by the court that Tuesday, the second day of this term be set apart for the transaction of court business.

(p-176) Monday 5th January Term 1835.

Catharine R. Davidson this day returned to court an additional account of sales of the estate of Andrew W. Davidson, deceased, which was ordered to be received & recorded.

Ordered by the court that Jubilee M. Bedford & William B. Porter be appointed commissioners to settle with William W. Watson, administrator of David Brown, deceased.

Joel H. Dyer, Attorney General of this court, having failed to attend and prosecute the Pleas of the State, it is ordered by the court that Felix Parker, Jr., one of the attornies of this court, be appointed Attorney General pro tem, for the present term. Who thereupon took the oath prescribed by law.

Ordered by the court that Franklin Longley be appointed overseer on the road leading from Brownsford on Reelfoot Lake to the Mississippi River in the place of Richard T. Merriwether, resigned, and that he work the same distance & bounds of land and that he keep the same in good repair.

William W. Edmonds records his stock mark as follows, to wit: A smooth cross off the left ear.

(p-177) Nicholas L. Allen)
         To            )
         Abram Henning )

A deed of conveyance from N. L. Allen to Abraham Henning for two hundred acres of land was this day produced in open court and the execution thereof duly proven by the oaths of Abraham Pursell and Daniel Brown the subscribing witnesses thereto and ordered to be so certified for registration.

Thereupon court adjourned until tomorrow morning at nine o'clock.

John Harpole, J. P. (Seal)
Willis Caldwell, J. P.
John Parr, J. P.

Tuesday January 6th, January Term A. D. 1835.

Court met pursuant to adjournment. Present the worshipful John Parr, John Harpole, Willis Caldwell, Wilford Farris, James Henderson, William Downey, and Jesse Daugherty and proclamation being made the court then proceeded to business.

This Jesse Daugherty tendered his resignation as a Justice of the Peace of Obion County to the court which was received by the court.

D. Armour & Moran)
Vs            ) Trespass on the case.
Joseph Meadows )

This day came the plaintiff into open court and say that he intends no further to prosecute their suit, and thereupon came the defendant into open court, and assumed upon himself the payment of the cost in this suit.

It is therefore considered by the court that (p-178) plaintiff recover of the defendants their costs by them about their suit in this behalf expended & that execution issue &c.

Ordered by the court that William Harpole be appointed Guardian of Susan Adaline Graves Dickson, minor heir of Robert Dickson, deceased.

Ordered by the court that Charles McAlister, James M. Porter and William W. Watson be appointed revenue commissioners for Obion County for the next ensuing four years.

Ordered by the court that John C. Wilson former Trustee of Obion County, have a release of twenty dollars and twenty five cents for insolvences who have posted strays in Obion County and are unable to pay the valuation of said strays, to wit: Jacob B. Summers $3.00, Sarah Baxter $3.00, Robert Dickerson $3.00, Alexander Starrett $3.00, Charles Hodges $4.75, W. Jackson $3.50.

State of Tennessee)
Vs            ) Affray.
David W. Pound )

This day came the Attorney General and by leave of the court, enters a nollk proseque in this cause, and it appearing to the satisfaction of the court that it was either a frivolous or malicious prosecution. It is therefore ordered by the court that James McNeely, prosecutor in this case, be taxed with the costs of this prosecution and that execution issue &c.

(p-179) This day Joel S. Enloe, high sheriff of the County of Obion, returned into court the venire facias issued from this court at its last term and returnable to the present term, execution on the following persons, good and lawful men, householders or free holders of this county, to wit:

1. James H. Guy
2. James N. Cullum
3. William Harpole
4. William A. Maxwell
5. George White
6. Samuel Curlin
7. John Stanford
8. James Wilson
9. Adram Marbry
10. James Wadkins
11. Jerome Wadkins
12. Ezekiel Carter
13. Francis Taylor
14. Samuel Reeves
15. James Reeves
16. Robert Harper
17. James S. Brown
18. Horace Head
19. James B. Hogue
20. Benjamin Garrison
21. William B. Partee
22. Thomas Allen
23. Benjamin Sheeks
24. Anson A. Cunningham

To serve as Grand and Petit Jurors at this term all of whom appeared accordingly, except James N. Cullum, Thomas Allen, Benjamin Sheeks, John Stanford, James B. Hogue, William B. Partee, James Wadkins, out of whom was drawn according to the Statue in that case made and provided the following persons to serve as a Grand Jury at this term, to wit:

1. William A. Maxwell (Foreman)
2. James Wilson
3. Jerome Wadkins
4. George White
5. Francis Taylor
6. Horace Head
7. William Harpole
8. James S. Brown
9. Benjamin Garrison
10. Samuel Reeves
11. James H. Guy
12. Anson A. Cunningham
13. Samuel Curlin

Who after having been empannelled sworn and charged, retired to consider of indictments and presentments under the care of James Caldwell (p-180) an officer sworn to attend them.

John Parr, Willis Caldwell and James Henderson was this day elected to serve as quorum court for the present year, and John Parr was then elected chairman of said court.

State of Tennessee )
Vs )
Gideon Kirksey & ) Obstructing legal process.
Dolly Kirksey )

This day came the Attorney General and by leave of the court entered a nolle prosique in this cause.

State of Tennessee )
Vs ) Breaking Jail.
Gideon Kirksey )

This day came the Attorney General and by leave of the court entered a nolle prosique in this cause.

State of Tennessee )
Vs ) Forfeiture of Recognisance.
David W. Pound )

On motion of the defendants supported by the oath of the party it is ordered by the court that the forfeiture in this case be set aside.

State of Tennessee )
Vs ) Forfeiture of Recognisance.
James M. Pound )

On motion of the defendants supported by the oath of the party it is ordered by the court that the forfeiture in this case be set aside.

Ordered by the court that the following be the Tavern rates for Obion County for the year A. D. 1835, to wit: (p-181) For each Diet twenty five cents, for lodging twelve and a half cents, for horse feed twenty five cents, for horse per night thirty seven and a half cents, for half pint of whiskey twelve and a half cents, for rum, gin, brandy or wine each, twenty five cents for half pint.

Ordered by the court that the following rates of ferriage at Fentress' ferry, to wit: For man and horse, twelve and a half cents, for footman or single horse six and a fourth cents, for each waggon and team fifty cents, for each carryall, thirty seven and a half cents, for each cart and team, twenty five cents, for each four wheel pleasure carriage &c fifty cents, for each gig &c twenty five cents, for cattle, hogs or sheep, three cents per head, for the present year.

Ordered by the court that Felix Parker, Jr. one of the practicing attornies of this court, be allowed the sum of thirty seven dollars and fifty cents for exofficio services rendered by him as attorney general pro tem of this court during the year A. D. 1833, and at the present term of this court, and that the county Trustee pay the same out of any monies in his hands not otherwise appropriated.
(Issued 9th June)

Ordered by the court that James Caldwell, a constable of Obion County, be appointed to wait on the Grand Jury during the present term of this county who thereupon took the oath required by law.

(p-182) This day being Tuesday, the second day of January Term of the County Court of Obion County, said court proceeded to hold an open and free election for Clerk of said court to fill the vacancy occasioned by the resignation of Samuel D. Wilson, former Clerk of this court, the chairman of said court having on Monday the first day of the present term publicly advertised on the Courthouse door of said County that said court would on this day proceed to elect a clerk to fill said vacancy, the Sheriff of said county having first made proclamation for all candidates to come forward and make themselves known, the court proceeded to hold said election, and on calling and counting out the votes, it appeared to the court that William S. S. Harris was duly, constitutionally and unanimously elected Clerk of Said Court, who therefore entered into bond and security for the faithful performance of his dutys as Clerk of said Court which bond is in the words and figures as follows, to wit:

State of Tennessee)
Obion County      )

Know all men by these presents that William S. S. Harris, James M. Porter, Horace Head, John Linn, George W. L. Marr and Theodore Staley all of the County and State aforesaid are held and firmly bond unto William Carroll, governor of the state aforesaid and his successors in office in the sum of five thousand dollars, for the payment of which well and truly to be made we bind ourselves, our heirs, executors and administrators jointly and severally firmly by (p-183) these presence, sealed with our seals and dated this sixth day of January 1835.

The condition of the above obligation is such that whereas the said William S. S. Harris was this day duly and constitutionally appointed Clerk of the County Court for the County of Obion of said Court, now if the said William S. S. Harris shall safely keep the Records of said Court and shall faithfully discharge all the duties of his said office, then the said obligation to be void, otherwise to remain in full force & virtue this date above.

William S. S. Harris (Seal)<br>
James M. Porter (Seal)<br>
Horace Head (Seal)<br>
John Linn (Seal)<br>
G. W. L. Marr (Seal)<br>
Theodore Staley (Seal)

And the said William S. S. Harris, thereupon took the several oaths prescribed by law, and entered on the duties of his said office of Clerk of said County Court.

Ordered by the Court that the following be the rate of Taxes for the County of Obion for the year A. D. 1835, to wit:

For County Contingences:

| | |
|---|---|
| On each 100 acres of land | .12½ cts. |
| On each town lot | .25 " |
| On each white pole | .12½ " |
| On each slave | .25 " |
| On each Stallion half amount season of 1 mare | |
| On each Tavern with license | $5.00 |
| On each retail store | $5.00 |
| On each Jack half the season of 1 mare | |
| (p-184) On each 4 wheel pleasure carriage | $4.00 |
| On each 2 wheeled Do Do | .50 cts. |

For Courthouse Tax

| | |
|---|---|
| On each 100 acres of land | .18 3/4¢ |

| | |
|---|---|
| On each town lot | .37½ |
| On each white pole | .12½ |
| On each slave | .25 |
| On each stud horse or jack half the season the season of 1 mare | |
| On each retail store | $ 5.00 |
| On each tavern with license | 5.00 |
| On each four wheeled pleasure carriage | 1.00 |
| On each 2 Do Do Do | .50 |

For the payment of Jurors.

| | |
|---|---|
| On each 100 acres of land | .06¼ |
| On each slave | .12½ |
| On each stallion or jack one fourth the season of one mare | |
| On each retail store | $ 2.50 |
| On each Tavern | 1.50 |
| On each 4 wheel pleasure carriage | 1.25 |
| On each 2 Do Do Do | 1.50 |

On each suit $1.00 to pay the quorum court.

And thereupon the court adjourned until tomorrow morning at nine o'clock.

           John Parr, J. P.
           Willis Caldwell, J. P.
           James Henderson, J. P.
           John Harpole, J. P. (Seal)

(p-185) January 7th Wednesday Morning.

Court met pursuant to adjournment present John Parr, Willis Caldwell and James Henderson, Justices of the Peace.

Cornelius Sheeks &)
Jesse Sheeks )
Vs      ) Case
Robert White )

This day came the parties by their attorneys and by his consent and agreement this cause ordered to be transferred to the Circuit Court of Obion County.

Littleton Hubbard)
Vs      ) Case
Samuel H. Cole )

By this consent of the parties and with the assent of the court, this case is ordered to be transferred to the Circuit Court of Obion County

Rosanna Harper         )
Vs                )
Richard B. Brown; Joel S. Enloe & R. D. Brown) Debt
Admrs. of James M. Ross, dec'd.     )

This day came the parties by their attorney and by their consent of agreement it is ordered by the court that this cause stand for trial at next term with leave for each party to avail themselves of all legal advantages as tho the cause was reviewed and the pleadings made up the present term within party, waiving anything.

Machbaum & Norville)
Vs                      ) Case
Charles McAlister )

By consent of parties this cause is ordered to be transferred to the Circuit Court of Obion.

(p-186) Monday.

William W. Lea, Assignee)
Vs                             ) Debt
Moses Parr                  )

This day came the parties by their attorneys and thereon came also a jury of good and lawful men, to wit: James Wadkins, Jesse Sheeks, Ezekiel Carter, Abram Mearkry, W. H. Guy, W. F. Smith, B. H. Linn, W. Minton, W. A. Brown, G. Colyear, W. C. Edwards & H. Applewhite who were elected, tried and sworn the truth to speak upon the issue joined upon their oaths do say that the defendant has not paid the debt in the declaration mentioned after his plea is alledged, and that the defendant owes the plaintiff the sum of one hundred and ninety six dollars and forty six cents, and they assess his damages therefore to the sum of eighteen dollars and sixty two cents. It is therefore considered by the court that the plaintiff recover of the defendant the said sum of one hundred and ninety six dollars and forty six cents his debt aforesaid and also the further sum of eighteen dollars and sixty two cents his damage, and the costs in this behalf from which the defendant prayed and obtained an appeal to the next Circuit Court of Obion County and entered into bond with security conditioned as the law directs.

James Hogge        )
Vs                       ) Case
Angus M. L. McBean)

This day came the parties by their attorneys and thereon came also a jury of good and lawful men, to wit: James Wadkins, Jesse Sheeks, Ezekiel Carter, Abram Mearkry, W. H. Guy, W. F. Smith, B. H. Linn, W. Minton, W. A. Brown, G. Colyear, W. C. Edwards and Henry Applewhite, who were elected, tried (p-187) and sworn the truth to speak upon the issue joined upon their oaths do say that the defendant did assume and undertake in manner and form as stated in the plaintiff's declaration and they assess the plaintiff's damage by reason of the non performance thereof to the sum of three hundred and eighty five dollars and ninety cents. It is therefore considered by the court that the plaintiff recover of the defendant the said sum of three hundred and eighty five dollars and nineteen cents his damage aforesaid assessed & also the costs in this behalf.

Henry L. Douglas & Larkin F. Wood)
Merchants &c in trade under the )
Style of Douglas S. Wood         )   Debt
Vs                               )
Daniel W. Pound & James W. Neely )

      This day came the parties by their attorneys and the defendants in Court withdrawn their pleading in this behalf plead, and suffers judgment to pass against them in this behalf by nil dicit, for the sum of one thousand and thirty four dollars and ten cents debt, and the further sum of one hundred and seventy dollars & sixty one cents damages for the detention thereof. It is therefore considered by the Court that the plaintiff recover of the defendant the sum of one thousand and thirty four dollars and ten cents debt, and the further sum on one hundred & seventy dollars and sixty one cents the damages aforesaid and the costs in this behalf.


David Sheeks                  )
Vs                            )
Little Hubbard, John Parr)    )   Debt.
And William Carmack           )

      This day came the parties by attorneys and thereon came also a Jury of good and lawful men, to wit: James Wadkins, Jesse Sheeks, (p-188) Ezekial Carter, Adram Marbry, W. A. Guy, William F. Smith, Benjamin A. Linn, William Minton, William A. Brown, George Colyear, William C. Edward & Henry Applewhite, who were elected, tried and sworn the truth to speak upon the issue joined upon their oaths do say, that the defendants have not paid the debt in the declaration mentioned, and that they owe the plaintiff the sum of one hundred and ninety five dollars & three cents debt, and they assess his damages to the sum of thirty one dollars fifty four cents damages for the detention thereof and also the costs in this behalf.

      It is therefore considered by the court that plaintiff recover of the defendant the sum of one hundred & ninety five dollars three cents, the debt and the further sum of thirty one dollars fifty four cents the damages & the costs in this behalf.


John Mc Clure        )
Vs                   )   Appeal from a Justice.
William S. S. Harris )

      This day came the parties by their attorneys and the defendant files his affidavit for a continuance and for the reasons disclosed therein it is ordered to be continued until next court.


James H. Guy                   )
Vs                             )
Robert B. Harper, Admr. of)    )   Assumpsit.
Andrew Linn, Deceased.         )

This day came the parties by their attorneys and by their consent and agreement, this cause is ordered to stand over till next court with leave for the parties to plead & try next court.

William W. Wilson, Admr. of )
David Taylor, deceased )
Vs ) Scire Facias
Jordan Hassell, Admr. of )
Jonathan C. Haughton, deceased)

This day came the parties by their (p-189) attorneys and defendant here say he cannot gainsay but that the plaintiff shall have judgment against him of his proper goods and chattels, lands & tenements for the sum of eighty three dollars and twenty five cents, the amount of the judgment in the Scire Facias and also the sum of six dollars and twenty two cents in trust and confessed judgment therefore.

It is therefore considered by the court that the plaintiff recover of the defendant said sum of eighty three dollars and twenty five cents and the -- their sum of six dollars and twenty two cents damages for the detention thereof and the cost in this behalf the plff. stayed execution three months.

The grand jury came into court and returned a bill of indictment for an assault & battery against John Fentress, a true bill which was recorded by the court & then retired.

Solomon D. Catoe )
Vs ) Appeal from a Justice.
John Hubert )

This day came the parties by their attorneys and thereon came also a jury of good and lawful men, to wit: James Wadkins, Jesse Sheeks, Ezekiel Carter, Adner Mearkry, Wm. H. Guy, Wm. F. Smith, Benjamin A. Linn, William Menton, Wm. A. Brown, George Colyear, Wm. C. Edwards & Henry Applewhite who were elected, tried and sworn the truth to speak upon the matter in dispute, upon their oaths do say they find that the defendant owes the plaintiff the sum of twenty eight dollars and they assess his damages for the detention thereof to the sum of one dollar and fifty cents. It is therefore considered by the court that the plaintiff recover of the defendant the sum of twenty eight dollars his debt aforesaid and also the sum of one dollar and fifty cents damages aforesaid (p-190) and also the costs in this behalf, and the defendant tendered a bill of execution to the opinion of the court, which was signed, sealed & made part of the record in this case.

Tyre Dabney )
Vs ) Certiorari Supercedeas
John Linn )

This day came the parties by their attorneys and by their consent and agreement and with the assent of the court, this cause is ordered to be transferred to the Circuit Court of Obion County.

James M. Porter & William B. Partee )
Merchants &c trading under the firm ) Attachment.
of Porter & Partee )

    This day came the plaintiff by consent and the defendant was called to come into court to replevy the property attached to give special bail & plead to the action, came not, but was in default. It is therefore considered by the court that the plaintiffs recover of the defendant his damages sustained in this behalf, but as it does not appear to the court what said damages are. It is ordered by the court that a Jury come here at next term to inquire of & assess what said damages are.


John Polk )
Vs ) Debt.
Thomas Allen )

    This day came the parties by their attorneys and by their consent it is ordered by the court that parties plead & try at next term, saving all exceptions to both parties.


(p-191) Wednesday.


John Polk ) Debt.
Vs )
Alexander Farris )

    This day came the parties by their attorneys and by their consent and agreement it is ordered by the court that the parties have leave to plead & try next court. Saving all exceptions to both parties.


Samuel A. Smith )
Vs ) Covenant.
James Hogge )

    This day came the parties by their attorneys and by their consent & agreement leave is given the parties to plead & try at next court, saving all exceptions to both parties.


State of Tennessee )
Vs ) A. & B.
John Fentress )

    This day came the Solicitors for the state and the defendant in person, who here says he is guilty in manner & form as charged in the indictment & for his deliverance puts himself on the favors of the court and for such his assinee, it is ordered by the court that he make his peace with the state by paying a fine of twenty five cents & the costs of the prosecution.

    It is therefore considered by the court that the State recover of the defendant the sum of twenty five cents & the costs of the prosecution & thereon William G. Fentress came into court & confessed Judgment jointly with the defendant for the fine & costs, and it is therefore considered by the court that the State recover against him the fine & costs aforesaid jointly with the defendant.

(p-192)   This day Charles Mc Alister one of the revenue commissioners appointed on yesterday came into court and entered into bond with Joel S. Enloe and James H. Guy his securities in the sum of one hundred dollars conditioned as the law directs.

This day James M. Porter, who was on yesterday appointed one of the revenue commissioners came into court and entered into bond in the sum of one hundred dollars with Robert Harper and James Henderson his securities conditioned as the law directs.

William W. Watson who was on yesterday appointed one of the revenue commissioners came into court and entered into bond in the sum of one hundred dollars conditioned as the law directs with Jerome Miller and Francis Taylor his securities.

William Harpole who was on yesterday appointed Guardian of Susan Adaline Gruves Dickson came into court and entered into bond in the sum of five hundred dollars conditioned as the law directs, with John Harpole and William A. Maxwell his securities and took the oath prescribed by law.

(p-193)   Mary Harper      )
          Vs               )
          Thomas M. Harper )

A bill of sale from Mary Harper to Thomas M. Harper for negro slave, Easter, was this day produced in open court and the execution thereof duly proven by the oaths of William Miller and Willis A. Hogge, the subscribing witnesses thereto and ordered to be so certified for registration.

Mary Harper      )
To               )
Thomas M. Harper )

A bill of sale from Mary Harper to Thomas M. Harper for negro slave, Henry, was this day produced in open court, and the execution thereof duly proved by the oaths of William Miller and Willis A. Hogge, the subscribing witnesses thereto, and ordered to be so certified for registration.

Ordered by the court that the following persons good and lawful men be summoned by the Sheriff of Obion County to hold the ensuing election for the ratification of the amended constitution of the State of Tennessee, at the different precincts in this county, to wit: John S. Doxey, William A. Maxwell and James B. Holloman at the precinct at J. B. Hollomons, John Parr, Willis Caldwell & Charles Mc Alister at the Courthouse in Troy. James Henderson, Hugh A. Shelton and John Williams at the precinct at John Williams, and William Downey, Richard Keathley and Henry Phillips at the precinct at Norrids old place and Richard T. Merriwethers, Stephen Mitchell & Franklin Longley at the precinct at Richard Merriwethers.

(p-194) Ordered by the court that the following persons good and lawful men, householders and free holders of Obion County be summoned by the Sheriff of said County to attend at the next Term of the Circuit Court as Grand and Petit Jurors, to wit:

1. Benjamin Totten
2. John Harpole
3. Abraham Herring
4. James L. Mills
5. John C. Outlaw
6. David Thompson
7. Willis Caldwell
8. Lewis Zachrey
9. David Sheeks
10. John Parr
11. William Wilkinson
12. William M. Wilson
13. William Downey
14. Stephen Mitchell
15. James Henderson
16. Wilford Farris
17. Evan Shelby
18. Richard B. Brown
19. Robert F. Chester
20. William Hutchinson
21. Henry J. P. Westbrook
22. John Williams
23. Henry Phillips
24. Thomas Spight
25. William Miller
26. Alfred Harget

And that said Sheriff also summons James Caldwell and Daniel St. John constables, to attend on the Circuit Court at its next term.

Ordered by the Court that the following persons, good and lawful men, householders and free holders of Obion County be summoned by the Sheriff of said County to attend at the next Term of the County Court as Grand and Petit Jurors, to wit:

1. James B. Holloman
2. Elisha Parker
3. Wyett Bettis
4. Issac Walker
5. Benjamin Evans
6. Edward Jones
7. Andrew B. Mills (p-195)
8. Jonas Bedford
9. Obediah Roberts
10. James Harper, Sr.
11. Samuel Hutchinson
12. Benjamin Sheeks
13. Thomas Buchanan
14. Sanford Bramblett
15. John P. Wright
16. Samuel Simpson
17. Harry Applewhite
18. Hugh A. Shelton
19. William F. Smith
20. Thomas A. Polk
21. Norton Oaks
22. Richard Keathley
23. William Miles
24. John Hubert
25. Hugh A. Caruthers
26. Stephen S. Calhoun

And that said Sheriff also summons William Calhoun and Charles Sinkler, Constables, to attend on the County Court at its next term.

Samuel L. Teater)
Vs            ) Trespass on the case.
Robert B. Harper)

This day came the parties by their attorneys and by their consent and agreement, it is ordered by the court that the parties have leave to plead and try at next court, saving all exception to both parties.

Solomon P. Catoe )
Vs ) Appeal, in the nature of error.
John Hubert )

This day came the defendant into court & entered into bond with security conditioned as the law directs and prayed an appeal in the nature of a suit of errors to the Circuit Court of Obion County, from a Judgment rendered against him in this cause, which is granted.

David Sheeks )
Vs )
Littleton Hubbard, ) Debt.
John Parr & William Carmac )

This day came the defendant and entered into bond & security, conditioned by the law directs & prayed an appeal to the Circuit Court of Obion County from the Judgment rendered in thei cause, which is granted.

(p-196) Wednesday.

David Armour & James H. Morans, Merchants &c )
Trading under the style of D. Armour & Moran )
Vs ) Scire Facias
George W. Wood & Angus M. L. Mc Bean, )
Admrs. of Andrew C. Pagan, Deceased. )

This day came the plaintiff by the consent, and the defendants were called to come into Court and defend the suit, came not but was in default, and from the record & proceedings in this cause, it appeared to the court that the plaintiff obtain judgment against the defendants as administrators of Andrew C. Pagan, dec'd, for the sum of fifty dollars debt & fifty cents costs of suit before Richard B. Brown, Justice of the Peace for Obion County, on the 10th of April 1834, and that the defendants had wasted the effects of the intestate.

It is therefore considered by Court that the plaintiff recover of the defendants said sum of fifty dollars & fifty cents and also the further sum of three dollars the interest in this behalf & costs of this proceedings.

The court then adjourned till court in course.

John Parr, J. P.
Willis Caldwell, J. P.
James Henderson, J. P.

(p-197) April A. D. 1835.

State of Tennessee ) Court of Pleas and Quarter Sessions
Obion County ) April Term A. D. 1835.

Be it remembered that a a Court of Pleas and Quarter Sessions begun and held at the Courthouse in the Town of Troy, County of Obion and State of Tennessee on the first Monday in April A. D. 1835 and 59th year of American Independence it being the 6th day of said month present the worshipful Benjamin Totten, John Harpole, Willis Caldwell, John Parr, William Wilkinson, James Henderson and William Downey, Justices of the Peace, commissioned and assigned to hold said Term of said Court, proclamation being made, the Court then proceeded to business.

Thomas D. Moseley came into Court and took the oath prescribed by law as a practicing attorney, it is therefore ordered by the Court that said Mosley be authorized to practice as an attorney in this court.

Ordered by the Court that the following hands be added to the hands under John Williams, to wit: Jesse Daugherty & hands and Joseph Sheeks, & that they work under him.

(p-198)  Monday 8th April Term 1835.

Abner Davis this day came into court and proved by his oath the killing of one wolf over four months old within the limits of this county. It is therefore ordered by the court & six Justices of the Peace that he be allowed agreeable to the statutes in such case made and provided & that the Treasurer of the Western District of Tennessee pay the sum out of any monies in his hands not otherwise appropriated.

Jesse Farmer produced in court two wolf scalps over four months, and by his own oath proved the killing of the same within the limits of this county. It is therefore considered by the court & six Justices of the Peace being present that he be allowed agreeable to the statues in that case made and provided and that the treasurer pay the same out of any monies ni his hands not otherwise appropriated.
(Issued to S. D. Wilson)

Henry Applewhite produced in court one wolf scalp over four months old, and proved the killing of the same within the limits of this county. It is therefore ordered by the court & six Justices being present that he be allowed agreeable to the statute in that case made and provided, and that the Treasurer pay the same out of any monies in his hands not otherwise appropriated.

Samuel Hutchinson produced in court one wold scalp over 4 months old and proved the killing of the same within the limits of this county. It is therefore ordered by the court six Justices being present that he be allowed agreeable to the statute in that case made and provided and that the Treasurer pay the same out of any monies in his hands not otherwise appropriated.
(Issued to S. D. Wilson)

Henry J. P. Westbrook and William Hutchinson, commissioners appointed at January term 1835 of  (p-199)  this court, to lay off and set apart one years provision for Clany Hanna, widow of Andrew Hanna, deceased, this day made their return into court as follows, to wit: Agreeable to an order to us directed we have this day met and laid off the provisions for Clany Hanna, widow of Andrew Hanna, deceased, for one year, to wit: One hundred bushels of corn, 400# pork, 20# coffee & 50# brown sugar, 100# salt.

It appearing to the satisfaction of the court that David Durham departed this mortal life on the day of February A. D. 1835 that at the time of his death he was a citizen of Obion County & that he left no last will and testament. William B. Partee thereon moved the court to appoint him administrator of said intestate, he being the highest creditor & no other person applying to administer on the same. It was therefore ordered by the court that said William B. Partee be appointed administrator of all and singular the goods and chattels, rights and credits which were of said David Durham, deceased, and thereon said William B. Partee entered into bond with John C. Wilson, Jubilee M. Bedford and A. W. O. Totten, his securities, and took the oath prescribed by law.

Robert Edmonds produced in court one wolf scalp over four months old, and proved the killing of the same within the limits of this court. It is therefore ordered by the court, six Justices being present, that he be allowed agreeable to the statute in such cases made and provided and that the Treasurer pay the same out of any monies in his hands not otherwise appropriated.

Lewis Stanley produced in court one wolf scalp over four months old, and proved the killing of the same within the limits of this county. It is therefore (p-200) ordered by the court, six Justices being present that he be allowed agreeable to the statute in that case made and provided and that the Treasurer pay the same out of any monies in his hands not otherwise appropriated.

Thomas Taylor produced in court one wolf scalp over four months old, and proved the killing of the same within the limits of this county. It is therefore ordered by the Court, six Justices being present, that he be allowed agreeable to the statute in that case made and provided and that the Treasurer pay the same out of any monies in his hands not otherwise appropriated.

It appearing to the satisfaction of the court that the late change made by John William in the road leading from Troy to Dyersburg is nearer and on better ground than where said road formally run. It is therefore ordered by the court that the overseer on said road work it where it now runs and that said road run where it now does.

Ordered by the court that James Faris be appointed overseer on the road leading from Troy to Dresden in the place of Thomas Harper, and that he have the same hand to work under him.

William Hutchinson returned here into court his list of Taxable property in Captain Darnals company, which is received by the court and ordered to be recorded.

Ordered by the court that the Sheriff receive and receipt for the Taxes due on 440 acres of land entered by Henry Rutherford, No. of entry 18993 in Range 7 and Section 6 & 7 on Clover Lick Creek, in the name of John L. Johnson.

(p-201)  The following order and return thereon was made to court, to wit:

99

State of Tennessee)  Court of Pleas and Quarter Sessions
Obion County    )  Oct. Term 1834

In pursuance to a petition of sundry citizens of Obion County, it is ordered by the Court that William A. Maxwell, George W. Maxwell, Martin Tally, Alfred Mc Daniel, John S. Doxey, John Jones and George White be appointed Jury of review to report whether the road from the state line to Dresden cannot be so altered and laid off from the Reelfoot Bridge to the state line as to run through the plantation of James L. Mills in a different way, without detriment to said Mills plantation so as to make it run on as good ground as it now runs on and that they report to the next Term of this Court.

W. S. S. Harris, Clerk J. P.

State of Tennessee)
Obion County    )

We, the jury, after being duly sworn & empannelled reviewed the road from Reelfoot Bridge to the state line and we believe that it may be altered running on better ground and equally near to leave the Dresden road when the Moscow road crossed said road, and running thence Northwest to the State line, so as to leave the house of Jas. L. Mills to the north side.

William A. Maxwell
George White
Martin Tally and
George W. Maxwell

And it is therefore ordered by the court that the overseer on said road cut out the road agreeable to the review.

(p-202) Ordered by the court that Joel S. Enloe, Sheriff & Collector, be released from accounting for the taxes on eleven thousand acres of land listed in the name of John G. & Thomas Blount for the year 1834, it appearing to the satisfaction of the court that there is no such land.

Ordered by the court that Thomas N. Buchannon, William Carmack, A. A. Cunningham & John Gore be appointed a Jury of review to straighten the Mills point road near the house of Jubilee M. Bedford, and that they report to next court.

Ordered by the court that Jesse Sheeks be appointed overseer on the road leading from Nelms ferry to Mills point in the place of John J. Taylor, and that the same hand work under him & that he work the same distance.

James Caldwell was this day duly and constitutionally elected constable for Captain Henry's company.

Jacob Long was this day duly and constitutionally elected constable for the Town Company.

Ordered by the court that Alfred Harget take charge of Barbary Andrews, a pauper until the next term of this court.

Ordered by the court that John B. Hubbard, William B. Partee and Daniel St. John be appointed to settle with Samuel D. Wilson former clerk of this court for the year 1834.

(p-203) Norton Cakes was this day duly and constitutionally elected constable for Obion County in Captain Glisson's company, and came into court and took the oath of office and entered into bond with Alfred Harget, James M. Spight, William T. White, Wm. Downey, C. Mc Alister and Richard Keathley his securities, conditioned as the law directs.

William Carter produced in court one wolf scalp over four months old, and proved the killing of the same within the limits of this county. It is therefore ordered by the court that he be allowed agreeable to the statue in that case made and provided and that the Treasurer pay the same out of any monies in his hands not otherwise appropriated.
(Issued to S. D. Wilson)

Ordered by the court that Daniel St. John be appointed a commissioner in trust for the Town of Troy.

Ordered by the court that Samuel D. Wilson, former clerk of this court, be allowed the sum of ten dollars for furniture furnished the clerks office of this court and that the Trustee pay the same out of any monies in his hands not otherwise appropriated.
(Issued)

Ordered by the court that Samuel D. Wilson be allowed twelve dollars and fifty cents for issuing & recording Jurors tickets for the year 1834, and that the Trustee pay the same out of any monies in his hands not otherwise appropriated.
(Issued)

Ordered by the court that the following persons, to wit: James Harper, sons & hands, John Long (p-204) Thomas Russell and Henry Long be added to the hands under Samuel Hutchinson & that they work under him.

Ordered by the court that the following persons, to wit: Mr. Lomax, John D. Dickey, Seweils Russel, Nathan Morris, A. Vincent, James Guy, Wm. H. Guy, Thos. G. Jones, Moses D. Harper, Saml. Nelms, -- Fulks, -- Powel be added to the hands of and work under Johathan Whitesides.

Ordered by the court that James M. Porter and William B. Partee be appointed commissioners to settle with William W. Watson, administrator of David Brown, deceased, & that they report to the next term of this court.

Ordered by the court that Thomas Taylor work under William O. Linsey on the Dresden road, and that F. Taylor release him from working under him.

William Wilkinson returned here into court his list of Taxable property, taken in Captain Heads company & the same is received by the court and ordered to be recorded.

William Downey returned here into court his list of taxable property taken in Captain Watson's old company which is received by the court and ordered to be recorded.

It appearing to the satisfaction of the court that the quorum court of January term 1835 served as such 3 days and that no ticket has been issued for the same, it is therefore ordered that they be allowed for three days service at (p-205) said term, and that the Trustee pay the same out of any monies in his hands not otherwise appropriated.

Ordered by the court that William Calhoun be allowed two dollars for attending on the Circuit Court at November term 1834 as constable in place of James Caldwell who had been summoned for that purpose and that the Trustee pay the same out of any monies in his hands not otherwise appropriated.

Ordered by the court that William Calhoun be allowed four dollars for furnishing wood and keeping up fires for the court at January term 1835 and that the Trustee pay the same out of any monies in his hands not otherwise appropriated.

Ordered by the court that James Caldwell be allowed two dollars for furnishing wood and keeping up fires for the grand jury at January term 1835, and that the Trustee pay the same out of any monies in his hands not otherwise appropriated.

Ordered by the court that the persons taking the tax list of taxable property & rolls for the year 1835 be allowed five dollars for each captains company, that he may have been appointed in, and that the Trustee pay the same out of any monies in his hands not otherwise appropriated and that the clerk give to each a certificate for each captains company.

It appearing to the satisfaction of the court that Henry Applewhite and John Williams are overseers of roads, it is ordered that they be released from attending as Jurors (p-206) at this term of this court.

Wm. W. Watson and Clancy Hanna, Administrators & Administratrix of the estate of Andrew Hanna, deceased, returned hereinto court an inventory of said intestates personal property which was sworn to as the law prescribed, & received by the court as ordered to be recorded.

William S. S. Harris records his stock mark which is as follows, to wit: A swallow fork and under bit on the right ear, and an under slope & split in the left.

The court then adjourned until tomorrow morning at 9 o'clock.

John Parr, J. P.<br>
James Henderson, J. P.<br>
Willis Caldwell, J. P.

Court met pursuant to adjournment this 7th April 1835.

Daniel St. John, who was on yesterday appointed commissioner in trust for the Town of Troy, this day came into court and took the oath of office and entered into bond conditioned as the law directs with James Davis and S. S. Calhoun his securities which was received by the court and ordered to be recorded.

It appearing to the satisfaction of the court that Edward Jones one of the original pannel summoned to attend this court as a Juror could not attend without great injury to himself, therefore it is ordered by the court that said Jones be excused from attending this court.

It appearing to the satisfaction of the court that (p-207) Sanford Bramblett, who has been summoned as one of the original pannel of this court, should be released. It is therefore ordered by the court that said Bramblett be released as a Juror from attending this court.

Joel Henry, Dyer Attorney General of this Court, having failed to attend and prosecute and prosecute the pleas of the State, it is therefore ordered by the court that Felix Parker, Jr., one of the practising attorneys of this court be appointed Attorney General pro tem for the present term of this county, who thereupon took the oath prescribed by law.

It appearing to the satisfaction of the court that Samuel Hutchinson is an overseer of a road & that he has been summoned one of the original pannel for this court, it is therefore considered by the court that said Hutchinson be released from serving as a Juror at this court.

This day Joel S. Enloe, high sheriff of this county, returned here into court the venire facias issued from the January term of this court and returnable to the present term executed on the following persons, good and lawful men, householders and free holders of this county, to wit:

1. James B. Holloman
2. Elisha Parker
3. Wyett Bettis
4. Benjamin Evans
5. Edwards Jones
6. Jonas Bedford
7. Obediah Roberts
8. James Harper
9. Samuel Hutchinson
10. Benjamin Sheeks
11. Thomas Buchannan
12. Sanford Bramblett
13. John P. Wright
14. Samuel Simpson
15. Henry Applewhite
16. Hugh A. Shelton

(p-208)

17. William F. Smith
18. Thomas A. Polk
19. Norton Oates
20. Richard Keathley
21. William Miles
22. Hugh A. Caruthers
23. Stephen Calhoun

To serve as grand and petit jurors at this term, all of whom appeared accordingly except James B. Holloman, Elisha Parker, Wyett Bettis, Edward Jones, Sanford Bramblett, who being called came not, and out of those present was drawn accordingly to the statute in that case made and provided, the following persons to serve as a grand jury at this term, to wit:

1. John P. Wright (Foreman)
2. Stephen S. Calhoun
3. Hugh A. Shelton
4. Benjamin Sheeks

5. Richard Keathley
6. Samuel M. Simpson
7. Thomas A. Polk
8. James Bedford
9. William F. Smith
10. Thomas N. Buchannah
11. Hugh A. Caruthers
12. Obediah Roberts
13. William Miles

who after having been empannelled, sworn and charged, retired to consider of indictment and presentments, under the leave of William Calhoun an officer sworn to attend them.

James Caldwell who was on yesterday elected constable for this county in Captain Henry's company came into court and took the oath of office and entered into bond conditioned as the law directs, with Jacob Long, Wm. W. Watson and Joel S. Enloe his securities which was received by the court and ordered to be recorded.

Jacob Long, who was on yesterday elected constable for this county in the Town Company, came into court and took the oath of office, and entered into bond conditioned as the law directs with Jonas Caldwell, Joel S. Enloe, Jonathan Whitesides (p-209) and Wm. Miller his security was received by the court and ordered to be recorded.

Samuel T. Teater)
Vs ) Assumpsit.
Robert B. Harper)

This day came the parties by their attorneys and by their consent and agreement and by the assent of the court, it is ordered by the court that this cause be transferred to the next Circuit Court of Obion County.

State of Tennessee)
Vs ) Assault
John Foust )

It was ordered by the court that this cause be striken from the docket, and that the County pay the cost.

James H. Guy )
Vs )
Robert B. Harper, executor) Assumpsit
of A. Linn, Deceased. )

This day came the parties by their attornies, and thereupon came a jury of good and lawful men, to wit: William H. Hoard, William T. Whiteside, Noah C. Johnson, Benjamin Evans, Alexander F. Polk, Fletcher G. Edwards, Ambrose Forbus, John Fary, Elisha Parker, William Buchannan, Ishmael Hamilton, Abner Harris, who being elected, tried and sworn, the truth to speak, upon the issues joined, upon their oaths do say that the defendant testator did assume and undertake in manner and form as the plaintiff is declaring hath alledged and that the defendants testator hath not kept and performed his said several promises and undertakings, but hath broken the same, and they do assess the plaintiffs damage by reason thereof, to the sum (p-210) of thirty five dollars.

It is therefore considered by the court that the plaintiff recover of the defendant the aforesaid sum of thirty five dollars the damages aforesaid in forms aforesaid and also his costs in this behalf expended, to be levied of the goods and chattels, rights and credits of the defendants testator in the hands of said defendant his executor to be administered.

Rosanna Harper )
Vs )
Richard B. Brown in his own right, ) In Debt.
Joel S. Enloe & against Richard B. Brown)
Admrs. of James M. Ross, Deceased. )

This day came the parties of their attorneys, and thereupon the defendants Richard B. Brown as administrator demand to the scire facias issue in this case came on to be agreed and thereupon all the matters and things arising thereon being fully understood by the court, it is considered by the court that the demand be overruled and that this cause be reviewed against said Brown, administrator of James M. Ross.

And said Richard B. Brown excepted to the review of said cause and said Richard B. Brown as such administrator declining to file any other pleas than those in which issue were made up in the lifetime of said intestate and thereupon came the following jury, to wit:

1. William H. Hoard
2. N. C. Johnson
3. B. Evans
4. F. G. Edwards
5. A. F. Polk
6. A. Foster
7. J. D. Dickey
8. B. Sheeks
9. J. Hamilton
10. J. E. Farr
11. Wm. Edward
12. W. T. Whiteside

Who being duly elected, empannelled and sworn the truth to speak (p-211) upon the issues joined, upon their oath do say that the defts., Enloe & Brown and said James M. Ross in lifetime did not pay the defts. in the declaration mentioned and in pleading they hath alledged and do assess the defts. damages to the sum of sixty eight dollars and twenty five cents ($68.25). It is therefore considered by the court that the plaintiff recover against said defts. said sum of seven hundred dollars ($700) in the declaration mentioned and said sum of $18.25 the damages of the Jury assessed together with the costs of this suit to be and of the proper goods and chattels, land & tenements of said Richard B. Brown and Joel S. Enloe and of the goods and chattels of said James M. Ross in the hands of said Richard B. Brown take administered & that execution issue thereof.

John Polk )
Vs ) In Debt.
Thomas Allen)

This day came the parties by their attorneys and thereupon came a jury of good & lawful men, to wit:

1. Jno. F. Wright
2. S. S. Calhoun
3. H. A. Shelton
4. B. Sheeks

5.  R. Keathly
6.  J. M. Simpson
7.  Jonas Bedford
8.  T. W. Buchannan
9.  Hugh A. Caruthers
10. Obediah Roberts
11. Wm. Miles
12. H. M. Daniel

Who being elected, tried and sworn the truth to speak, upon their oaths do say that the defendant hath not paid the debt in the declaration mentioned (p-212) except the sum of $11.91 and that the balance of the debt detained amounts to 733.09 and assess the damages for the detention to $25.00. It is therefore ordered by the court that the plaintiff recover of the defendant said sum of seven hundred and thirty three dollars and nine cents with said sum of twenty one dollars and 25 cents the damage aforesaid assessed with the costs of this suit for which execution shall issue.

Rosanna Harper )
Vs             )  In Debt.
Brown & Enloe  )
And Brown, Admr.)

In this case defendants pray an appeal in nature of a writ of error to the next Circuit Court and entered into bond in pursuance of the statutes with W. B. Partee, Charles Sinkler and Wm. A. Brown as their security with appeal in nature of a writ of error is granted.

Partee and Partee )
Vs                )  Attachment on writ of Inquiry
A. M. L. Mc Bean  )

This day came the plaintiff by his attorney and thereupon came the following jury of good and lawful men, to wit:

1.  Wm. Hoard
2.  W. C. Johnson
3.  B. Evans
4.  G. G. Edward
5.  A. T. Polk
6.  A. Forster
7.  J. R. Farr
8.  E. Parker
9.  Wm. Buchannan
10. J. Harper
11. Wm. Whiteside
12. J. Hamilton

Who being (p-213) elected, tried and sworn well and truly to inquire of the damages upon their oaths do say they assess the plaintiff damages to the sum of two hundred and fifteen dollars and 92 cents. It is therefore considered by the court that the plaintiffs recover against said defendant said sum of $215.92 together with the costs of this suit.

Jno William      )
Vs               )  Apl. J. P.
Wm. S. S. Harris )

This day came the parties by their attornies and therefore came the following jury of good and lawful men, to wit:

R. B. Harper, R. C. Andrews, B. Evans, F. G. Edwards, A. F. Polk, A. Forbus, C. Sheeks, J. Hamilton, F. E. Farr, W. C. Edward, Wm. T. Whiteside and M. H. Hoard who being elected, tried & sworn the truth to speak upon the matter in dispute upon their oaths do say the fine for the plaintiff the sum of $58.17 debt and assess his damages to $7.83 therefor considered by the court that the plaintiff recover of the deft. the said sum of $66, together with the cost of this suit.

Defendant moved the court for a new trial which the court referred to which opinion of the court deft. accepts and promoted a bill of exceptions which is signed & sealed by the court & much a part of the record of this case (p-214) and the court then adjourned until tomorrow at 10 o'clock.

                                                                   John Parr, J. P.
                                                                   James Henderson, J. P.
                                                                   Willis Caldwell, J. P.

Wednesday 8th April term 1835.

        Court met pursuant to and

Ordered by the court that James Caldwell be released from paying the double tax on 5000 acres of land for the years 1833 & 1834 entered Robert Martin by grant No. -- in this county, by his paying the single taxes, costs and charges on the same.

Saml. H. Smith, asignee)
Vs                          )  Covenant.
James Hogge        )

This day came the parties by their attornies and thereupon came the following jury of good and lawful men, to wit:

1. E. Parker             7. C. Fields
2. B. Evans              8. Wm. T. Whiteside
3. J. Harper             9. Jno. Polk
4. John Hoard           10. Jno. Linn
5. Wm. Miller           11. A. F. Polk
6. M. Chamberlin        12. David Lyon

Who being elected, tried and sworn the truth to speak upon the issue joined upon their oaths do say fined for the defendant and it is therefore considered of the court that the defendant recover of the plaintiff the costs of this suit & the plaintiff in -- from which the plaintiff -- appeal to the next Circuit Court which is granted and thereupon Joel S. Enloe came into court and acknowledged himself the plff. security to present said appeal with effect (p-215) from failure thereof to pay all such costs as may be allowed for failure thereof.

D. F. John and Catharin Ingram,)
Admr. of B. Ingram, Deceased  )
Vs                             )
Wyatt Bells                    )

    This day came the plaintiff by their attorney the defendant being solemnly called to come into court and defend his suit, came not, it is therefore considered by the court that the plaintiff recover of the defendant the damage by them in this behalf sustained but because it is unknown to the court what damages the plaintiff have sustained, it is ordered that a jury come at next court and inquire of the damages.

John Polk       )
Vs              )   Debt.
Alexander Faris )

    This day came the parties by their attornies and by their consent and agreement, it is ordered by the court that this cause stand continued until the next term of this court, and that either party have leave to take depositions by giving the opposite party legal notice.

Seth Bedford, Assignee &c            )
For the use of Joel H. Wilson        )
Vs                                   )   Debt.
Henry Applewhite & Ezekiel Carter    )

    This day came the plaintiff by his attorney and also the defendant, Applewhite, in proper person came into open court and says that he cannot gainsay the plaintiffs action and freely confesses judgment for the (p-216) sum of one hundred dollars debt, and the further sum of seven dollars and seventy three cents damages, by reason of the detention thereof. It is therefore considered by the court that the plaintiff for the use of James H. Wilson, recover of the defendant said sum of one hundred dollars and the further sum of seven dollars and seventy three cents damages as aforesaid and also the costs in this behalf expended, and execution issue.

John Polk      )
Vs             )   Debt - Appeal in nature of a writ of errors.
Thomas Allen   )

    This day came the parties by their attornies and thereupon the defendant tendered here in court bond and security and prayed an appeal in the nature of a writ of error to the next Circuit Court to be holden for Obion County in May next, and thereon said appeal in nature of a writ of error was granted accordingly.

David B. Dickson )
Vs               )   Case
Daniel W. Pound  )

    This day came the plaintiff by his attorney and on motion it was ordered that this cause be continued until the next term of this court.

Francis Taylor )
Vs            ) Debt.
Samuel Edmonds )
& Jesse Meacham )

This day came the parties by their attorneys and by their consent and agreement and by the assent of the court, this cause is ordered to be continued until the next term of the court without prejudice to either party.

(p-217) Samuel D. Wilson )
        Vs             ) Debt.
        James Hogge    )

This day came the parties by their attorneys, and also the plaintiff in proper person who says here in open court that he intends no further to prosecute his said suit, and assumes upon himself the costs in this suit. Therefore it is considered by the court that the defendant recover of the said plaintiff his cost in this behalf expended and that execution issue &c.

James Hogge      )
Vs               ) Capias ad respond.
Solomon Stoddard )

This day came the plaintiff here in open court by his attorney and says that he intends no further to prosecute his said suit, and assumes upon himself the costs of this suit, it is therefore considered by the court that the defendant recover of the plaintiff his costs by him in this behalf expended & execution issue &c.

Thomas W. Crabb    )
Vs                 ) Ca Sa
Gideon Harr etals  )

In this cause there appearing no plaintiff to prosecute, and for further reason shown the court, it is ordered by the court this cause be stricken from the docket and that the county pay the cost.

The court then adjourned until tomorrow 8 o'clock.

               Willis Caldwell, J. P.
               John Parr, J. P.
               James Henderson, J. P. (Se

(p-218) Thursday 9th April Term 1835.

This day before the worshipful Willis Caldwell, John Parr & James

Henderson, Justices of the said Obion County sitting and holding a court of pleas and quarter sessions for said Obion County comes into open court Joel S. Enloe, Sheriff and collector of the public taxes of Obion County and makes and presents here to the court a report in due form of law of sundress tracts of land and parts of tracts of land and town lots lying and being in the said county of Obion, which have been given in for Taxes in said county for the year A. D. 1834 the taxes upon which remain due and unpaid for said year and wherefore the respective owners or claimants thereof have no goods or chattels in said county, on which to distrain for said taxes, which report is here received by the county, and it is ordered that the clerk of this court receive & record said report which is done accordingly and is in words and figures as follows:

I, Joel S. Enloe, Sheriff and collector of the public taxes for the County of Obion, do hereby report to court the following tracts and parts of tracts of land and town lots, the taxes upon which for the year A. D. 1834, remain due and unpaid and the respective owners or claimants thereof have no goods or chattels in my county on which I cam distrain for said taxes, to wit:

John Bosley, one hundred acres entry No. 329, lying in range 3 and section 6 & 7, 13th district, taxes 56 cents, clerks fees (p-219) $1.40, Sheriffs fees $1.00, Printers fees $1.50.

Elizabeth Childress heirs, 611 acres, taxes $3.43, Clerks fees $1.40, Sheriff fees $1.00, Printers fees $1.50.

Elizabeth Childress heirs, 1000 acres, taxes $56$\frac{1}{2}$, Clerks fees $1.40, Sheriffs fees $1.00, printers fees $1.50.

Andrew Barnet and individual part or balance consisting of 802 acres of a tract of a 1002 acres, entry No. 102, lying in Range 5, Section 9, 13th District. Balance of tract paid by J. C. McLemore. Taxes $4.51, Clerks fee $1.40, Sheriff fee $1.00, Printers fees $1.50.

John R. Eatons being one tract of 1000 acres granted by the State of North Carolina to Adner Nash, by grant No. 147, dated 10th day of July 1788, lying in 3 &4 ranges & 7th section, 13th district. Taxes $56¢, Clerks fees $1.40, Sheriffs fee $1.00, printers fee $1.50.

John R. Eatons heirs, one tract of 1318 3/4 acres, granted by the State of North Carolina No. 150, dated 10th July 1788, lying in Ragnes 3 & 4 section 8, & 13th district. Taxes $7.41, Clerks fee $1.40, Sheriffs fee $1.00, printers fee $1.50.

Thomas B. L. Eaton one tract of 1000 acres, granted by the State of North Carolina to Adner Nash by grant No. 143, dated 10th July 1788, lying in range 3 & 4 and section 8 & 13th district. Taxes 56¢, (p-220) Clerks fee $1.40, Sheriffs fee $1.00, printers fee $1.50.

Sarah and Susan C. Eaton one tract of 1278 acres granted by the State of North Carolina, for 1000 acres to abner Nash, by grant No. 138, dated 10th July 1788, lying in Ranges 3 & 4, section 8, 13th district. Taxes $7.18, Clerks fees $1.40, Sheriffs fees $1.00, printers fees $1.50.

Sarah and Susan C. Eaton, one tract of 1000 acres, granted by the State of North Carolina to Abner Nash by grant No. 146, dated 10th July 1788, lying in range 3 & 4, section 8, 13th district. Taxes $5.62, Clerks fees $1.40, Sheriffs fee $1.00, printers fees $1.50.

Thomas R. L. Eaton one tract of 1175 acres, granted by the State of North Carolina to Abner Nash, for 1000 acres, by grant No. 152, dated 10th July 1788, lying in range & section, 13th district. Taxes $6.60, Clerks fees $1.40, Sheriffs fees $1.00, printers fees $1.50.

Pleasant Hunter, 400 part of James Martins 5000 acre tract lying in 3 & 4 range & 5 section, 13th district. Taxes $2.25, Clerks fees $1.50, Sheriffs fees $1.00, printers fees $1.50.

Andrew S. Harris one tract of 640 acres, granted by the State of North Carolina to Edward Harris by grant number 332, lying in -- range & -- section, 13th district. Taxes $3.60, Clerks fees $1.40, Sheriffs fees $1.00, printers fees $1.50.

Andrew S. Harris one town lot in the town of (p-221) of Troy, No. 10, taxes $1.12½, clerks fees $1.40, sheriffs fees $1.00, printers fees $1.50.

Andrew S. Harris one town lot in Town of Troy, No. 29, Taxes $1.12½, Clerks fees $1.40, Sheriffs fees $1.00, printers fees $1.50.

Thomas Henderson, one tract of 640 acres entry No. 648, lying in range 5 & section 7 & 8, 13th district. Taxes $3.60, Clerks fees $1.40, Sheriffs fees $1.00, printers fees $1.50.

Heirs of John C. Hamilton, 1128 acres out of Hugh Martins 5000 acre tract entry No. 119, 5 range, 9 & 10 section, 13th district. Taxes $6.32, Clerks fees $1.40, Sheriffs fees $1.00, Printers fees $1.50.

Heirs of John C. Hamilton, 250 acres formally Thomas Old. Taxes $1.40, Clerks fees $1.40, Sheriffs fees $1.00, Printers fees $1.50.

Heirs of John C. Hamilton, 640 acres entry No. 430 in the name of Willis Scoggins, in range 6 & section 8, 13th district. Taxes $3.60, Clerks fees $1.40, Sheriffs fees $1.00, printers fees $1.50.

Heirs of John C. Hamilton 140 acres entry No. 716 in the name of David O. Williams lying in 7th range & 7th section, 13th district. Taxes 78 cents, Clerks fees $1.40, Sheriffs fees $1.00, printers fees $1.50.

Heirs of John C. Hamilton, 130 acres part of Wycoff & Clarks grant, grant No. 82, for 390 acres lying in 9th range, 7th section. Taxes 73 cents, Clerks fees $1.40, (p-222) Sheriffs fees $1.00, printers fees $1.50.

Heirs of John C. Hamilton, 133½ acres part of Wycoff & Clarks grant No. 57 for 400 acres lying in range 9, section 7, 13th district. Taxes 75 cents, Clerks fees $1.40, Sheriffs fees $1.00, Printers fees $1.50.

John C. Hamiltons heirs 3360 acres out of a tract of 3840 acres entry number 630 in the name of B. Stedman, lying in 10th range, 6th section, 13th district. Taxes $18.90, Clerks fees $1.40, Sheriffs fees $1.00, Printers fees $1.50.

M. C. & E. E. C. Lockett one town lot in the town of Troy No. 39, Taxes $1.12½, Clerks fees $1.40, Sheriffs fees $1.00, Printers fee $1.50.

John Payne one tract of 524 acres part of a tract of 955 acres, entered in the name of Searcy Payne and Mc Lemore by entry number 575, in range 6, sections 7 & 8, 13th district. Balance paid by Moore and Mc Lemore. Taxes $2.93, Clerks fees $1.40, Sheriffs fees $1.00, printers fees $1.50.

Samuel Levingston 250 acres, Reelfoot Creek. Taxes $140, Clerks fees $1.40, Sheriffs fees $1.00, Printers fees $1.50.

Samuel Levingston 160 acres, State line. Taxes 70 cts., Clerks fees $1.40, Sheriffs fees $1.00, Printers fees $1.50.

Joel Swindle, 230 acres in grant No. 15, granted to Edward Harris by the (p-223) State of North Caroline, and dated 10th day of July 1788, range --, section --, 13th district. Taxes $1.29, Clerks fees $1.40, Sheriffs fees $1.00, Printers fees $1.50.

Jonathan Wyatt, 160 acres, range 4, section 9, taxes 70 cents, Clerks fees $1.40, Sheriffs fees $1.00, Printers fees $1.50.

Edward Write, 112 acres of land on Clover Creek. Taxes 63 cents, Clerks fees $1.40, Sheriffs fees $1.00, printers fees $1.50.

Charles White 185½, taxes $1.18, Clerks fees $1.40, Sheriffs fees $1.00, Printers fees $1.50.

Fountain Winston 500 acres on Reelfoot. Taxes $2.81, Clerks fees $1.40, Sheriffs fees $1.00, Printers fees $1.50.

Fountain Winston 160 acres, State line. Taxes 70 cents, Clerks fees $1.40, Sheriffs fees $1.00, printers fees $1.50.

              Joel S. Enloe, Sheriff &
              Collector for Obion County.

Whereupon it duly appearing to the satisfaction of the court here that Justices of the Peace, one for each captains company, in said county had been duly appointed to take and receive lists of taxable property and poles within said county for the year 1834, that said Justices so appointed respectively proceeded accordingly to take and receive the same and made due return thereof into said court and that the same have been duly recorded by the clerk of (p-224) this court, and it furthermore appearing here to the satisfaction of the court, from an inspection of the records so made by the clerk as aforesaid, that the foregoing tracts of land and parts of tracts of land and town lots are upon and form a part of said recorded lists and were by the respective owners or claimants thereof given in for taxes in said county for the year 1834, and are lying and being in the said County of Obion and that the Clerk of this court has within the time and in the manner prescribed by law made out and delivered to said

Sheriff and collector, a list of taxable property and polls, from the said record lists, containing said lands and lots, and that said lands and lots are liable to the several amounts of taxes, costs and charges on each and all other matters and things required by law in this behalf to be done and performed appearing here to the satisfaction of the court to have been duly done and performed it is considered by the court, that judgment be and it is hereby entered against the aforesaid tracts and parts of tracts, of land and town lots, in the name of the State for the sums annexed to each, being the amount of Taxes, costs and charged due severally thereon for the year 1834, and it is ordered by the court that said several tracts of land and parts of tracts of land and town lots, or so much thereof as shall be sufficient of each of them to satisfy the taxes, costs and charges annexed to them severally be sold as the law directs.

(p-225) Thursday 9th April Term 1835.

And also here before the Justices aforesaid setting and holding a court as aforesaid comes Joel S. Enloe, Sheriff and collector of the Public Taxes for the County of Obion and makes and presents here into court a report in due form of law of sundry tracts and parts of tracts of land and town lots lying and being in said county of Obion which were omitted to be given in for the taxes for the year 1834, and are liable for double taxes for said year, which double taxes remain due and unpaid, wherefor the owners or claimants thereof have no goods or chattels in said county on which to distrain for said double taxes, which said report is received by the court, and it is ordered by the court that the clerk receive & record said report which is done accordingly, and is in words and figures as follows, to wit:

I, Joel S. Enloe, Sheriff and Collector of the Public Taxes of the County of Obion, do hereby report to court the following tracts of land and parts of tracts of land and town lots as having been omitted to be given in for the taxes for the year 1834; that the same is liable to double taxes; that the double taxes thereon remain due and unpaid and the respective owners or claimants thereof have no goods or chattels within my county on which I can distrain for said double taxes, to wit:

Heirs of Isham Boyce, one tract of land containing 640 acres entry number 711 in the name of John Terrill, lying in ranges 8 and 9 section 9, 13th district. Taxes $7.20, Clerks fees $1.40, Sheriffs fees $1.00, Printers fees $1.50.

(p-226) Heirs of Isham Boyce, one tract of land containing 640 acres. Entry number 712 in the name of John Terrill, lying in range 8, section 9, 13th district. Taxes $7.20, Clerks fees $1.40, Sheriffs fees $1.00, Printers fees $1.50.

John Shaw 800, an undivided part or balance of a tract of 1000 acres entry number 427 lying in the 10th range & 7th section, 13 district. Balance paid by Mc Lemore & Vaught. Taxes $9.00, Clerks fees $1.40, Sheriffs fees $1.00, printers fees $1.50.

Robert Haul, 1800 acres, an undivided part or balance of a tract of

2500 acres entry number 535, lying in ranges 10 & 11, section 6, 13th district, balance paid by James Caruthers. Taxes 20 25/100, Clerks fees $1.40, Sheriffs fees $1.00, Printers fees $1.50.

William Fowler 640 acres, entry number 613, lying in range 11, section 6, 13th district. Taxes $7.20, Clerks fees $1.40, Sheriffs fees $1.00, printers fees $1.50.

David Ross one tract of 135 acres, entry number 611, lying in range 11, section 6, 13th district. Taxes $1.25, Clerks fees $1.40, Sheriffs fees $1.00, Printers fees $1.50.

William B. Lewis, 100 acres part of 200 acres entered in the name of Hogge & Mc Daniel by entry 22, lying in range 7, section 6, 13th district. Taxes $1.12½, Clerks fees $1.40, Sheriffs fees $1.00, printers fees $1.50.

Robert C. Williams, one tract of (p-227) 101 acres, entry number 62, lying in range 7, section 6, 13th district. Taxes $1.12, Clerks fees $1.40, Sheriffs fees $1.00, printers fees $1.50.

William L. Williams, 80 acres entry number 79, lying in range 7, section 6 & 7, 13th district. Taxed $81, Clerks fees $1.40, Sheriffs fees $1.00, printers fees $1.50.

William Murfree, 1398 acres, the balance of a tract of 1500 acres, entry number 432, lying in ranges 7 & 8, section 7, 13th district after deducting 102 acres paid by Mc Lemore & Vault. Taxes $15.68, Clerks fees $1.40, Sheriffs fees $1.00, printers fees $1.50.

Frederick Miller, one tract of 4000 acres granted by the State of North Carolina to said Miller by grant number 158, lying in ranges 8 & 9, sections 7 & 8, 13th district, after 440 acres paid by Samuel Crockett, and 745 acres paid by John W. Campbell, which leaves 2815 acres hereby reported. Taxes $31.70, Clerks fees $1.40, Sheriffs fees $1.00, printers fees $1.50.

One tract of land containing 640 acres entered by the heirs of Michael Hockley, by entry number 670, lying in the 5 & 6 range and 6 section, 13th district. Taxes $7.20, Clerks fees $1.40, Sheriffs fees $1.00, printers fees $1.50.

One tract of land containing 640 acres, entry number 743, in the name of Cullin Andrews, lying in the 6th range & 6th section, 13th district. Taxes $7.20, Clerks fees $1.40, Sheriffs fees $1.00, printers fees $1.50.

(p-228) Thomas Hopkins, one tract of land containing 5000 acres, entered on the 6th of December 1820, by entry number 7, in the names of John C. Mc Lemore and Thomas Hopkins, lying in the 5th & 6th ranges and 6 & 7 section, 13th district. Taxes $56.25, Clerks fees $1.40, Sheriffs fees $1.00, printers fees $1.50.

Thomas H. Williams, 250 acres, entry number 714, lying in range 5, section 8, 13th district. Taxes $2.81, Clerks fees $1.40, Sheriffs fees $1.00, printers fees $1.50.

C. Strong, one tract of 640 acres, entry number 469, lying in range 4 & 5, section 9, 13th district. Taxes $7.20, Clerks fees $1.40, Sheriffs fees $1.00, printers fees $1.50.
(Paid)

One tract of land containing 640 acres entered by the Trustees of Cumberland College by entry number 653, lying in the 6th range & 8th section, 13th district. Taxes $7.20, Clerks fees $1.40, Sheriffs fees $1.00, printers fees $1.50.

One tract of 5000 acres, entered in the name of Joseph Winston by entry number 386, lying in range 6, sections 9 & 10, 13th district. Excepting out of this report, Joseph Williams 400 acres, Mrs. Daulton 500 acres, 500 acres reported for single tax in the name of Fountain Winston, 500 acres paid by Lewis Winston, J. Blakemores 1000 acres, Isaac Parker 200 acres (p-229) and R. Crowders 300 acres, H. B. Sweeneys 212 acres, and R. Grimes 100 acres, which leaves 1288 acres of the original tract hereby reported. Taxes $14.75, Clerks fees $1.40, Sheriffs fees $1.00, printers fees $1.50.

One tract of 5000 acres entered by Henry Rutherford, by entry number 214, lying in range 7, section 6, 13th district, excepting out of this report, Pillows 2666, Garrett & Gardner 225, Woodridge 75 acres, and Whites 444 acres, which leaves 1590 acres of the original tract hereby reported. Taxes $17.88, Clerks fees $1.40, Sheriffs fees $1.00, Printers fees $1.50.

One tract of land containing 640 acres, entered by the heirs of Edward Hickman, by entry number 487, lying in the 5th range & 8 section, 13th district. Taxes $7.20, Clerks fees $1.40, Sheriffs fees $1.00, Printers fees $1.50.

One tract of land containing 200 acres entered in the name of Thomas Wilson, by entry number 387, lying in 5th range & 9th section, 13th district. Taxes $2.25, Clerks fees $1.40, Sheriffs fees $1.00, Printers fees $1.50.

Overton & Cage, 420 acres, entry number 328, lying in 5th range, 8 & 9 section, 13th district. Taxes $4.95, Clerks fees $1.40, Sheriffs fees $1.00, printers fees $1.50.

Wilson Cage 133 1/3 acres, entry number 390, lying in the 5 & 6 ranges, 9th section, 13th district. Taxes $1.40, Clerks fees $1.40, Sheriffs fees $1.00, printers fees $1.50.

(p-230) One tract of land containing 1500 acres granted by the State of North Carolina to William T. Lewis of grant number 330 lying in the 4 range and 9 & 10 section, 13th district excepting out of this report, Martha Mc Daniel 160 acres, Lewis Winston 160 acres, Fountain Winston 160, Sarah Daulton 160 acres, David Johnson 160 acres which leaves 700 acres of the original tract hereby reported. Taxes $7.87, Clerks fees $1.40, Sheriffs fees $1.00, minutes fees $1.50.

One tract of land containing 294 acres, entry number 661, in the name of Benjamin Grimes. Taxes $3.12, Clerks fees $1.40, Sheriffs fees $1.00, Printers fees $1.50.

One tract of 2000 acres, granted by the State of North Carolina to Jane Davidson by grant number 52, dated 10th July 1788, lying in the 5th range, 6 section, 13th district. Clerks fees $1.40, Sheriffs fees $1.00, Printers fees $1.50, Taxes $22.50.

One tract of 2000 acres, granted by the State of North Carolina to Mary Davidson by grant number 115, dated 10th July 1788, lying in the 5th range and 6 & 7 section, excepting out of this report 620 acres including one fourth of the bluff, paid by Stith and Clouston, which leaves 1380 acres of the original tract hereby reported. Taxes $15.50, Clerks fees $1.40, Sheriffs fees $1.00, Printers fees $1.50.

One tract of land containing 3000 acres granted by the State of North Carolina to (p-231) Thomas Davidson by grant number 44, dated 10th July 1788, lying in the 4 & 5 range, 6 & 7 section, 13th district. Taxes $34.62, Clerks fees $1.40, Sheriffs fees $1.00, Printers fees $1.50.

Ephriam McLean 800 acres being that part of a tract of 2500 acres granted by the State of North Carolina, by grant number 159, which lies in Obion County, in ranges 8 & 9, and sections 5 & 6, 13th district. Taxes $9.00, Clerks fees $1.40, Sheriffs fees $1.00, Printers fees $1.50.

Hardy Murphy, one tract of 640 acres, entry number 364, being in 7 range & 9th section, 13th district. Taxes $7.20, Clerks fees $1.40, Sheriffs fees $1.00, Printers fees $1.50.

John P. & E. Hickman, one tract of 600 acres, entry number 480, lying in range 4, section 6, 13th district. Taxes $6.75, Clerks fees $1.40, Sheriffs fees $1.00, Printers fees $1.50.

Archibald Henderson, 72 acres entry number 466, in 3 range, 7th section, 13th district. Taxes 80 cents, Clerks fees $1.40, Sheriffs fees $1.00, Printers fees $1.50.

One tract of land containing 277½ acres, being that part of an entry of 555 number 300, in the name of B. & G. Love & John C. McLemore, which lies in Obion County in ranges 3 & 4, section 7, 13th district. Taxes $3.12, Clerks fees $1.40, Sheriffs fees $1.00, Printers fees $1.50.

(p-232) One tract of land of 1000 acres, entered by entry number 640, by the Trustees of Cumberland College, being in the 7th range & 7th section, 13th district. Taxes $11.25, Clerks fees $1.40, Sheriffs fees $1.00, Printers fees $1.50.

Robert Holm, 1200 acres, granted by the State of North Carolina of grant number 371 being in 3 & 4 range, 5 & 6 section, 13th district, excepting out of this report 122½ acres paid by R. Keathley, which leaves 1077½ acres hereby reported. Taxes $12.12, Clerks fees $1.40, Sheriffs fees $1.00, Printers fees $1.50.

Alexander Read, 600 acres granted by the State of North Carolina by grant No. 33, being in 3 range & 5 & 6 section, 13th district. Taxes $6.75, clerks fees $1.40, sheriffs fees $1.00, printers fees $1.50.

Oliver D. Williams, one tract of 120 acres, entry number 713, in the 4 range and 6 section, 13th district. Taxes $1.35, clerks fees $1.40, sheriffs fees $1.00, printers fees $1.50.

James Taylor, one tract of 1000 acres granted by the State of North Carolina, to Abram Bush by grant number 141 dated 10th day of July 1788, lying in the 3 & 4 ranges & 8th section, 13th district. Taxes $11.25, clerks fees $1.40, sheriffs fee $1.00, printers fees $1.50.

One undivided part consisting of 4166 2/3 acres of a tract of 5000 acres entered by John C. McLemore by grant number 426, lying in the 9 & 10 ranges & 6 & 7 section, 13th district, balance paid by John C. McLemore. Taxes $48.00, clerks fees $1.40, sheriffs fees $1.00, printers fees $1.50.

(p-233)  One tract of land granted by the State of North Carolina to John G. & Thomas Blount by grant number 226, dated the 10th day of July 1788 for 1000 acres, lying in the 7th range, 8th section, on Indian Creek. Taxes $11.25, clerks fees $1.40, sheriffs fees $1.00, printers fees $1.50.

One tract of land containing 1000 acres granted by the State of North Carolina to J. G. & Thos. Blount by grant number 327, dated 10th day of July 1788. Taxes $11.25, clerks fees $1.40, sheriffs fees $1.00, printers fees $1.50.

One tract of land of 1000 acres granted by the State of North Carolina to J. G. & Thos. Blount by grant number 217, dated 10th July 1788, lying the 5th Range & 6th Section, 13th District. Clarks fees $1.40, Sheriffs fees $1.00, printers fees $1.50 four fifths paid Taxes $2.25.

One tract of land containing 1000 acres granted by the State of North Carolina to J. G. & Thomas Blount, by grant number 240, dated the 10th July 1788, lying in the 5th range & 6th section, 13th district. Clerks fees $1.40, Sheriffs fees $1.00, printers fees $1.50 fout fifths paid, Taxes $2.25.

One tract of land containing 1000 acres, granted by the State of North Carolina to J. G. & T. Blount by grant number 189, dated 10th July 1788. Clerks fees $1.40, Sheriffs fees $1.00, printers fees $1.50 four fifths paid, Taxes $2.25.

One tract of land containing 1000 acres granted by the State of North Carolina  (p-234)  to John G. & Thos. Blount, by grant number --, dated 10th July 1788. Clerks fees $1.40, Sheriffs fees $1.00, Printers fees $1.50, four fifths paid, taxes $2.25.

One tract of land, containing 3000 acres, granted by the State of North Carolina to J. G. & T. Blount by grant number 254, dated 10th

July 1788, lying in the 3 & 4 range, 5 & 6 section, 13th district, one fifth of this tract only reported. Taxes $6.75, Clerks fees $1.40, Sheriffs fees $1.00, printers fees $1.50.

One tract of land containing 1000 acres granted by the State of North Carolina to John G. & Thos. Blount by grant number 246, dated 10th July 1788, lying in the 5th range, 5th & 6th section, 13th district. Taxes $4.50, Clerks fees $1.40, Sheriffs fees $1.00, printers fees $1.50. One fifth of this tract only reported.

One tract of 1000 acres, granted by the State of North Carolina to J. G. & Thos. Blount by grant number 250, dated 10th July 1788, lying in range --, section --, 13th district. One fifth of the tract only reported. Taxes $2.25, Clerks fees $1.40, Sheriffs fees $1.00, printers fees $1.50.

One tract of land containing 1000 acres granted by the State of North Carolina to J. G. & T. Blount, by grant number 328, dated 10th July 1788, lying in range --, section --, 13th district. One fifth part of this tract only reported. Taxes $2.25, Clerks fees $1.40, Sheriffs fees $1.00, printers fees $1.50.

(p-235) One tract of land containing 1000 acres granted by the State of North Carolina to J. G. & T. Blount, by grant number 172, dated 10th July 1788, lying in range --, section --. 13th surveyors district, one fifth of this tract only reported. Taxes $2.25, Clerks fees $1.40, Sheriffs fees $1.00, printers fees $1.50.

One tract of 1000 acres, granted by the State of North Carolina to J. G. & T. Blount by grant number 252 dated 10th July 1788, lying in 4th range & 6th section, 13th district. One fifth of this tract only reported. Taxes $2.25, Clerks fees $1.40, Sheriffs fees $1.00, printers fees $1.50.

One tract of land containing 1000 acres, granted by the State of North Carolina to J. G. & T. Blount, by grant number 174, dated 10th July 1788, lying in 4 range & 6 & 7 section, 13th district. One fifth of this tract only reported. Taxes $2.25, Clerks fees $1.40, Sheriffs fees $1.00, printers fees $1.50.

One tract of land containing 1000 acres, granted by the State of North Carolina to J. G. & T. Blount, by grant number 236, dated 10th July 1788, lying in the 5th range, 6th section, 13th district. One fifth part of this tract only reported. Taxes $2.25, Clerks fees $1.40, Sheriffs fees $1.00, printers fees $1.50.

One tract of 1000 acres of land granted by the State of North Carolina to J. G. & T. Blount, by (p-236) grant number 227, dated 10th July 1788, lying in the 5th range, 6th section, 13th district. One fifth part of this tract only reported. Taxes $2.25, Clerks fees $1.40, Sheriffs fees $1.00, printers fees $1.50.

One tract of land containing 5000 acres granted by the State of North Carolina to J. G. & T. Blount, by grant number 232, dated 10th

July 1788, lying in the 5 & 6 range, & 6th section, 13th district. One fifth part of this tract only reported. Taxes $11.25, Clerks fees $1.40, Sheriffs fees $1.00, printers fees $1.50.

One tract of land containing 1000 acres, granted by the State of North Carolina to Edward Harris by grant number 8, dated 10th July 1788, lying in the 3 range, 9 & 10 section, 13 district. One fifth part of this tract only reported. Taxes $11.25, Clerks fees $1.40, Sheriffs fees $1.00, printers fees $1.50.

One tract of land containing 196 acres, it being lot No. 1 in grant number 4, granted by the State of North Carolina to Edward Harris, dated 10th July 1788, on Clover Lick Creek. Taxes $2.20, Clerks fees $1.40, Sheriffs fees $1.00, printers fees $1.50.

One tract of land containing 166 2/3 acres, it being lot No. 2 in grant number 4, granted by the State of North Carolina to Edward Harris by grant No. 4, dated 10th July 1788 on Clover Lick Creek. Taxes $1.87, Clerks fees $1.40, Sheriffs fees $1.00, printers fees $1.50.

One tract of land containing 250 acres (p-237) it being the lot laid off to Robert Sloan and Martha, his wife, part of grant number 16 granted by the State of North Carolina to Edward Harris, dated 10th July 1788, lying on Reelfoot Lake. Taxes $2.81, Clerks fees $1.40, Sheriffs fees $1.00, printers fees $1.50.

One tract of land containing 1000 acres, granted by the State of North Carolina by grant No. 10, dated 10th July 1788 in the 7th range & 7th section, 13th district. Taxes $11.25, Clerks fees $1.40, Sheriffs fees $1.00, printers fees $1.50.

One tract of land containing 1000 acres granted by the State of North Carolina to Edward Harris by grant number 6, dated 10th July 1788, lying in range 7, section 6, 13th district. Taxes $11.25, Clerks fees $1.40, Sheriffs fees $1.00, printers fees $1.50.

One tract of land containing 1000 acres, granted by the State of North Carolina to Edward Harris by grant No. 7, dated 10th July 1788, lying in the 7 & 8 range, 6 & 7 section, 13th district. Taxes $11.25, Clerks fees $1.40, Sheriffs fees $1.00, printers fees $1.50.

Heirs of Eli Harris, one tract of land containing 168 acres being lot No. 11, laid off by decree of the Chancery Court to heirs of Eli Harris at Paris out of a grant of 1000 acres granted to Edward Harris by the State of North Carolina by grant No. 15, lying in the 7 & 8 range, (p-238) 6th section, 13th district. Taxes $1.88, Clerks fees $1.40, Sheriffs fees $1.00, printers fees $1.50.

Heirs of Eli Harris, one tract of land containing 250 acres, being lot number 11 laid off to them by a decree of Chancery Court at Paris, part of 1000 acres granted by the State of North Carolina to Edward Harris of grant number 11, dated 10th July 1788 in Range --, Section --, 13th District. Taxes $2.81, Clerks fees $1.40, Sheriffs fees $1.00, printers fees $1.50.

Samuel Harris, one tract of land containing 250 acres, laid off by decree of the Chancery Court at Paris, to said Harris part of a 1000 acre tract granted by the State of North Carolina to Edward Harris by grant No. 16, dated 10th July 1788, 13th District. Taxes $2.81, Clerks fees $1.40, Sheriffs fees $1.00, printers fees $1.50.

Robert McCord, one tract of land containing 250 acres laid off to said McCord and wife by lot No. 6 by decree of the Chancery Court at Paris, out of a tract of 1000 acres granted by the State of North Carolina to Edward Harris, by grant No. 6, dated 10th July 1788, 13th district. Taxes $2.81, Clerks fees $1.40, Sheriffs fees $1.00, printers fees $1.50.

One town lot in Town of Troy, owner unknown, No. 9. Taxes $2.25, Clerks fees $1.40, Sheriffs fees $1.00, printers fees $1.50.

Madison G. Johns, one town lot in the Town (p-239) of Troy, No. 38. Taxes $2.25, Clerks fees $1.40, Sheriffs fees $1.00, Printers fees $1.50.

One town lot in the Town of Troy number 40, owner unknown. Taxes $2.25, Clerks fees $1.40, Sheriffs fees $1.00, Printers fees $1.50.

One town lot in the Town of Troy number 71, owners unknown. Taxes $2.25, Clerks fees $1.40, Sheriffs fees $1.00, printers fees $1.50.

John Polly, one town lot in the Town of Troy number 67. Taxes $2.25, Clerks fees $1.40, Sheriffs fees $1.00, printers fees $1.50.

One lot in the Town of Troy, owner unknown, number 83. Taxes $2.25, Clerks fees $1.40, Sheriffs fees $1.50.

One lot in the Town of Troy, owner unknown, number 89. Taxes $2.25, Clerks fees $1.40, Sheriffs fees $1.00, Printers fees $1.50.

                                              Joel S. Enloe,
                            Sheriff and Collector of Obion County.

Whereupon it is considered by the Court, that Judgment be, and it is hereby entered against the aforesaid tract of land and parts of tracts of land, and town lots, in the name of the State for the sums annexed to each, being the amount of double taxes, costs and charges due severally thereon for the year 1834 and it is ordered by the Court that said several tracts of land and parts of tracts (p-240) of land and town lots or so much thereof as shall be sufficient of each of them to satisfy the double taxes, costs and charges annexed to them severally, be sold as the law directs.

It appearing to the satisfaction of the Court here that the following lands, to wit: Henry A. Garrett 100 acres, Garrett & Gillespies 866 2/3, J. C. Hamilton heirs 333 1/3 acres, J. C. Hamiltons heirs 350 acres, J. S. Hamiltons heirs 217 acres and John C. Hamiltons heirs 202 acres and Garrett & Gillespies 200 acres, have been wrongly reported for the single taxes &c for the year 1834. It is therefore ordered by the court that the Sheriff and Collector (Joel S. Enloe) be released from accountability for said taxes, costs & charges for sd. year.

This day Jubilee M. Bedford, chairman of the Trustees of Obion County Academy fund, presented here in open court the bonds of the several Trustees appointed by the County Court of said County for that purpose, and the Court having carefully examined said bonds and approving of the same.

It is ordered by the Court that the Clerk receive said bonds, and certify the same agreeable to the statutes in that case made and provided.

Ordered by the Court that the following persons (good and lawful men) householders and freeholders of Obion County be summoned by the Sheriff of said County to attend at the next term of this Court as Grand and Petit Jurors, to wit: (p-241)

1. Tidwell Davis
2. James Snow
3. Benjamin F. McWherter
4. Elijah Reeves
5. Hansel McCaleb
6. James Johnson
7. John L. Williams
8. John Hoard
9. Howe Legate
10. Wiley Legate
11. Thomas Linson
12. James Read
13. James Lyons
14. William Jones
15. George Read
16. Terrell L. Camp
17. Noah C. Johnson
18. Benjamin Parmer
19. James Byron
20. Sion Hill
21. John Carter
22. James Crow
23. William Enloe
24. George W. Fentress
25. William T. Norrid
26. Andrew Moore

And that said Sheriff also summons Jacob Long and Norton Oakes, Constables, to attend on said Court at its next term.

And the Court then adjourned until Court in Course.

Willis Caldwell, J. P.
John Parr, J. P.
James Henderson, J. P.


(p-242) July: A. D. 1835.

State of Tennessee)   Court of Pleas and Quarter Sessions,
Obion County      )   July Term A. D. 1835

Be it remembered that at a Court of Pleas and Quarter Sessions begun and held at the Courthouse in the Town of Troy, County of Obion and State of Tennessee on the first Monday in July A. D. 1835 and the 60th year of American Independance, it being the 6th day of said month present the worshipful John Parr, William Wilkinson, Richard B. Brown, Willis Caldwell & William M. Wilson, Justices of the Peace in and for said County of Obion, Commissioned and assigned to hold said term of said court, proclamation being first made the Court then proceeded to business.

It appearing to the satisfaction of the Court that at the December Term A. D. 1830, of said County Court, allowances were improperly made to the solicitor, sheriff and clerk of said county said allowance or appropriation having been twice made when it was the intention of the said court to have made said allowances but once. It is therefore ordered by the court, present the worshipful John Parr, William Wilkinson, Richard B. Brown, Willis Caldwell and William M. Wilson, Esquires, all voting in the affirmative that one of said orders to said solicitors, sheriffs and clerks be revoked and made null and void.

William Cunningham produced in court three wolf scalps under four months old and proved the killing of the same within the limits of this County. It is therefore ordered (p-243) by the court, five Justices being present, that he be allowed agreeable to the Statutes in that case made and provided and that the Treasurer pay the same out of any monies in his hands not otherwise appropriated.

John Carter, Jr., produced in court one wolf scalp over four months old, and proved the killing of the same within the limits of this county, it is therefore ordered by the court, five Justices being present, that he be allowed agreeable to the Statutes in that case made and provided, and that the Treasurer pay the same out of any monies in his hands not otherwise appropriated.
(Issued 17th Dec. 1835.)

William C. Edwards produced in court three wolf scalps under four months old, and proved the killing of the same within the limits of this county. It is therefore ordered by the court, five Justices being present, that he be allowed agreeable to the Statutes in that case made and provided and that the Treasurer pay the same out of any monies in his hands not otherwise appropriated.

Greenberry Collier produced in court one wolf scalp over four months old, and proved the killing of the same within the limits of this County. It is therefore ordered by the court, five Justices being present, that he be allowed agreeable to the statutes in that case made and provided, and that the Treasurer pay the same out of any monies in his hands not otherwise appropriated.
(Issued 17th Dec. 1835.)

Frederick Taylor returned into court his road order. It is therefore ordered by the court (p-244) that he be released from further services as overseer of the Dresden Road.

Ordered by the court that Larkin Morrid be appointed overseer on the Dresden Road in place of Frederick Taylor, resigned, and that he work the same distance and bounds & hands as the former overseer, and keep the same in repair as a first class road.

Ordered by the Court that Tyron P. Nicholson be appointed overseer on the Dresden road in the place of William O. Lindsey, and that he work the same distance and bounds of hands as the former overseer, and keep the same in repair as a first class road.

Ordered by the Court that Randolph Stone be appointed overseer on the road from Troy to Reelfoot Lake, and that he cut out said road from the narrows of said Lake near James N. Stones to intersect the Dyersburg road near the 10 mile post or John Williams and that the following hands work under him, to wit: Daniel Miller, John Newton, Robert Newton, Isham Newton and all his hands, Joseph Speaks, Jesse Daugherty, James N. Stone, Elijah Reeves and all hands in those bounds, and that he keep the same in repair as a second class road.

Ordered by the court that Archibald H. Hogue be appointed overseer on the Mills Point road that runs by said Hogues in place of James B. Hogue, removed, and that he work the same distance and bounds of hands as the former overseer and keep the same in repair as a second class road.

(p-245) Ordered by the court that Abraham Marbury be appointed overseer on the Iron Banks road in the place of Owen Gissie, resigned, and that he work from the Mills Point road to James Wilsons and have the same bounds of hands as the former overseer and keep the same in repair as a second class road.

Ordered by the court that Joseph C. Culberson be appointed overseer on the Mills Point road in the place of John Brown, resigned, and that he work the same distance and bounds of hands as the former overseer and keep the same in repair as a first class road.

Ordered by the court that Henry Pryor be appointed overseer on the Trenton road from the three mile post to the Obion River in the place of Thomas K. Polk, and that he work the same distance and bounds of hands as the former overseer and keep the same in repair as a first class road.

The Jury of View who was appointed at April Term 1835 of this court to view out and straighten the Mills Point road from near J. M. Bedford, came into court and made the following return, to wit:

We, the undersigned Jury of Review being summoned & qualified according to law, do say the road shall be straightened from a certain white oak tree designated by us on the side of the road to the east mouth of the lane to go straight.

John Gore  
Wm. Carmack  
A. B. Cunningham

It is therefore ordered by the court that the (p-246) overseer on said road cut out the same agreeable to said review and make said alteration.

It is ordered by the court that the following hands work under James Farris on the Dresden road in addition to the hands already under him, to wit: ------ and that he keep the same in repair as a first class road.

This day a petition from sundry citizens of Obion County was presented to the court, praying that a road may be opened or a jury of view appointed to view out a road from Troy to the Reelfoot Lake as near a place called Davidsons Camp, to run near the present trail to said part as convenient. It is therefore ordered by the court that James Reeves, Hiram Reeves, William Hutchinson, John L. Bartlett, George W. Cunningham, Richard Hill and Daniel Waling be appointed a Jury of view to view out and lay off said road, and that they report to the next term of this court.

This day the petition of G. W. Fentress was presented to court praying the court to grant a Jury of review to review out a road from W. Enloes across the Obion River at Mary Richardsons Bluff, running thence to the Dyer County line in a direction to meet a road cut out by citizens of Dyer County.

It is therefore ordered by the court that the following persons be appointed a Jury of review to review out said road, leaving the Trenton road at or near William Enloes running to (p-247) Mary Davidsons' Bluff on Obion River, thence through the Obion Bottom, thence to the Dyer County line to intersect said road in the direction of Dyersburg, to wit: Thomas Spight, Norton Oakes, Samuel Reeves, William Miles, George W. Fentress, John Polk and Henry Pryor be appointed said Jury, and that they report to the next term of this court.

This day the petition of H. J. P. Westbrook and William Hutchinson was presented to the court praying for an order for a road leading from Dyersburg to Mills Point, leaving the Dyersburg road between the 8 & 9 mile post, from thence to Reelfoot Creek where Larkin Eastridge now lives, from thence to Mills Point.

It is therefore ordered by the court that the following persons, to wit: Samuel McElyer, John B. Tanner, Jonathan Mix, Jesse Daugherty, Greenberry Collier, A. Floyd and William Hutchinson be appointed to view out said road and mark the same and that they report to the next term of this court.

Ordered by the court present the worshipful John Parr, Willis Caldwell, William Wilkinson, Richard B. Brown, William M. Wilson and James Henderson, Esqrs., all voting in the affirmative that Alfred Harget be allowed fifteen dollars for keeping Barbary Andrews, pauper, the last three months, and that the Trustee pay the same out of any monies in his hands not otherwise appropriated.

(p-248) John Parr, Willis Caldwell, William Wilkinson, Richard B. Brown, William M. Wilson and James Henderson, all voting in the affirmative that Barbary Andrews, pauper, be let out by the sheriff of said county to the lowest bidder for the next ensuing twelve months on tomorrow at 12 o'clock.

This day before the worshipful Willis Caldwell, John Parr, William M. Wilson, William Wilkinson and Richard B. Brown, being more than one third of the Justices of said County of Obion, sitting and holding a County Court, Lucinda Coats by her council came into court and moves the court to grant her letters of administration on the estate of Austin M. Coats, deceased, and it appearing to the satisfaction of the court that said Austin M. Coats departed this life out of the limits of this State, and left said Lucinda Coats, his widow and relict, and at the time of his death departed out of the limits of this state and had and was seized of lands and real estate within the limits of this estate, to wit: A certain tract of land lying and being within the limits of said County, and that he had not at the time of his death any goods, chattels, effects or real estate within any other county in estate. It is therefore ordered by the court that letters of administration issue to the said Lucinda Coates on the estate of the said Austin M. Coats, deceased, on her entering into bond in the sum of two thousand dollars and security as required by law and it is further ordered by the court that said Lucinda be permitted to file said bond with sufficient security against next term of this court and that the (p-249) oath of administration before some Justice of the Peace of the State against the next term of this court, all of which shall be returned at next term of this court until which time said letters of administration shall not issue.

This day before the worshipful Willis Caldwell, John Parr, William Wilkerson, Richard B. Brown and William M. Wilson being more than one third of the Justices of said County of Obion, sitting and holding a County Court, comes into court in proper person James N. Stone, and moves the court to grant him letters of administration on the estate of John Zellers, deceased, and it appearing to the satisfaction of the court that said John Zellers had his place of residence in said County of Obion at the time of his death. It is therefore ordered by the court that letters of administration be issued to the said Stone upon all the goods and chattels rights and credits of said John Zellers, deceased, on his entering into bond and security as required by law.

This day Samuel C. Henry, administrator of the estate of Dempsey Allen, deceased, came into court and presented three receipts from the heirs of said D. Allen, deceased, as follows: One from George W. Haislip and Elizabeth Haislip for fifty three dollars and eighty eight cents, one from William Haislip and Tabitha Haislip for fifty three dollars and eighty eight cents and one from Samuel E. Allen for fifty three dollars and eighty eight cents, all of which was received by the court and ordered to be filed and recorded with the papers of said estate.

(p-250) This day Robert B. Harper, executor of the estate of Andrew Linn, deceased, came into court and returned an Inventory of Sundry notes of said estate, which is received by the court and ordered to be filed and recorded among the papers of said estate.

This day William W. Watson, one of the administrators of the estate of Andrew Hanna, deceased, came into court and returned an account of the sales of the property of said estate as sold on the 25th day of April 1835, which is received by the court and ordered to be filed and recorded with the papers of said estate.

Frederick Taylor )
To              )
Thomas Hampton  )

A deed for fifty acres of land on Little Richland Creek in Obion County, Tennessee, from Frederick Taylor to Thomas Hampton was acknowledged in open court by said Taylor and ordered to be so certified for registration.

William Haselip )
To            )
John B. Allen )

Deed of conveyance for his interest in one hundred and seventy five acres of land being the same belonging to the heirs of Dempsey Allen, deceased, was this day acknowledged in open court by said William Haselip, and ordered to be so certified for registration.

George W. Haselip )
To              )
John B. Allen   )

Deed of conveyance for his interest in one hundred and seventy five acres (p-251) of land, being the same belonging to the heirs of Dempsey Allen, deceased, was this day proven in open court by the oath of Samuel C. Henry and William Haselip, and ordered to be so certified for registration.

Proclamation being first made the Court, present the worshipful John Parr, Willis Caldwell, William Wilkinson, Richard B. Brown, William M. Wilson and James Henderson proceded to elect Internal Improvement Commissioners for the County of Obion, agreeable to the statute in that case made and provided, whereupon on counting out the votes, it appeared that Thomas Spight, Richard B. Brown and William W. Watson unanimously and constitutionally elected said Internal Improvement Commissioners for the next ensuing twelve months.

The court then adjourned until tomorrow morning at 9 o'clock.

                                              John Parr, J. P.
                                              James Henderson, J. P.
                                              Willis Caldwell, J. P.

7th July, 1835.

Court met pursuant to adjournment proclamation being made &c.

St. John & Ingram            )
Admrs. of B. Ingram, Dec'd.) Trover
Vs                           )
Wyitt Bettis                 )

This day came plaintiff by attorneys and on motion, and for reasons appearing to the court, it is ordered that this cause and the writ of inquiry be continued to the next (p-252) term of this court, and that a Jury then come to assess the plaintiffs damages in the behalf.

John B. Hubbard   )
Vs                ) Assumpsit
Archibald K. Hogue)

This day came the parties by their attorneys and thereupon came a jury of good and lawful men, to wit:

| | | | |
|---|---|---|---|
| 1. | George W. Fentress | 7. | William L. Norrid |
| 2. | Benjamin Parmer | 8. | John Carter |
| 3. | James Snow | 9. | John L. Williams |
| 4. | George Read | 10. | James Pryor |
| 5. | Elijah Reeves | 11. | James Lyons |
| 6. | Ludwell E. Davis | 12. | Howe Legate |

Who being elected, tried and sworn the truth to speak upon the issue joined in this behalf on their oaths do say that the said defendant did assume and undertake in manner and form as said plaintiff in his declaration hath alledged, and they do assess the damages of the said plaintiff by reason of the non-performance of said assumpsit and undertaking to one one hundred and three dollars and fifty cents, besides costs.

It is therefore considered by the court that said plaintiff recover of said defendant one hundred and three dollars and fifty cents, the damages aforesaid by the jury aforesaid in manner and form aforesaid assessed and also his costs in and about his suit in this behalf expended and the defendant prayed & obtained an appeal to the Circuit Court.

Joseph Garwood )
Vs ) Debt
Thomas Spight )

This day came the parties by their attorneys and thereupon came a jury of good and lawful men, to wit:

(p-253)

| | | | |
|---|---|---|---|
| 1. | George W. Fentress | 7. | William L. Norrid |
| 2. | Benjamin Parmer | 8. | John Carter |
| 3. | James Snow | 9. | John L. Williams |
| 4. | George Read | 10. | James Pryor |
| 5. | Elijah Reeves | 11. | James Lyons |
| 6. | Ludwell E. Davis | 12. | Howe Legate |

Who being elected, tried and sworn the truth to speak upon the issues joined upon their oath do say that they find the issued for the plaintiff, to wit: That said defendant has not paid the debt in the declaration mentioned and that he has proved no set off against the same, but they find the defendant indebted to the plaintiff in the sum of one hundred and fifty dollars, as plaintiff hath alledged and they assess the damages by reason of non payment of the same to thirteen dollars and fifty cents.

It is therefore considered by the court that the plaintiff recover of the defendant one hundred and fifty dollars the debt aforesaid found to be due and oweing in manner and form aforesaid and thirteen dollars and fifty cents the damages aforesaid, assessed in manner and form aforesaid, and also the costs in and about his suit in this behalf expended.

John Polk )
Vs ) Debt
Alexander Faris )

This day came the parties by their attorneys, and thereupon came a jury of good and lawful men, to wit:

1. William Enloe
2. Benjamin F. McWherter
3. Sion Hill
4. James Read
5. James H. Guy
6. Henry Pryor
7. Thomas Hampton
8. William T. Whiteside
9. John Hoard
10. James Crow
11. John Boon
12. Philip Fields

(p-254) Who being elected, tried and sworn the truth to speak upon the issues joined, upon their oaths do say, they find that the defendant was on the fourteenth day of March 1829, indebted to the plaintiff seventy dollars as in the first court in the declaration mentioned, and that he gave his note thereof, and they do assess the plaintiffs damages by reason of the detention of said seventy dollars, to twenty six dollars and forty cents.

John Hutchinson )
Assignee &c )
Vs ) Debt
Henry Long & )
James Harper )

This day came the parties by their attornies and thereupon came a jury of good and lawful men, to wit:

1. Benjamin Enloe
2. William Enloe
3. Sion Hill
4. James Read
5. John Hoard
6. James Crow
7. Fletcher C. Edwards
8. Samuel Nelms
9. Henry J. P. Westbrook
10. Horace Read
11. James Good
12. Philip Fields

Who being elected, tried and sworn the truth to speak upon the issues joined, upon their oaths do say that they find for the plaintiff one hundred and forty dollars and eighty seven cents, and they do assess his damages to thirty six dollars and sixty one cents.

It is therefore considered by the court that the plaintiff recover of the defendants the sum of one hundred and forty dollars and eighty (p-255) seven cents, the debt in the declaration mentioned together with the sum of thirty six dollars and sixty one cents, the damages by the jury aforesaid assessed and also his costs by him about his suit in this behalf expended.

D. St. John & C. Ingram)
Admrs. of           )
Benjamin Ingram, Dec'd.)   Trover
Vs                  )
Samuel Wills        )

This day came the parties by their attorneys and thereupon came a jury of good and lawful men, to wit:

1. George W. Fentress
2. Benjamin Parmer
3. James Snow
4. George Read
5. Elijah Reeves
6. Ludwell E. Davis
7. William L. Norrid
8. John Carter
9. John L. Williams
10. James Pyron
11. James Lyons
12. Howe Legate

Who being elected, tried and sworn the truth to speak upon their oaths do say they find the issues in favor of the defendant.

It is therefore considered by the court that the defendant go hence without pay, and recover of the plaintiff his costs by him in and about his suit in this behalf expended and the plaintiffs pray an appeal to the next Circuit Court of this County, which is granted by the court.

(p-256) This day Joel S. Enloe, high sheriff of this county, returned here into court the States writ of venire facias, issued from the April Term of this court and returnable to the present term, executed on the following persons, good and lawful men, householders and freeholders of this county, to wit:

1. James Snow
2. Ludwell E. Davis
3. Benjamin T. McWherter
4. Elijah Reeves
5. Hansel McCaleb
6. James Johnson
7. John P. Williams
8. John Hoard
9. Howe Legate
10. James Read
11. James Lyons
12. George Read
13. Terrell L. Camp
14. Noah C. Johnson
15. Benjamin Parmer
16. James Pyron
17. Sion Hill
18. John Carter
19. James Crow
20. William Enloe
21. George W. Fentress
22. William L. Norrid
23. Andrew Moore

To secure a grand and petit jurors at this term, all of whom appeared accordingly, except:

1. Hansel McCaleb
2. James Johnson
3. N. C. Johnson

Who being called, came not. And out of those present was drawn according to the statute in case made and provided, the following persons to serve as grand jurors at this term, to wit:

1. Terrell L. Camp (Foreman)
2. George W. Fentress
3. Benjamin Farmer
4. James Snow
5. George Read
6. Elijah Reeves
7. Ludwell E. Davis
8. William L. Norrid
9. John Carter
10. John L. Williams
11. James Pyron
12. James Lyons
13. Howe Legate

Who after being empannelled, sworn and charged, retired to consider of indictments and presentments under the care of Jacob Long, an officer sworn to attend thence.

(p-257) Satisfactory reasons being shown to the court it is ordered that Andrew Moore, one of the original pannel summoned to serve as a juror at the court, be released from serving at this term.

Richard B. Brown, one of the commissioners in Trust for the Town of Troy, came into court and tendered his resignation as such, which was received by court.

Thomas Spight, who was on yesterday elected one of the commissioners of Internal Improvement, came into court and entered into bond as the law directs, with James M. Spight and William M. Wilson his securities and took the oath of office.

William W. Watson, who was on yesterday elected one of the commissioners of Internal Improvements, came into court and entered into bond as the law directs, to wit: Benjamin Sheeks and James Davis, his securities and took the oaths of office.

Richard B. Brown, who was on yesterday elected one of the Commissioners of Internal Improvements, came into court and entered into bond as the law directs, with William M. Wilson and Joel R. Enloe, his securities and took the oath of office.

James N. Stone, who was on yesterday appointed Administrator of all and singular the goods and chattels, (p-258) rights and credits of John Zellers, deceased, came into court and entered into bond conditioned as the law directs, with John Brown his security, which said bond was ordered to be recorded.

William B. Partee, who was at last term of this court appointed Administrator of the estate of David Durham, deceased, came into court and presented an Inventory of the effects of said estate, which is received by the court, and ordered to be filed and recorded.

Agreeable to an order on yesterday made the sheriff, proclamation being first made, proceeded to let out Barbary Andrews, pauper, for the next ensuing twelve months. Norton Oakes being the lowest bidder, she was (fair warning being given) bid off to him for ninety four dollars, it is therefore ordered by the court that he take the said pauper and give bond with sufficient security for the faithful maintenance of her for the (p-259) said term of twelve months, whereupon he came into court and entered into bond with Daniel St. John -- his security conditioned as the law directs, and the court then adjourned until tomorrow morning at 9 o'clock.

Willis Caldwell, J. P.<br>John Parr, J. P.<br>James Henderson, J. P.

Wednesday, 8th. July 1835.

Ordered by the court, present Willis Caldwell, John Parr, James Henderson, that Daniel St. John and James N. Cullem be appointed commissioners to settle with William Andrews, administrator of Enis Hay, deceased, and that they allow him a credit of twenty six dollars and seventy three cents, for cash expended for the benefit of said estate, besides whatever they may allow him on said settlement, and that they make report to the next term of this court.

John Polk )
Vs ) Debt
Alexr Faris )

This day came the parties by their attornies and thereupon came the plaintiff demurrer to the defendants plea of the statutes of limitations of three years to be argued which being seen and fully understood by the court it is considered that said demurrer be sustained.

It is therefore considered by the court that the plaintiff recover against the defendant (p-260) the sum of seventy dollars, found by the jury aforesaid and the sum of twenty six dollars and forty cents, the damages aforesaid by the jury aforesaid assessed together with the costs of this suit for the which execution shall issue.

This day Mary Smith came into court and moved the court to grant her an ordinary license, which the court granted. She giving bond and took the oath with Benjamin T. McWerter and William T. Whiteside her securities, conditioned as the law directs, all of which is accepted by the court, and said license ordered to be issued.

State of Tennessee )
Vs )
William Nellums )

The grand jury came into court and by their foreman returned into open court a presentment against said William Nelms for selling spiritous liquors without license.

State of Tennessee )
Vs )
Samuel Rodgers & )
Thomas M. Harper )

The grand jury came into court and by their foreman returned in to open court a presentment against said Samuel Rodgers and Thomas M. Harper for an affray.

State of Tennessee )
Vs )
Jerome Miller )

The grand jury came into open court and returned a bill of indictment, endorsed a true bill, and signed (p-201) by Terrell L. Camp, foreman of the grand jury.


Robert B. Harper )
Executor of A. Linn, Dec'd. )
Vs ) Appeal from a Justice of the Peace.
Samuel Nelms & Samuel Hutchinson )

This day came the plaintiff by his attorney, and the defendant being solemnly called came not, but made default. It is therefore considered by the court that the plaintiff Harper recover of the defendants Nelms & Hutchinson, the sum of eleven dollars and fifty two cents, the amount of the judgment below, and the further sum of fifteen cents the interest up to the date of this judgment and the costs of suit by him about his suit in this behalf expended and that execution issue &c.


Jno. Polk )
Vs ) In Debt.
A. Farris )

The defts. council presented a bill of exception which is signed & sealed by the court and made a part of the record in this case.


State of Tennessee )
Vs ) Recognisance
Abram Enloe )

This day came the attorney general on the part of the state, and the defendants in proper persons by his council moves the court to be discharged from his recognisance and an agreement was considered by the court that said deft. be discharged from his recognisance and that the court pay the costs of this proceedings.


State of Tennessee )
Vs ) Recognisance
James Hogge )

This day came attorney general on the part of the State and the defts. in proper person who was to be discharged from his recognisance whereupon it is considered by the court that the deft. be discharged from his recognisance and that the county pay the costs of this proceedings.

Ordered by the court that the following persons be appointed Judge of the execution held on the 1st. Thursday in August next, to wit at Troy.

        Jno. Hoard
        Jno. Par.
        B. B. Brown

A. Holloman precinct:

        William A. Maxwell
        Benj. Totten
        Jno. Whiteside

(Page 262 not noted)

(p-263) At Jno. Williams

        James Henderson
        H. Applewhite
        Hugh A. Shelton

At Merriwethers

        R. T. Merriwether
        Thurston Hornsby
        James Brown

At Nixons

        Jno. Holloman
        Thos. Spight
        James Mc Neely

Ordered by the court that the following persons, good and lawful men of the County of Obion, being householders and freeholders thereof be summoned by the sheriff of this court to attend on Tuesday of the next County Court to compose a Grand & Petit Jury for said Court, to wit:

1. Horace Allen
2. Jas. Dorris
3. Wm. Maxwell
4. Worthy Darkin
5. Jas. B. Holloman
6. Edmund Jones
7. Geo. White
8. Samuel G. Waford
9. Wm. Scott
10. Ezekiel Carter
11. Jno. Stanford
12. Andrew Moore
13. Jno. Le Gatt
14. Jas. Barham
15. Wm. Haslipp
16. Jonas B. Lyth
17. C. Sheeks
18. James Harper
19. T. Taylor
20. Jacob Yokum
21. Jesse Wilson
22. Thos. Haines
23. Jonathan Nix
24. Wm. Carter
25. Jno. Holloman
26. Jno. Hoard

(p-264) And that William Calhoun & Wm. Edmund, Constables, be appointed and summoned to attend upon the court and jury.

And that the following persons good and lawful men of Obion County, being householders and freeholders thereof be summoned by the Sheriff of this County to attend at the next Circuit Court in this County to form a Grand Jury ascending to the statutes in such cases made out and provided, to wit:

1. B. Totten
2. J. J. McCollum
3. Daniel Brown
4. Jno. Harper
5. Jesse Maxwell
6. Jno. Panky
7. A. R. Mills
8. Alfred McDaniel
9. Jno. Mosier, Sr.
10. Stephen Mitchell
11. Thurston Hornsby
12. Francis Taylor
13. Jno. Parr
14. A. L ---
15. Robt. Harper
16. Wm. Downey
17. Edward Norrid
18. Jas. Henderson
19. Wm. M. Wilson
20. H. J. P. Westbrook
21. J. C. Wilson
22. Jesse Daugherty
23. Wm. Wilkinson
24. R. B. Brown
25. Wilford Farris
26. Willis Caldwell

And that Daniel St. John & James Caldwell be appointed and summoned to attend the Court and Jury.

The Court be adjourned until Court in course.

Willis Caldwell, J. P.
John Parr, J. P.
James Henderson, J. P.

THE END

-A-

ABINGTON,
 JOHN F., 94
 JOHN T., 94
ADAIR,
 WILLIAM, 100
ADAM,
 CAPTAIN, 175
ADAMS,
 —, 14, 26
 LYSANDER, 48,
 86, 87
 WILLIAM, 134
ADAMS & BEDFORD,
 14
ALLEN,
 ALEXANDER, 29
 D., 249
 DEMPSEY, 249,
 250
 HORACE, 97, 263
 JOHN B., 250
 N.L., 177
 NICHOLAS L., 177
 SAML. E., 47
 SAMUEL E., 249
 THOMAS, 5, 150,
 169, 179(2),
 190, 211, 216
 THOS., 151
ALLISON,
 THOMAS, 20, 44,
 111, 120, 152,
 153, 156, 157
 THOS., 149, 156
ANDERSON,
 ARCHIBALD G., 64
 JOHN, 70
 WILLIAM E., 69
ANDREW,
 WILLIAM, 97
ANDREW B.,
 EDWARD, 195
ANDREWS,
 BARBARY, 202,
 247, 248, 258
 CULLIN, 227
 R.C., 213
 WILLIAM, 17, 90,

100, 134, 135,
 155, 259
ANTHONY,
 JOSIAS, 68
APPLESHINE,
 HARRY, 117
APPLEWHITE,
 EHNRY, 215
 H., 186, 263
 HARRY, 118, 139
 HENRY, 6, 109,
 110, 118, 119,
 120, 186, 188,
 189, 195, 198,
 205, 207
ARMAN,
 B., 145
ARMOUR,
 D., 177, 196
 DAVID, 112, 196
ASBROOK,
 CAPT., 5
ASHBROOK,
 CAPT., 6
AULD,
 COLIN, 132

-B-

BADGET,
 JONATHAN, 85
BADGETT,
 JONATHAN, 13,
 21, 27, 34, 106
BALDRIDGE,
 WILLIAM F., 110
 WILLIAM T., 30
BAPHAM,
 ELI, 2
 JAMES, 2
BARHAM,
 JAS., 263
BARNER,
 ISHAM, 98
BARNET,
 ANDREW, 219
BARNETT,
 ANDREW, 64
BARTLETT,
 JOHN L., 246
BAXTER,
 SARAH, 178
BEDFORD,
 —, 14, 26
 ADAMS, 21
 J. M., 11, 37,
 46
 J.M., 245
 JAMES, 34, 208
 JAMES F., 18,

135

23, 29, 38
 JONAS, 21, 28,
 86, 87, 195,
 207, 211
 JUBILEE M., 11,
 12, 21(2), 22,
 93, 98, 174,
 176, 199, 202
 JUBILLE M., 174
 SETH, 1, 5, 6,
 11, 18, 21(2),
 22, 23, 25, 26,
 27, 48, 86, 87,
 142(2), 168,
 174, 215
BEDFORE,
 JUBILEE M., 240
BEDJFORD,
 SETH, 152
BEGG,
 LAMAS STEPHEN,
 97
BELLS,
 WYATT, 215
BENNETT,
 C.M., 149
BERRYHILL,
 WILLIAM M., 71
BETTIS,
 WYATT, 169
 WYETT, 194, 207,
 208
 WYITT, 251
BEZZY,
 A.S., 98
BIRD,
 —, 28
 WIDOW, 97
BLAKEMORE,
 J., 228
BLOUNT,
 J.G., 56, 57,
 58, 233, 234,
 235(2), 236
 JOHN G., 57, 59,
 60, 72, 78, 202,
 233, 234(2)

 T., 56, 57, 234,
 235(2), 236
 THOMAS, 57, 58,
 59, 60, 72, 78,
 202, 233
 THOS., 233,
 234(2)
BLOUNTS,
 J.G., 56
 T., 56
BLUFF,
 MARY DAVIDSONS,

247
MARY
 RICHARDSONS, 246

BOOD,
 JAS., 156
BOON,
 JOHN, 253
BOSLEY,
 JOHN, 218
BOTTOM,
 OBION, 247
BOYCE,
 ISHAM, 72, 225, 226
BRAMBLET,
 SANFORD, 6
BRAMBLETT,
 SANFORD, 174, 195, 207, 208
BRASFIELD,
 GREEN, 147
BRIDGE,
 GROVE CREST, 129
 REELFOOT, 132
BROACH,
 GEORGE W., 171
BROCKWELL,
 E.T., 134, 149
 EDWARD T., 97, 157
 EDWIN, 123
 EDWIN T., 100, 153, 156(2)
 WILLIAM, 97
BRONW,
 JOHN, 173
 RICHARD B., 251
BROWN,
 B.B., 261
 BRICHARD B., 247
 CAPT., 5(2), 6
 D. B., 30
 DANIEL, 35, 37, 100, 134, 135, 264
 DAVID, 123, 155, 176, 204
 JAMES, 263
 JAMES A., 157
 JAMES L., 9(2), 15, 47, 169
 JAMES S., 18, 19(2), 23, 153, 156, 179(2)
 JAMES T., 3
 JOHN, 245, 258
 R. B., 3, 5, 6, 9, 30, 33, 35, 49, 143
 R.B., 89, 102, 105(2), 106, 122, 124, 145, 146, 151, 164, 166, 168, 169, 185, 264
 R.S., 133
 RICAHRD B., 242
 RICHARD, 91, 210
 RICHARD B., 1, 5, 9, 23, 28, 30, 38, 39, 85, 112, 138, 168, 185, 194, 196, 210(2), 211(2), 242, 248(2), 249, 251, 257(2)

 W.A., 186(2)
 WILLIAM A., 105, 157, 188
 WM. A., 16, 189, 212
BROWN & ENLOE, 212
BUCHANAN, 173
 JOHN M., 100, 135, 136, 155
 THOMAS, 195
BUCHANNAN,
 T.W., 211
 THOMAS, 207
 THOMAS N., 208
 WILLIAM, 209
 WM., 212
BUCHANNON,
 THOMAS, 3
 THOMAS N., 202
BUCKANAN,
 JOHN M., 134
BUIN,
 JAMES, 80-
BUSH,
 ABRAM, 232
BUY,
 W.H., 186
BYRD,
 JOHN W., 98
 LUCY, 40
 WIDOW, 97
BYRON,
 JAMES, 241

-C-

CAGE,
 WILSON, 229
CALDWELL,
 AJEMS, 194, 202
 D.T., 117
 JAMES, 100, 101, 179, 181, 205(2), 208, 214, 264
 JONAS, 208
 W., 168(2)
 WILLIE, 8
 WILLIS, 1, 5(2), 6, 13, 18, 20, 22, 23, 25, 26, 27, 28, 30(2), 31, 35, 38, 39, 49, 51, 83, 88, 89, 100, 101, 115, 121, 122, 131, 145, 146, 151, 164, 169, 170, 175, 177(2), 180, 184, 185, 193, 194, 196, 197, 206, 214, 217, 218, 241, 242(2), 247, 248(2), 249, 251(2), 259, 264

CALHOON,
 WILLIAM, 37, 125
CALHOUN,
 S.S., 149, 206, 211
 SAMUEL S., 137
 STEPEHEN S., 208
 STEPHEN, 208
 STEPHEN S., 195
 WILLIAM, 29, 137, 169, 195, 205(2), 208, 264

CAMP,
 DAVIDSON, 246
 TERRELL L., 241, 256(2), 261
CAMPBELL,
 G. W., 54
 GEORGE W., 65
 JOHN W., 227
CARMAC,
 JOHN, 97
 WILLIAM, 195
 WM. C., 79(2)
CARMACH,
 WILLIAM, 39
CARMACK,
 WILLIAM, 28, 40, 41, 42, 43, 44, 174, 187, 202
 WM., 245
CARROLL,
 WILLIAM, 137,

182
WILLIAM, GOV., 102
CARTER,
 ELIZABETH, 100
 EZEKIAH, 169
 EZEKIAL, 188
 EZEKIEL, 20, 28, 179, 186(2), 189, 215, 263
 JOHN, 241, 252, 253, 255, 256(2)
 JOHN, JR., 242
 WILLIAM, 9(3), 15, 18, 19(2), 23, 91, 95, 100, 134, 149, 153, 156(2), 157, 203
 WM., 263
CARUTHERS,
 ELERSION, 171
 HUGH A., 195, 208(2), 211
 JAMES, 226
 JAS., 11
CASSADY,
 —, 45
CASSEDY,
 —, 17
CATHEY,
 WILLIAM, 81
 WILLIS, 5
CATOE,
 SOLOMON D., 189
 SOLOMON P., 105, 115, 136, 195
CHAMBERLIN,
 M., 214
CHEEKS,
 CORNELIUS, 42
CHESTER,
 ROBERT F., 194
CHIGER,
 HENRY, 48, 49
CHILDRESS,
 ELIZABETH, 219(2)
CLARK,
 GEO. W., 169
CLEAR,
 JOHN, 100
CLOAH,
 JOHN, 173
COATS,
 AUSTIN M., 248
 LUCINCA, 248
COCHRAN,
 DENNIS, 5

COLE,
 MADISON, 2
 SAMUEL H., 42, 139, 185
 SAMUEL W., 145
COLLEGE,
 CUMBERLAND, 228, 232
COLLIER,
 GREENBERRY, 242, 247
COLYEAR,
 G., 186(2)
 GEORGE, 188, 189
COLYER,
 G.B., 171
COMPANY,
 TOWN, 202, 208
COOK,
 JEFFERSON, 98
 JESSE, 29, 36
 LEVI, 29, 39, 40, 41, 42, 43, 44, 47
 LEWIS, 97
COOKE,
 JESSE, 36, 98
 LEVI, 36
CORNELL,
 WILLIAM, 104
COUNTY LINE,
 WEAKLEY, 2
CRABB,
 THOMAS W., 217
CREEK,
 CANE, 95
 CLAY, 97
 CLOVER, 223
 GROVER, 97
 HOOSIER, 97, 123, 126
 INDIAN, 96, 131
 LITTLE RICHLAND, 250
 MUD, 128
 REELFOOT, 222, 247
CROCKETT,
 SAML., 22
 SAMUEL, 16, 227
CROW,
 JAMES, 241, 253, 254, 256
CROWDERS,
 R., 229
CULBERSON, 128
 JOSEPH C., 245
CULLEM,
 JAMES N., 259
CULLEN,

JAMES N., 97, 169
CULLUM,
 JAMES N., 179(2)
CULPERSON,
 JOSEPH C., 38
CUNNINGHAM,
 A. A., 36(2)
 A.A., 169, 202
 A.B., 245
 ANDERSON A., 29
 ANSON A., 179(2)
 GEORGE, 137
 GEORGE W., 246
 WILLIAM, 18, 96, 242
CURLEN,
 SETH, 97
CURLIN,
 SAMUEL, 169, 179(2)
 SETH, 97

-D-

DABNEY,
 FINEY
 MATHEW, 68
 PETE, 68
 THOMAS, 68
 TYRA, 48, 107
 TYRE, 190
DALTON,
 SARAH, 67
 WIDOW, 2
DANIEL,
 H.M., 211
DARKIN,
 WORTHY, 263
DARNALL,
 CAPTAIN, 175
DARNALS,
 CAPTAIN, 200
DAUGHERTY,
 JESSE, 1, 9, 101, 170, 171, 172, 177(2), 197, 244, 247, 264
DAULTON,
 MRS., 173, 228
 SARAH, 230
DAVIDSON,
 ANDREW T., 91
 ANDREW W., 124, 176
 CATHARIN B., 91
 CATHARINE R., 124, 176
 JANE, 77, 230

MARY, 124, 230
THOMAS, 77, 231
UMPHREY, 165
WIDOW, 28
DAVIS, 117
ABNER, 198
HAMES H., 98
JAMES, 2, 100,
  104, 174, 206,
  257
JAMES H., 8, 12,
  27, 93, 123(2),
  125, 131
JAS. H., 21
JOHN S., 132
JONAS, 107
JOSEPH, 98
LUDWELL E., 252,
  253, 255, 256(2)

PORTER A., 29,
  36, 97, 123
RICHARD, 92,
  137(2)
SAMUEL, 98
TIDWELL, 241
DAVISON,
  RICHARD, 92
DEAN,
  THOMAS, 171
  THOMAS W., 29,
  36(2)
DICKERSON,
  —, 2
  ROBERT, 27, 29,
  178
  ROBERTSON, 106
DICKEY,
  J.D., 210
  JOHN D., 85, 99,
  204
DICKINSON,
  ROBERT, 85
DICKISON,
  ROBERT, 2
DICKSON,
  DAVID B., 216
  ROBERT, 178
  SUSAN ADALINE
    GRAVES, 178
  SUSAN ADALLINE
    GRAVES, 192
DIGG,
  EDMUND, 70
DOCKSEY,
  JOHN S., 37
DOFFEL,
  BERRY, 175
DORRIS,
  JAS., 263

DOUGLAS,
  HENRY L., 187
DOWNEY,
  WILLIAM, 1, 5,
  6, 28(2), 33,
  101, 175, 177,
  193, 194, 197,
  204
  WM., 89, 203,
  264
DOXEY,
  JOHN, 97
  JOHN L., 6, 101
  JOHN S., 28, 97,
  193, 201
DRESDEN, 128
  Town of, 91
DUNLAPP,
  WHITE, 78
DUNN,
  DANIEL, 97
DURHAM,
  DAVID, 199(2),
  258
DYER,
  JESSE H., 101
  JOEL H., 36,
  133, 176
DYERSBURG, 127

-E-

EACHBAUM,
  WILLIAM A., 145
EASTRIDGE,
  LARKIN, 92, 137,
  247
  WILLIAM, 137
EATON,
  JOHN R., 51, 219
  SARAH, 220(2)
  SARAH A., 52(2)
  SUSAN, 52(2)
  SUSAN C., 220(2)
  THOMAS B.L., 219
  THOMAS R. L., 52
  THOMAS R.L., 220
EATONS,
  JOHN R., 219
EDMINSON,
  JESSE, 5
EDMOND,
  JOHN, 85
EDMONDS,
  ROBERT, 199
  SAMUEL, 216
  WILLIAM, 101
  WILLIAM W., 176
EDMONDSON,
  JESSE, 23

EDMUND,
  J.G., 79(2)
  WM., 264
EDMUNDS,
  ALEXANDER, 12
EDWAARDS,
  JOSEPH R., 100
EDWARD,
  G.G., 212
  W.C., 213
  WILLIAM C., 100,
  126, 151, 188
  WILLIAM G., 102
EDWARDS,
  ELIAS, 2
  F.G., 210
  FLETCHER C., 254
  FLETCHER G., 209
  JOSEPH R., 134,
  135, 155
  W.C., 186(2)
  WILLIAM, 150
  WILLIAM C., 102,
  134, 135, 155,
  242
  WM. C., 1, 189
EDWARRD,
  WM., 210
EDWDARDS,
  F.G., 213
ELDER,
  JAMES, 29, 36(2)
ENCHBAM & NORRELL,
  106
ENLOE,
  —, 5
  ABRAM, 261
  BENJAMIN, 254
  JOEL, 81
  JOEL S., 141
  JOEL A., 45
  JOEL L., 5
  JOEL S., 7,
  9(2), 11, 15,
  21(2), 23(2),
  27, 34, 49, 51,
  59, 60, 61, 93,
  94, 98, 99,
  102(2), 105,
  107, 116(2),
  127, 130, 142,
  143, 144, 168,
  179, 185, 192,
  202, 207,
  208(2), 210,
  211, 214,
  218(2), 223,
  225(2), 239,
  256, 257
  W., 246

WILLIAM, 241,
246, 253, 254,
256
ENLOE & BROWN, 211
ENLOSE,
JOEL S., 142
ESTRIDGE,
TULLY, 2
EVANS,
B., 210, 212,
213, 214
BENJAMIN, 194,
207, 209

-F-

FARIS,
ALEX'R, 259
ALEXANDER, 215,
253
BENJAMIN, 40
JAMES, 200
RICHARD, 171
FARLEY,
DAVID, 93, 95
FARMER,
BENJAMIN, 165,
241
JESSE, 95, 198
FARR,
F.E., 213
J.E., 210
J.R., 212
JOHN, 23, 103,
209
FARRIN,
WILFORD, 122
FARRIS,
A., 261
ALEXANDER, 191
BENJ., 29, 44,
47
BENJAMIN, 36,
39, 41, 42, 43
DAVID W., 127,
171
JAMES, 246
W., 146
WILFORD, 101,
170, 177, 194,
264
FAULK,
JACOB, 171
FAUST,
JOHN, 149
FENTRESS,
G.W., 246
GEORGE, 16
GEORGE W., 47,
241, 247, 252,
253, 255, 256(2)

JOHN, 191
WILLIAM G., 191
FERRIAGE,
rates, 181
FERRY,
FENTRESS, 92, 95
KENTEN'S, 7
NELM'S, 7
NELMS, 94, 99
TERRIELS, 92
FIELD,
PHILIP, 20
FIELDS,
C., 214
PHILIP, 253, 254
PHILLIP, 30,
110, 153, 156(2)

FILIECAND,
KY, 96
FISHER,
WILLIAM B., 123
WILLIAM R., 97
FLEMING,
WILLIAM, 52
FLEMMING,
WILLIAM, 52
FLOYD,
A., 247
FORBUS,
A., 213
AMBROSE, 209
FORD,
BROWNS, 176
FORK,
HARRIS, 97(2)
HOOSIER, 98
FORSTER,
A., 212
FOSLER,
A. A., 36
FOSLLEN,
A. A., 36
FOSTER,
A., 210
FOUST,
JOHN, 209
LEWIS, 9(2), 12,
15, 18, 19(2),
40
FOWLER,
WILLIAM, 226
FULK,
JOSEPH, 171
FULKS, 204

-G-

GARRETT,
H.A., 151
HENRY A., 240
GARRETT & GARDNER,
229
GARRETT &
GILLESPIE, 240
GARRISON,
BENJ., 15, 19(2)
BENJAMIN, 9, 18,
23, 169, 179(2)
BENJAMINE, 9
GARWOOD,
JOSEPH, 252
GATT,
JNO. LE, 263
GENE,
JOHN, 149
GIBSON,
G. W., 79(4)
JNO. T., 79
GILLES,
OWEN, 117
GISSIE,
OWEN, 245
GLISSON,
CAPTAIN, 203
GOOD,
G. W., 20, 45
JAMES, 104, 153,
156, 254
GORE,
JOHN, 28, 202,
245
GRIMES,
BENJAMIN, 230
R., 229
GUY,
JAMES, 204
JAMES H., 29,
36, 39, 40, 41,
42, 43, 44, 169,
179(2), 188,
192, 209, 253

W.A., 188
W.H., 186
WILLIAM H., 16
WM. H., 189, 204

-H-

HACKETT,
ISIAH P., 72
HACKNEY,
MICKEL, 65
HAINES,
THOS., 263
HAISLIP,
ELIZABETH, 249

GEORGE W., 249
TABITHA, 249
WILLIAM, 36, 249
HALL,
  MARTIN, 132
HAMILTON,
  —, 12
  ISHMAEL, 209
  J., 210, 212, 213
  J.C., 240(2)
  JOHN C., 52, 70, 221(5), 222(2), 240
  RUBEN, 98
  WILLIAM, 20
HAMPTON,
  JONATHAN, 71
  THOMAS, 100, 134, 135, 250(2), 253
HANNA,
  ANDREW, 173, 199, 206, 250
  CLANEY, 206
  CLANY, 199
  CLARA, 173
HANNAH,
  CLAY, 172
HARGET,
  ALFRED, 92, 194, 202, 203, 247
HARPER,
  J., 212, 214
  JAMES, 3, 20, 37, 207, 254, 263
  JAMES, SR., 195
  JHAMES, 203
  JNO., 146, 264
  JROBERT, 192
  MARY, 193(2)
  MOSES D., 1, 9(3), 15, 19, 23, 91, 204
  R.B., 213
  ROBERT, 8, 9(2), 16, 19, 20, 169, 179
  ROBERT B., 37, 82, 99, 157, 166, 188, 195, 209(2), 250, 261
  ROBT., 3, 264
  ROSANAH, 168
  ROSANNA, 185, 210, 212
  ROSANNAH, 23, 105

THOMAS, 138, 200
THOMAS M., 28, 193(2), 260
WIDOW, 3
WILLIAM, 96, 97
HARPOLE,
  JAMES, 101
  JOHN, 1, 5, 23, 28(2), 31, 33, 89, 100, 101, 122, 133, 170, 177(2), 184, 192, 194, 197
  JOHN, JR., 8
  WILLIAM, 169, 178, 179(2), 192

HARR,
  GIDEON, 217
HARRIS,
  A. L., 9
  A. S., 21(3)
  A.L., 66
  A.S., 130(2), 159
  ABNER, 209
  ANDREW C., 122
  ANDREW S., 16, 146, 159, 220(2), 221
  EDWARD, 52(2), 72, 73(2), 74(2), 76, 220, 222, 236(3), 237(2), 238(3)
  EDWIN, 75
  ELI, 74, 75, 237(2), 238
  JAMES, 76
  S.S., 109
  SAMUEL, 75, 238
  W.S.S., 37, 46, 47, 81, 151, 159(2), 201
  WILLIAM, 75
  WILLIAM S.S., 103, 139, 150, 155, 182(2), 183(2), 188, 206

WILLIAM S.S.S, 147
WM. S.S., 213
HASELIP,
  GEORGE W., 250
  WILLIAM, 250, 251
  WM., 36
HASLIP,
  WILLIAM, 29

HASLIPP,
  WM., 263
HASSEL,
  JOURDAN, 46
HASSELL, 163
  —, 33
  JORDAN, 159(3), 161(2), 188
  JOURDAN, 33
HAUGHLETT,
  WILLIAM, 52
HAUGHTON,
  JONATHAN C., 159(4), 161, 188

HAUL,
  ROBERT, 226
HAUSER,
  NOAH B., 156
HAY,
  BETTY, 123
  ELISAH, 123
  ELIZAH, 97
  ENIS, 259
  ENNIS, 172
  ENOS, 90
  WYETT, 123
HEAD,
  CAPT., 5, 6(2), 33
  CAPTAIN, 175
  HORACE, 16, 41, 117, 118, 120, 169, 171, 179(2), 183, 254

HEADS,
  CAPTAIN, 204
HENDEJRSON,
  JAMES, 251
HENDERSON,
  ARCHIBALD, 52, 231
  JAMES, 5, 28, 31, 33, 89, 101, 122, 146, 175, JAS., 264
  THOMAS, 69, 221
HENNIN,
  ABRAHAM, 44
HENNING,
  ABRAHAM, 177
  ABRAHAMN, 101
  ABRAM, 36, 177
HENRY,
  CAPT., 5, 6
  CAPTAIN, 175, 202, 208
  JOEL, 207
  S.S., 87

SAML., 29
SAMUEL, 36
SAMUEL C., 36,
    249, 251
HERRIN,
    ABRAHAM, 39, 41
    ABRAM, 42
HERRING,
    ABRAHAM, 40, 43,
    97, 194
    ABRAM, 29, 96
HEY,
    ENOS, 17
HICKMAN,
    E., 52, 231
    EDWARD, 52, 229
    I. P., 52
    JOHN P., 231
HILL,
    CAPT., 5, 6, 33
    CAPTAIN, 175
    LION, 29
    RICHARD, 246
    SION, 36, 39,
    40, 41, 42, 43,
    44, 98, 241,
    253, 254, 256
HITLY,
    WILLIAM, 71
HIX,
    JONATHAN, 247
HOARD,
    JNO, 263
    JNO./, 261
    JOHN, 214, 241,
    253, 254, 256
    M.H., 213
    WILLIAM H., 209,
    210
    WM., 212
HOCKLEY,
    MICHAEL, 227
HODGES,
    CHARLES, 178
HOGGE,
    A. K., 20
    JAMES, 19, 23,
    119, 147(2),
    153, 186, 191,
    214, 217(2), 261

    JAMES B., 3,
    9(2), 15, 18,
    23, 26, 48, 49,
    169
    WILLIS, 9, 16,
    20, 138
    WILLIS A.,
    193(2)
HOGGE & McDANIEL,

    226
HOGGE & WILSON,
    105
HOGGS,
    ARCHIBALD K., 99
HOGUE,
    ARCHIBALD, 244
    ARCHIBALD K.,
    251
    JAMES B., 19,
    179(2), 244
HOLLOMAN,
    A., 261
    JAMES B., 9, 12;
    193, 194, 207,
    208
    JAS. B., 263
    JNO, 263
    JNO., 263
    JOHN, 9(2), 15,
    18, 19(2), 23
HOLLOMONS,
    J.B., 193
HOLM,
    ROBERT, 232
HOLMES,
    HUBERT, 71
HOLOMAN,
    JAMES B., 101
HOLOMONS,
    JAMES B., 97,
    129
HOPKINS,
    THOMAS, 228(2)
HORD,
    JOHN, 171
HORNSBY,
    ALBERT, 97
    JOHN, 97
    THURSTON, 263,
    264
HORTON,
    J.C., 46
    JOHN C., 37
HOUGHTON,
    J. C., 33
HOUSER,
    H.B., 106
HUBARD,
    LITTLETON, 139
HUBB,
    BETTY, 97
    MARK, 97
HUBBARD,
    -, 140
    JOHN B., 202,
    251
    LITTLE, 187
    LITTLETON,
    16(2), 42, 145,

    185, 195
HUBERT,
    A. C., 16
    DAVID, 100, 134,
    149, 153, 155,
    156, 157
    JOHN, 115, 136,
    189, 195(2)
HUBLETT,
    D. PORTER, 54
    JOHN, 46
    WILLIAM, 52
HUNTER,
    PLEASANT, 220
HUNTSMAN,
    ADAM, 172
    SELAM, 116
HUTCHINSON,
    JOHN, 159, 254
    SAML., 15
    SAMUEL, 9(2),
    18(2), 22,
    23(2), 39, 40,
    41, 42, 43, 44,
    99, 195, 198,
    204, 207(2), 261

    WILLIAM, 92(2),
    171, 172, 194,
    198, 200, 246,
    247(2)
    WM., 7(2), 175
HUTCHISON,
    SAMUEL, 37
    WILLIAM, 137
HUZZA,
    JOHN, 28
HUZZY,
    JOHN, 97

    -I-

INGRAM,
    B., 215, 251
    BENJAMIN, 172,
    255
    C., 255
    CATHARIN, 215
    CATHARINE, 172
IVINE,
    B., 129

    -J-

JACKSON,
    W., 178
    WILLIAM, 9
JANES,
    EDWARD, 128
JOHN,

141

D.F., 215
M.G., 79
JOHNS,
FREDERICK,
43(2), 49, 50(2)

MADISON G., 23,
238
JOHNSON, 78
DAVID, 230
GEORGE, 171
JAMES, 241,
256(2)
JOHN L., 200
N.C., 210
NOAH C., 209,
241, 256
W.C., 212, 256
JONES,
EDMUND, 263
EDWARD, 28, 194,
206, 208
EDWARDS, 207
JAMES, 2, 23
JNO., 132
JOHN, 29, 36,
40, 41, 42, 43,
47, 97, 123, 201

THOS G., 204
WILLIAM, 241

-K-

KEATHLEY,
RICHARD, 193,
195, 203, 208(2)

KEATHLY,
R., 211
KELTON,
JOHN H., 43(2),
49, 50(2)
KERKSEY,
DOLLAY, 119
KERR,
JOSEPH, 72
KETHLEY,
R., 232
KIGER,
HENRY, 26
KINDRED,
J.C., 89, 90
KINKANNON,
A. A., 30
KIRKSEY,
DOLLY, 163, 180
GIDEON, 9, 20,
153, 156(2),
157, 163, 180(2)

LINDEN, 114

-L-

LAKE,
REELFOOT, 96,
176, 244, 246
LAMAR,
ALFRED, 99
LAUDETTES,
JOEL, 66
LAW,
DANIEL, 92
LEA,
WILLIAM W., 186
LEGATE,
HOWE, 241, 252,
253, 255, 256(2)

WILEY, 241
LEVINGSTON,
SAMUEL, 222(2)
LEWIS,
JAMES, 14
WILLIAM B., 226
WILLIAM T., 59,
71, 230
LIEMAN,
ANDREW, 82
JNO., 79
JOHN, 79
LUKE, 78
LILNN,
JOHN, 190
LINDSEY,
WILLIAM O., 94,
244
LINELL,
JOHN, 72
LINN,
A., 92, 99, 157,
209, 261
ANDREW, 3, 8,
92, 99, 166,
188, 250
B. H., 47
B.H., 186(2)
BENJAMIN A.,
188, 189
JANE A., 8, 45,
94
JNO., 214
JOHN, 29, 48,
107, 150, 151,
153, 156(2),
158, 183
LINSEY,
WILLIAM O., 204
LINSON,

THOMAS, 241
LITTLE,
A., 55
LOCKETT,
ARCHIBALD, 16,
20
E.E.C., 222
M.C., 222
LOGAN,
B. D., 2, 38
BENJ. D., 29
H. D., 38
H.D., 21, 101
HENRY, 96
HENRY D., 1, 6,
11, 29(2), 118
LOGAN & HUBERT,
105
LOMAX,
ALFRED, 28, 99,
102, 126
MR., 204
LONG,
HENRY, 204, 254
JACOB, 202,
208(2), 241, 256

JOHN, 20, 39,
44, 203
LONGLEY,
FRANKLIN, 176,
193
LORNAX,
ALFRED, 6
LOVE,
B., 231
G., 231
LYNN,
ANDREW, 37
JOHN, 37
LYON,
DAVID, 214
LYONS,
JAMES, 241, 252,
253, 255, 256(2)

LYSANDER,
ANDERSON, 149
LYTH,
ARCHIBALD, 74
JONAS B., 263
LYTHE,
WILLIAM, 52

-M-

McADAMS,
JOHN, 52
McALISTER,
C., 168, 203

CHARLES, 16, 22,
  38, 85, 104,
  109, 145, 178,
  185, 192, 193
McALLISTER,
  CHARLES, 106
McBAIN,
  A.M.L., 146,
    147, 150
  ANGUS W.L., 145
  W.L., 88
McBEAN,
  —, 103
  —, 23
  A.M.L., 20(2),
    23, 41, 44, 109,
    110, 111, 112,
    118, 119(2),
    120(2), 155,
    157, 164, 212

  A.S.M., 45
  ANGUS L.M., 152
  ANGUS M. L., 118
  ANGUS M.L., 112,
    117, 118, 123,
    186, 196
McCALEB,
  HANSEL, 241, 256
  MANSEL, 256
McCLURE,
  JOHN, 47, 81,
    103, 155, 188
McCOLLUM,
  J.J., 264
  JAMES I., 2, 3
  JAMES J., 171
  JAMES L., 169
McCOLUM,
  JAMES, 75
  JAMES & MAY, 74
McCORD,
  ROBERT, 76, 238
McDANIEL,
  ALFRED, 101,
    132, 201, 264
  JOHN, 22, 83, 84
  MARTHA, 230
  SAML. L., 13
  SAMUEL, 100, 134
  SAMUEL L., 34,
    59
McDONALD,
  JOHN S., 113
McELYER,
  SAMUEL, 247
McEWING,
  —, 17
  —, 45
MACEY,

GEORGE W., 2
STEPHEN, 3
McGEE,
  JOHN, 28
McINTOSH,
  BENJAMIN W., 142
McKINLEY,
  DANIEL, 69
McLAIN,
  EPHSIUM, 70
McLAUREN,
  M., 161, 162
McLEAN,
  EPHRIAM, 231
McLEANN,
  MICHIEL, 52
McLEMORE, 72, 222
  H. & VAUGHN, 74
  I.C., 52
  JOHN C., 228,
    231, 232(2)
  JOHN C. & WIFE,
    65
McLEMORE & VAUGHT,
  226
McLEMORE & VAULT,
  227
McNEELY,
  JAMES, 178, 263
  JOHN, 126
McWERTER,
  BENJAMIN T., 260
McWHERTER,
  BENJAMIN F.,
    241, 253
  BENJAMIN T., 256
McWREY,
  THOMAS, 64
MAHAN,
  JOHN, 97
MANN,
  J.H., 145
MANSFIELD,
  GEORGE, 101
  GRASTLY, 16,
    100, 135
  GRASTY, 134, 155
MARBARY,
  ABRAM, 169
MARBRY,
  ADAM, 179
  ADRAM, 188
MARBURY,
  ABRAHAM, 245
MARR,
  —, 5
  G.W.L., 25, 49,
    52, 171, 183
  GEORGE W. L.,
    26, 39, 49

MARTIN,
  HUGH, 52
  JAMES, 220
  ROBERT, 214
MARTINS,
  HUGH, 221
MASON,
  DANIEL, 68
MATHENEY,
  JOHN, 129
MATHENY,
  JOHN, 23
MATHEWS,
  JOHN P., 52
MAUL,
  ROBERT, 72
MAXEY,
  STEPHEN, 171
MAXWELL,
  GEO. W., 132
  GEORGE W., 96,
    201(2)
  JESSE, 264
  WILLIAM A., 5,
    6, 97, 132,
    179(2), 192,
    193, 201(2), 261

  WM. A., 169
MEADOWS,
  JOSEPH, 28, 100,
    134, 135, 155,
    177
MEARKRY,
  ABRAM, 186(2)
  ADNER, 189
MEECHAM,
  JESSE, 216
MENTON,
  WILLIAM, 189
MEREWETHER,
  RICHARD T., 101
MERRIWETHER,
  R.T., 263
  RICHARD, 28
  RICHARD T., 95,
    171(2), 176
MERRIWETHERS, 263
  RICHARD, 193
  RICHARD T., 193
MEXWELL,
  WM., 263
MILES,
  WILLIAM, 195,
    208(2), 247
  WM., 211
MILLER,
  DANIEL, 244
  FREDERICK, 227
  JAMES L., 157

JAS. L., 156
JEROME, 93, 95,
  102, 104,
  123(2), 134,
  135, 155, 192,
  260
JERROME, 100
WILLIAM, 8,
  9(3), 15, 18(2),
  19, 23, 45, 92,
  93, 95, 99, 101,
  102, 193(2), 194

WILLIAM M., 101
WM., 209, 214
MILLS,
  A.R., 264
  JAMES, 100, 134
  JAMES L., 128,
    132, 153, 158,
    194, 201
  JAS. L., 155,
    201
MILLS POINT,
  KY, 92, 137
MINTON,
  W., 186
  WILLIAM, 149,
    188
MITCHELL,
  STEPHEN, 101,
  171, 193, 194,
  264
MMINTON,
  W., 186
MONTGOMERY,
  DANIEL, 63
MOORE, 222
  ALBERT, 21
  ANDREW, 2, 241,
    256, 257, 263
  DANIEL F., 9
  JAMES, 2
  STANCEL, 31
  STANCIL, 46
MORAN, 177
  JAMES H., 112
MORANS,
  JAMES H., 196
MORRIS,
  JAMES S., 156
  NATHAN, 204
MOSELEY,
  THOMAS D., 197
MOSES,
  JOHN, 2
  SAMUEL, 2
  WASHINGTON, 2
MOSIER,
  JNO. SR., 264

JOHN, 34, 137
JOSH, 92
SAM'L, 137
SAMUEL, 91, 92
MUNSFIELD,
  GRASTY, 97
MURFREE,
  WILLIAM, 227
MURIEL,
  C.C., 145
MURPHY,
  WILLIAM, 72
MURPHY],
  HARDY, 231

-N-

NASH,
  ABNER, 51, 52,
    56, 220(3)
  ADNER, 219
NEELY,
  JAMES W., 187
NELLUMS,
  WILLIAM, 260
NELM,
  CAPT., 5, 6
  CAPTAIN, 175
NELMS,
  ALFRED, 92
NELM'S,
  CAPT. Company,
    125
NELMS,
  JOSHIA, 92
  RICHARD, 95
  SAM'L, 106, 204
  SAMUEL, 92, 156,
    173, 254, 261
NELMS,
  SAMUEL, 173
NELMS,
  THOMAS, 94
  WILLIAM, 260
NELSON,
  SAMUEL, 40
NEWTON,
  ISHAM, 170, 244
  JOHN, 244
  ROBERT, 244
NICE,
  CHARLES, 2
  JONATHAN, 100
NICHOLSON,
  TYRON P., 244
NIX,
  JONATHAN, 134,
    135, 263
NIXONS, 263
NORRID,

—, 28
EDWARD, 9(2),
  15, 18, 19(2),
  23, 28, 100, 264

JEREMIAH, 28,
  95, 101
LANFORD, 9
LARKIN, 95, 244
WILLIAM L., 252,
  253, 255, 256(2)

WILLIAM T., 241
NORRIDS,
  old place, 193
NORVELL,
  EACHBAUM, 85
NORVILLE,
  EACHBAUM, 185
NULLS,
  JAMES, 149
NUTON,
  L, 31

-O-

OAKES,
  NORTON, 203,
  241, 247, 258
OAKS,
  NORTON, 195
OATES,
  NORTON, 208
OLD,
  THOMAS, 221
OUTLAW,
  JOHN C., 194
OVERTON & CAGE,
  229

-P-

PAGAN,
  -, 111
  A.C., 44, 112,
    120, 123, 147,
    150, 155
  ANDREW C., 112,
    152, 164, 196
  ANDRU C., 145
  H.C., 147
  JOHN, 156
PAGE,
  JOHN, 55
PANKEY,
  JOHN, 129
PANKY,
  JNO., 264
PARKE,
  ELISHA, 9

PARKER,
 E., 212, 214
 ELISHA, 9, 15,
  18, 19(2), 23,
  101, 194, 207,
  208, 209
 FELIN, JR., 36
 FELIX, JR., 176,
  181, 207
 ISAAC, 77, 228
PARKS,
 ISAAC, 67
PARMER,
 BENJAMIN, 252,
  253, 255, 256(2)

 P., 52
PARR,
 JAMES, 89, 90
 JNO., 264
 JNO./, 261
 JOHN, 1, 5(2),
  13, 18, 20(2),
  28, 31, 32, 39,
  45, 49, 51, 82,
  85, 88, 89, 101,
  115, 121, 122,
  126, 141, 142,
  143, 150, 155,
  164, 170, 175,
  177(2), 180,
  184, 185, 187,
  193, 194, 195,
  196, 197, 206,
  214, 217, 218,
  241, 242(2),
  247, 248(2),
  249, 251(2),
  259, 264
 JOHN, JR., 89
 JOHN, SR., 89
 MOSES, 186
 POLLY, 32, 94
 WILLIAM, 32,
  89(2), 90, 94
PARTEE,
 —, 3
 W.B., 212
 WILLIAM B.,
  179(2), 190,
  199(2), 202,
  204, 258
 WM. B., 169
PATE,
 JOHN, 168, 174
PAYNE,
 ANDERSON C., 88
 JOHN, 84, 113,
  114, 153, 156,
  222

SEAREY, 222
 WILLIAM, 171
PERVIS,
 STARKEY, 28
PHILLIPS,
 HENRY, 193, 194
PILLOW,
 GIDEON, 78
PILLOWS, 229
PINSON,
 JOEL, 18
 NATHAN G., 18
POLK,
 A.F., 210, 213,
  214
 A.T., 212
 ALEXANDER, 16
 ALEXANDER F.,
  209
 JNO., 149, 214,
  261, 80-
 JOHN, 29, 36,
  39, 40, 41, 42,
  43, 44, 47, 101,
  190, 191, 211,
  215, 216, 247,
  253, 259
 THOMAS, 95
 THOMAS A., 195,
  208(2)
 THOMAS K., 245
POLLY,
 JOHN, 239
PORTER,
 —, 3
 JAMES M., 41,
  100, 102(2),
  134, 135, 155,
  175, 178, 183,
  190, 192, 204
 WILLIAM B., 176
 WM. B., 175
PORTER & PARTEE,
 3, 190
POST,
 WM., 79
POUND,
 DANIEL W., 216
 DAVID W., 48,
  111, 166, 167,
  178, 180
 JAMES M., 111,
  167
POUNT,
 DANIEL W., 187
POUOND,
 JAMES M., 180
POWEL, 204
PROVINCE,
 A., 77

PRYOR,
 ALLEN, 97
 HARRY, 36
 HENRY, 29, 36,
  245, 247, 253
 JAMES, 252, 253,
  255
PURSELL,
 ABRAHAM, 177
PURVIS,
 STARKEY, 93
PYRON,
 JAMES, 256(2)

-R-

RAFORD,
 SAMUEL G., 263
RAGSDALE,
 SAMUEL, 77
RATCLIFF,
 WM., 79
 WM. P., 159
RATCLIFT,
 WILLIAM P., 159
RATLIFF,
 AMY, 80-
READ,
 ALEXANDER, 232
 GEORGE, 253,
  255, 256(2)
 JAMES, 241, 253,
  254, 256
REED,
 GEORGE, 171,
  241, 252
REEVES,
 ELIJAH, 241,
  244, 252, 253,
  255, 256(2)
 HIRAM, 246
 ISAC, 96
 JAMES, 169, 179,
  246
 SAML., 19
 SAMUEL, 9(2),
  15, 18, 19, 23,
  93, 169, 173,
  179(2), 247
 URIAS, 93
RICHARDS,
 WILLIAM, 146
RITCHEY,
 HUGH, 59, 60
RITCHEYS,
 HUGH, 56(2), 57,
  58(2)
RIVER,
 MISSISSIPPI, 176
 OBION, 95, 99,

247
OBION - NORTH
FORK, 97, 132
ROAD,
DRESDEN, 91,
94(2), 95, 138,
173, 200, 201,
204, 244, 246
DYERSBURG, 3,
137, 171, 200,
244, 247
from REELFOOT
BRIDGE, 201
IRON BANK, 96
IRON BANKS, 117,
245
MILLS POINT, 2,
3, 96, 97(2),
99, 123, 128,
173(2), 202(2),
244, 245(3), 247

MILLS PONT, 117
MOSCOW, 201
NELMS FERRY, 202
TOTTEN, 97, 98
TRENTON, 92,
95(2), 172, 245
ROBBINS,
EDWARD, 149, 158
ROBERTS,
EDWARD, 46
OBEDIAH, 28,
195, 207, 208,
211
ROBERTSON,
ELDRIDGE B., 94
ROBINS,
EDWARD, 16
RODGERS,
SAMUEL, 260
ROLINS,
EDWARD, 108
ROLL,
WILLIAM B., 97
ROSBROUGH,
M., 77
ROSS,
A. W., 3
ALFRED W., 100,
123(2), 134,
135, 155
BENJ., 47
DAVID, 226
I. M., 17
I. S., 17
JAMES M., 9, 23,
45, 90, 91,
105(2), 124,
168(2), 185,

210, 211(2)
JESSE M., 95
JESSE S., 33,
34, 45
JOHN, 16
W., 3
ROSSITT,
JORDAN, 37
RUSSELL,
SESEILS, 204
THOMAS, 204 -
RUTHERFORD,
HENRY, 200, 229

-S-

St. JOHN,
D., 255
ST. JOHN,
DANIEL, 5, 9,
27, 29, 37
St. JOHN,
DANIEL, 101,
107, 172(2),
194, 202,
259(2), 264
St. jOHN,
DANIEL, 206
St. JOHN & INGRAM,
251
SAUNDERS,
WILLIAM, 2
SCOGGINS,
WILLIAM, 68
WILLIS, 221
SCOTT,
W. P., 9
WILLIAM F., 100,
129, 134, 135,
155
WILLIAM P., 9
WM., 263
SEACOAT,
JEREMIAH, 171
SHAW,
JOHN, 226
SHEEKS,
B., 211
BENJ., 29, 43,
44, 47
BENJAMIN, 36,
39, 40, 41, 42,
169, 179(2),
195, 207, 208,
257
C., 210, 213,
263
CORNELIUS,
16(2), 39, 40,
41, 43, 44, 47,

85, 108, 113,
114, 148, 154,
185
DAVID, 187, 194,
195
JESSE, 29, 36,
148, 149, 154,
185, 186(2),
187, 189, 202
JOSEPH, 197
SHELBY,
EVAN, 194
SHELLY,
EVAN, 28
SHELTON,
H.A., 211
HUGH, 20
HUGH A., 28,
193, 195, 207,
208, 263
WASHINGTON, 55,
116
SHELY,
EVAN, 101
SIMPSON,
J.M., 211
SAMUEL, 28, 195,
207
SAMUEL M., 127,
208
SINKLER,
CHARLES, 6, 9,
29, 100, 102,
171, 195, 212
SKEGGS,
WILLIE, 2
Slave,
EASTER, 193
HENRY, 193
SLAVE -,
CHARLES, 89
EMMALIN, 90
PEGGY, 90
SLOAN,
MARTHA, 237
ROBERT, 237
SMITH,
JOEL R., 55, 74
MARY, 260
MAURY, 104
SAM'L H., 214
SAMUEL A., 191
W.F., 186(2)
WILLIAM F., 95,
153, 156(2),
188, 195, 208(2)

WM. F., 189
WM.L., 157
SNIDER,

147

JOHN, 2
WILLIAM, 2
SNOW,
  JAMES, 241, 252,
    253, 255, 256(2)

SPEAKS,
  JOSEPH, 244
SPIGHT,
  JAMES M., 172,
    203, 257
  SIMON B., 130
  THOMAS, 130,
    194, 247, 251,
    252, 257
  THOS., 263
SPRIGHT,
  THOMAS, 127
STALEY,
  THEODORE, 7(2),
    29, 36(2), 182,
    183
STANFORD,
  JNO., 263
  JOHN, 2, 169,
    179(2)
STANLEY,
  LEWIS, 199
STARRETT,
  ALEXANDER, 178
STEDMAN,
  B., 222
STEPHENSON, 77
STITH & CLOUSTON,
  230
STODDARD,
  SOLOMON, 217
STONE,
  JAMES N., 244,
    257
  R. W., 28
  RANDOLPH, 244
STONES,
  JAMES N., 244
STRONG,
  C., 228
STROUD,
  SETH, 18
SUMMER,
  JACOB B., 178
SWAMP,
  BLACK, 96, 128
SWEDEN,
  WILLIAM, 96
SWEENEY,
  H.B., 229
SWINDLE,
  JOEL, 222

-T-

TALLEY,
  M., 129
TALLY,
  MARTIN, 28,
    201(2)
TANNER,
  BERYL, 28
  JOHN B., 247
  THOMAS, 29,
    36(2), 171
TART,
  JOHN, 98
TAVERN,
  rates, 181
TAX,
  rate, 183, 184
TAYLOPR,
  DAVID, 159
TAYLOR,
  A., 55
  CLAYBOURN, 2
  DAVID, 159(2),
    161, 162, 188
  F., 204
  FRANCES, 96
  FRANCIS, 169,
    179(2), 192,
    216, 264
  FREDERICK, 28,
    94, 101, 242,
    244, 250(2)
  I. P., 55
  JAMES, 56, 232
  JOHN, 29, 36
  JOHN L., 36
  JOHN J., 202
  JOSEPH, 9, 94
  T., 263
  THOMAS, 29, 36,
    39, 40, 41, 42,
    43, 44, 47, 94,
    95, 200, 204
TEATER,
  S.L., 100
  SAMUEL L., 21,
    143, 150, 151,
    195
TEETER,
  SAMUEL T., 209
TERRILL,
  JOHN, 225, 226
TETTER,
  SAMUEL L., 37
THOMAS,
  —, 54
THOMPSON,
  DAVID, 28(2),
    43(2), 49,
    50(2), 194

W. L., 43
WM. L., 43, 49,
  50(2)
THURSLY,
  EDWARD, 55
THURSLYS,
  EDWARD, 56
TOTTEN, 97
  A.W.C., 168
  A.W.O., 6, 199
  B., 13, 22, 30,
    35, 49, 88, 97,
    100, 115, 121,
    126, 133, 145,
    146, 151, 164,
    168(2), 169, 264

B., JR., 8
BENJ., 1, 18,
  20, 25, 30, 49,
  261
BENJAMIN, 5, 22,
  23, 26, 27, 28,
  31, 37, 38, 39,
  51, 85, 89, 101,
  116, 122(2),
  172, 175, 194,
  197
BENJAMIN C.,
  133(2)
G.B., 96
JAMES L., 145
W.W., 102
TOWN OF TROY, 80-
TOWN OF TRY, 89
TOWNSEND,
  WILLIAM, 55
TROY, 127
  Courthouse at,
    193
  TOWN OF, 3
  Town of, 104,
    126, 130, 131,
    165, 170, 197,
    203, 206, 220,
    221, 222, 238,
    239, 242, 257
TRUST & McMILLAN,
  72

-U-

UNIV. OF NC,
  TRUSTEES, 68

-V-

VAUGHN,
  CAPT., 5, 6, 33
  CAPTAIN, 175

VINCENT,
  A., 204
  PERRY, 165

-W-

WADKINS,
  JAMES, 2, 169,
    173, 179(2),
    186(2), 187, 189

  JEROME, 2, 169,
    179(2)
WAFFORD,
  SAMUEL G., 100
WALING,
  DANIEL, 246
WALKER, 148
  ISAAC, 194
  JAMES, 13, 14,
    22, 83(2)
  LUCY D., 13
  RUBEN, 97
WALLACE,
  JOSEPH, 175
WALTON & CO.,
  LONSDALE, 19, 23
WARFORD,
  SAMUEL G., 134,
    136
WATKINS,
  JAMES, 96
WATSON,
  BRYANT, 68
  CAPT., 5, 6, 33
  CAPTAIN, 175,
    204
  LONSDALE, 46
  WILLIAM U., 21,
    27, 34, 46, 87,
    88, 102, 107,
    109, 117, 172
  WILLIAM W., 21,
    37, 45, 99, 123,
    125, 131, 139,
    145, 176, 178,
    192, 204, 250,
    251, 257
  WM. U., 166
  WM. W., 206, 208
WEAKLEY,
  COUNTY, 94
  COUTNY, 97
WEBB,
  AMOS, 35
WELL,
  TOTTENS, 96
WELLS,
  SAMUEL, 98
  TOTTENS, 2

WESTBROOK,
  A.C.P.
  H.I.P., 28(2),
    31
  H.J.P., 5,
    146(3), 264
  H.L.P., 122
  HENRY J.P., 101,
    147, 172, 194,
    198, 254
  J.P., 247
WESTCOTT,
  JERIMIAH, 79
WHEATON & LINDELL,
  74
WHEETON,
  CALLOW, 69
WHITE, 229
  CHARLES, 223
  GEN., 263
  GEO., 132
  GEORGE, 169,
    179(2), 201
  GOERGE, 201
  JOHN, 101
  ROBERT, 154,
    157, 166, 185
  WILLIAM T., 135,
    155, 203
WHITEHEAD,
  WILLIAM S., 100
WHITESELL,
  JAMES, 56
  WILLIAM T., 134,
    135(2)
WHITESHIDE,
  WM. T., 213
WHITESIDE,
  JNO., 261
  JONATHAN, 3,
    173, 204, 208
  W.T., 210
  WILLIAM T., 29,
    36(2), 209, 253,
    260
  WM., 212
  WM. T., 214
WHITESIDES,
  JOHN, 28
WILIAM,
  JOHN L., 255
WILKERSON,
  WILLIAM, 249
WILKINSON,
  WILLIAM, 1, 18,
    20, 25, 26, 27,
    28(2), 89, 101,
    122, 142, 175,
    194, 197, 204,
    242(2), 247,

    248(2), 251
  WM., 264
WILLIAM,
  —, 54
  JNO., 213
  JOHN, 171, 200
WILLIAMS,
  ALVIN D., 71
  DAVID O., 221
  HUGH, 56
  JESSE, 1
  JNO., 263
  JOHN, 1, 28,
    98(2), 100(2),
    124, 134,
    193(2), 194,
    197, 205, 244
  JOHN L., 241,
    252, 253, 256
  JOHN P., 256
  JOSEPH, 67, 228
  OLIVER D., 232
  ROBERT C., 226
  THOMAS H., 228
  WILLIAM L., 227
WILLIAMSON,
  HUGH, 57(2), 58,
    59, 60
WILLINGHAM,
  WILL, 79
  WM., 79
WILLS,
  SAMUEL, 255
WILLSON,
  WILLIAM M., 9
WILSON,
  GEORGE, 63
  J.C., 264
  JAMES, 9(2), 15,
    18, 19(2), 23,
    96, 117, 131,
    169, 179(2), 245

  JESSE, 263
  JOEL H., 215
  JOHN C., 12, 27,
    41, 82, 95, 100,
    105, 125(2),
    131, 134, 149,
    153, 157, 171,
    178, 199

  JOSEPH, 3, 14,
    29, 35, 36(2),
    40, 45, 101, 171
  S.D., 198(2),
    203
  SAMUEL D., 11,
    12, 15, 41, 87,
    91, 109, 122(2),

128, 138, 153,
181, 202,
203(2), 217
SAMUEL S., 162
THOMAS, 64, 229
W.M., 168
W.U., 168
WILLIAM M., 11,
21, 23, 142,
159(3), 161,
170, 171, 194,
242(2), 247,
248(2), 249,
251, 257(2)
WILLIAM W., 107,
188
WM. M., 6, 89,
161, 162, 264
WINFORD,
HARDY, 70
WINSTON,
FOUNTAIN, 66,
223(2), 228, 230
JOSEPH, 66, 67,
228
LEWIS, 66, 67,
228, 230
SAM'L L., 67
SAMUEL L., 65
WINTHROP,
HENRY, 78
WLYCOFF & CLERK,
78
WOOD,
—, 23
C.W.
DOUGLAS S., 187
ENUS W., 44
G. W., 20
G.W., 120
GEO. W., 150
GEORGE W., 111,
112, 118(2),
123, 152, 155,
164, 196
JAMES H., 68
JNO. W., 146
JOHN, 67
LARKIN F., 187
SCOTT, 88
WOODRIDGE, 229
WRIGHT,
JNO. P., 211
JOHN P., 1, 28,
171, 195, 207,
208
S.P., 171
THOMAS, 2
WRITE,
EDWARD, 223

WYATT,
JONATHAN, 223
WYCOFF & CLARK,
221
WYCOFF & CLARKS,
222

-Y-

YOKUM,
JACOB, 263
YOUNG,
MATHEW, 14, 86,
157

-Z-

ZACHERY,
LEWIS, 93, 95
ZACHREY,
LEWIS, 93, 194
ZELLERS,
JOHN, 249, 258

www.ingramcontent.com/pod-product-compliance
Lightning Source LLC
Chambersburg PA
CBHW020655300426
44112CB00007B/386